the state of the
GAME

DENNY CRUM
WITH BOB SCHALLER

THE STATE OF THE GAME

Denny Crum with Bob Schaller, The State of the Game

ISBN 1-887002-94-4

Cross Training Publishing
317 West Second Street
Grand Island, NE 68801
(800) 430-8588

This book is manufactured in the United States of America.

Library of Congress Cataloging in Publication Data in Progress.

Published by Cross Training Publishing
317 West Second Street
Grand Island, NE 68801
Website: crosstrainingpub.com
1-800-430-8588

Photo Credit:
University of Louisville Photography

TABLE OF CONTENTS

ACKNOWLEDGEMENTS

This book would never have happened without three people:

First of all, I would like to thank Denny Crum for making time for me on dozens of occasions, whether in his office, on the road or on the phone. Despite covering college sports for a dozen years, I had never met Coach Crum before. All I knew was that he had won an awful lot of college basketball games and had been coaching since I was 4 years old. Coach Crum spoke openly about issues and subjects that he had, in many cases, never spoken of before.

I did not feel like I knew Coach Crum until we had spoken a dozen or so times. At first Crum refused to talk about his various charity works, claiming that would fly in the face of the genuine, true intention and motivation of why he does the work in the first place: to help people, not his own image. With the incredible responsibilities involved in being a coach in the highly competitive Conference USA, Crum's generous efforts on this book are worthy of more than simple appreciation.

Secondly, the work of Gary Tuell can be found throughout this book. Tuell, a former Louisville athletic department worker and assistant to Crum, used the skills he developed as a sportswriter to pen the book, *Above the Rim*, a history of U of L basketball. Tuell, now the head basketball coach at Augusta (Ga.) State College, also graciously gave his thoughts for this book as well. Tuell's work can be found in the four chapters that document four key seasons for Crum. We picked just four seasons because a book that was only a chronology of Crum's career could have gone 600 pages, and it would not have delved as deeply into Crum's personal life, his philosophy on and off the court, and what makes him who he is.

The four seasons were picked for a number of reasons. The first season in this book, 1971-72, was Crum's initial season as U of L's coach, during which he took his team to the Final Four. The 1974-75 season was chosen because, among other reasons, that year's Final Four marked the last time Crum would face his mentor, John Wooden. The 1979-80 and 1985-86 seasons were picked because those were U of L's two national championship marches. Yet all four seasons were picked for another reason: All involved overcoming certain obstacles, whether it was team chemistry or rebounding from tough defeats, and players accepting their roles as the coaches worked to put the team in the best possible position to succeed. In short, there are life lessons to be learned in each of those seasons, and you will see subtle, and not so subtle, signs of those lessons as you read through each season.

Finally, this book would never have been started without the attention and care of Larry McCoy, who came up with the idea of doing the book as a fund-raiser for the Kentucky chapter of the Fellowship of Christian Athletes. In any book endeavor, there are critical hurdles that have to be cleared to keep the project on track. This book was more than a year in the making, and at every bump in the road, McCoy popped onto the scene, keeping the project moving forward through communication, hard work and a desire to raise money for a very good cause.

It was McCoy who first approached Crum about the book before contacting me about writing it. Crum, by his very nature of not turning down a charitable effort, immediately said he would offer any assistance or resources to help the project along. All of that assistance came on Crum's own time, and he is donating all of his author royalties from this book. Coach Crum is more giving of himself than those outside his tight inner circle could ever know. At least, until this book came out.

Lastly, I would like to convey my gratitude to Coach Crum's former assistant coaches and players and his personal friends, who agreed to be interviewed. In addition, thanks also go to the other college coaches who took time out during the 1998-99 season to offer their thoughts and insights about Coach Crum. Also, to the administrative staff in the U of L basketball office and sports information department for their hard work and patience.

The humor and personal stories add to a book that is geared toward success in life through lessons on the court, which will be Crum's legacy long after his Hall of Fame status, the incredible 600-plus wins, the national championships and Final Four appearances, and his longevity at U of L are all totaled.

Bob Schaller, author, March 1, 1999

Although I had many players under my supervision with the talent to become fine coaches, Denny Crum is the only one about whom I made this statement at the time he was playing for me:

He was born to coach.

This was the case for a number of reasons: Denny possesses a fine concept of the game, his love of the game is strong, he has a competitive nature, and his work habits and desire to learn are strong. Also, while he is a person of few words, he does have an engaging personality. He also has an inquisitive nature about all aspects of the game. He was the most inquisitive player—in the proper way—of any player ever under my supervision.

Denny wanted to know the reasoning for everything we did. We would do a fundamental drill, and Denny would ask what the drill was for primarily, and peripherally. If I made a strategical move, he wanted to know why, and what were the other implications of the move. He also noticed substitution patterns and always asked why I went this way or that way. His interest also extended to why certain players were kept on the bench, and he was always concerned with how players would best accept roles that would best benefit the team.

Denny also picked up on how important everyone was within the program, from administrators to his assistant coaches, support staff, trainers and managers. He established an immediate rapport with our media, alumni, parents and all others who were interested, or involved, in the program.

Furthermore, his experience as a player, assistant coach and head coach at the high school, junior college and Division I four-year level provide a unique experience few others possess.

Denny's book will be valuable to anyone interested in teaching the great sport of basketball. It also will enlighten those who want to learn more about the sport or simply allow someone to follow the trail this highly successful coach has blazed for three decades. I am proud of my association with Coach Crum. I take pride in hearing what he says when he credits me for his multiple successes, but the truth is simply this: Denny Crum is a great teacher—and has always been a great student—and that is why he has been so successful.

John Wooden, February 3, 1999

Denny Crum has been coaching at Louisville for almost 30 years. He proves that you only get better as you get older. He knows that as time goes on, there are more types of personalities to deal with. Denny has a wealth of experience to draw from. You get older, you get smarter. The older you are and the longer you have been at this, the more ways you figure out how to get things accomplished.

He's stayed at the college level when he has had a lot of other opportunities. But in college basketball, you, as the head coach, are your own personnel director. You are the general manager. You are, in fact, the steward of your team, although of course you do not own it. The other thing is that it's fun working with young guys. It is a lot of fun to make a difference in young guys' lives. You have more impact on them and more influence than you would on a professional level. To that end, Denny has really made a mark as a coach.

I have played against several of Denny's teams. The thing that always sticks out in my mind is Denny's extraordinary attention to detail. His teams have a lot of sets, but they seem to run them all with such precision, which is what makes it work.

Often when I think of Denny's teams, I think of the great guards he's had. He has had a lot of good, big men, too, but the guards are what I think of first. His teams are characterized by great guard play, really a cerebral approach.

He does UCLA basketball as well as UCLA used to do it when Coach John Wooden was there. Denny runs Coach Wooden's stuff, yet he has gone out on his own and added his own nuances to it. Coach Wooden had a profound influence on him. But Denny is also someone who has ideas of his own, and he has incorporated those ideas very well into his system.

Defensively, no one employs more extended defenses as well as Denny. You have to be prepared for the press changes. Another thing you face going up against Louisville is that Denny makes excellent adjustments during the game. He can coach in practices, he's a good game coach, a good preparer, a good late-in-the-game coach—in short, Denny is a coach for all seasons. He really enjoys basketball. I enjoy watching his teams play against other teams, to see what Denny will do, or how he will adjust to a certain situation

But he has kept a handle on the program. One thing I really appreciate is the way Denny cares about all of his players. He is very loyal to his current and former players and assistant coaches.

Rick Majerus, head basketball coach, University of Utah

CHAPTER 1

THE (LARRY) BIRD THAT FLEW THE COOP

B efore Larry Bird was "Larry Legend," he was in the small community of French Lick, Indiana, in the 1970s, playing high school basketball almost under a cloak of anonymity until his junior year.

"The recruiting services then weren't like they are now—there were only a few, and there were players who could slip through the so-called cracks, whereas today that would be almost impossible," recalls then Louisville assistant Bill Olsen. "Up until the end of Larry's junior year, we didn't have anything on him that said he was 6-foot-8."

Denny Crum remembers that, too.

"Last we had heard, Larry was something like 6-foot-1 or 6-2," Crum said. "We heard he had grown six or seven inches. With his ball-handling skills, we figured he would really be something else."

Only problem was, Bird was planning to head somewhere else.

"Once we found out Larry had grown and saw the new numbers, I was the one who was in charge of recruiting him," Olsen said. "I went up several times and saw him. We knew about, and recruited, a couple of other Indiana high schoolers, David Smith of Milltown and Curt Gilstrap out of Orleans. They were about 6-8 and we were looking at them. I saw Larry Bird play his senior year, and we moved him to the top of the list right away."

Crum agreed: Bird was priority No. 1.

"Larry, before the growth spurt, had been a guard," Crum said. "So he could handle the ball, shoot the ball, run the floor well and really had a sense of the game. With the added height, here was a 6-foot-9 kid who could do it all, and rebound."

Olsen, visiting French Lick, met with Bird and Bird's coach,

Gary Holland, at Spring Valley High School. Bird was as respectful off the court as he was dominating on it.

"To be honest sir, the only way I would go over the river (the Ohio River, from Indiana to Kentucky), would be if the University of Kentucky was to recruit me," Bird said. "My only interest in playing college basketball in the state of Kentucky is at UK."

"Could you at least come visit us, Larry?" Olsen asked.

Bird shook his head.

"No sir, but thank you," Bird said. "It would be a waste of your money and my time."

Olsen reported back to Crum that Bird did not want to visit, let alone contemplate signing with, Louisville.

"His dream is of playing at the University of Kentucky," Olsen told Crum. "If that doesn't happen, Knight (Indiana University Coach Bobby Knight) will get him."

"But it's just a short drive from French Lick to here," Crum answered to Olsen. "Not even a visit?"

Every other player Olsen had recruited at least agreed to visit Louisville. From there the sell got easier, with Crum's successful tenure and the rich basketball tradition at Louisville.

"Maybe, Coach," Olsen told Crum, "if you met with him, we could get him to visit."

"Set it up," Crum said. "Let's go over together."

A week later, Crum and Olsen drove to Spring Valley High School where they met with Holland and Bird in the coach's office.

"Larry, it's nice to meet you," Crum said, shaking Bird's hand.

"Thank you sir," Bird replied. "It's nice to meet you, too."

"That's great," Crum said. "Now Larry, we'd just like you to visit Louisville, no strings attached of course. We think you have a lot of talent—like a lot of other schools do—and we think our system would really fit your skills."

"I'm just not interested in Louisville sir," Bird said.

Crum looked at Olsen and Holland. Then, he looked at Bird.

"Larry, you're a pretty good shooter, aren't you?" Crum asked.

"Yes sir," Bird answered.

"So you probably think you could beat me in a game of horse, right?" Crum asked.

"Oh, yes sir," Bird answered.

"So, if we shot a game of horse, and I beat you, would you at least visit Louisville?" Crum proposed.

"Definitely sir," Bird said.

Holland got out two basketballs. Crum and Bird were both in their street clothes. Olsen sat with Holland in the first row of bleachers as Crum and Bird took a couple of practice shots each, with neither missing.

"I remember that being the darkest gym I'd been in," Crum said. "Later, when I saw the movie Hoosiers, I thought they'd filmed it in that gym."

Olsen chatted with Holland as Bird and Crum shot warmups without either missing a single shot.

"Coach Holland, is Larry really in this gym for hours on end?"

"Oh yeah," Holland said. "He's got his own key to the gym. He stays until midnight. In the evenings, the kids from town come down and shag for him because he'll put up hundreds of shots a day. In the morning, he's here when myself and the rest of the faculty get in. I always have to run out before the first bell and say, 'Larry, come on, it's time for class.' "

Holland continued.

"Coach Crum's got quite a shot," Holland said to Olsen.

"Incredible," Olsen said. "He doesn't usually miss, and he's got quite a repertoire of trick shots from impossible angles. I've never seen him lose a game of horse."

"Well then," Holland said with a smile, "watch this."

Crum looked at Bird.

"Are you warm and ready?" Crum asked.

"Yes sir," Bird said.

Olsen was making plans in his head for Bird's visit.

"I thought Denny would take over, and he was going to distract Larry," Olsen recalled. "I thought Coach Crum would beat him. I'd seen him do this with our players, and Denny would win. I had never seen him lose in a free throw shooting contest or a game of horse. He had a trick shot that no one else could execute. That was important in a game like horse."

So the game of horse was about to start.

"Do you want to shoot first Larry?" Crum asked. "Or should I?"

Bird did not look up.

"Go ahead, Coach," Bird said. "You go first."

Olsen could not believe it.

"Big mistake, Coach Holland," Olsen said with a grin. "He's got Larry now. Larry will be behind before he knows it. Larry should have gone first."

Olsen sat back and folded his hands across his lap. "I felt good," Olsen recalled. "I smiled and thought, 'We've got the advantage. This will be typical Denny Crum.' "

Crum shot first from near the free throw line.

Swish!

"Couldn't have been any more perfect," Olsen said.

Bird shot.

Swish!

"What a touch," Olsen whispered to Holland. "Perfect arc, soft touch. Hmmm."

"Yeah," Holland replied. "And that's how ALL of Larry's shot are."

"You mean he makes them all, or they all look that perfect?" Olsen asked.

"Both," Holland answered with a smile.

Crum headed to the corner, where the baseline meets the sideline. The hoop is not completely visible from there, just the front part of the hoop.

"Denny, on his second shot, was going to his trick shot," Olsen said. "I was surprised he went to the corner. He could have gone to his other shots first. But I was still comfortable because I'd seen Denny hit this shot maybe nine times out of 10 and never miss in a game of horse."

Crum dribbled the ball to the corner. To make the shot, he'd have to arc the ball over the squared off backboard and drop it clean into the cylinder.

"Denny has a ritual he goes to when he does that," Olsen said. "He pointed to the floor."

"Larry," Crum said. Bird turned and looked. Crum pointed at the floor. "Right here—this is where I'm going to shoot from. You have to make sure you are outside the sideline and the baseline— behind where the two lines meet."

Crum wound up and shot.

"I saw the ball arc perfectly, creep over the backboard," Olsen said. "He had lined it up perfectly."

Well, almost perfectly. The ball rimmed in and out.

"It was in the cylinder," Olsen said, "and it went around the rim and flew out. I couldn't believe it."

Bird went out near half-court. On the "old" style basketball courts, there is a hash mark a couple of steps past center court, on each side.

"Larry goes to where that hash mark hits the side-court line," Olsen said.

"Coach Crum," Larry said.

"Yes?" Crum said.

"Coach, see where my feet are?" Bird said, imitating Crum's ritual on the failed attempt. "Your feet have to be out of bounds and behind the mark here."

"Larry was not being disrespectful," Olsen said. "He had a sense of humor, and boy was that young man a competitor."

Olsen and Holland smiled at each other.

"You know, Coach," Olsen said to Holland, "this is not going to be funny if he misses."

"He won't miss, Coach," Holland replied to Olsen.

Bird told Crum, "It has to be a jump shot."

"You have to understand that Bird's jumpshot was not something like Jordan's, where he got a couple of feet off the ground or anything," Olsen said. "Larry got two inches off the ground."

But the shot was true.

"He was maybe a bit more than 40 feet out," Olsen said. Swish!

"The way he made it, it looked like a free throw," Olsen said. "I mean, the guy is at least 40 feet away, and he swishes it completely clean."

Olsen did not know at the time if that was a fluke.

"He doesn't really have that kind of range, does he?" Olsen asked Holland.

"That's not luck, that's Larry Bird," Holland answered. "Coach, if he goes to half-court, he will, I guarantee you, hit at least seven of 10 from the jump circle. And then he'd be mad about the three he missed, so he'd hit eight or nine of the next 10."

Olsen was amazed.

"I had never seen anything like that game before," Olsen said.

Crum was ready to try the shot to keep the game letter-less.

"Denny is strong, but he's not going to square up and just do a jumpshot," Olsen said. "He was lining up like a shotputter, to crank it like that."

The ball hit the front of the rim and fell harmlessly to the floor.

"Coach," Bird said, "you call that a jumpshot?"

"Larry, where I come from on the West coast, that's a jump shot," Crum said.

Bird moved to the other hash mark. Another 40-plus footer. Swish!

"Like a free throw again," Olsen said.

Crum's shot?

"It was really dark in there," Crum recalls with a grin.

"To be honest," Olsen said, "it was like a clinic. I don't know if Denny got the rim but one more time from there on out."

Bird went back and forth, across the court.

"Never closer than 40 feet, I can tell you that much," Olsen said. Swish! Swish! Swish!

Game over. Bird: Clean. Crum: H-O-R-S-E.

"Coach Holland, I don't know if I believe you," Olsen said.

"I'm sorry coach—about what?" Holland asked.

"If Larry went to the half-court circle, he would have made 10 of 10, wouldn't he?" Olsen asked with a smile.

"Yeah," Holland said. "He probably would. But it's something you have to see to believe. I can't tell coaches over the phone the range he has or describe the way he shoots. No one would believe me."

He would indeed head to Indiana for college before transferring back to a junior college by French Lick and then to Indiana State, where he would lead ISU to the NCAA Championship game against Magic Johnson's Michigan State team.

All that without going over the river to visit Louisville.

"I really thought we had him when he said he'd visit if Coach Crum could beat him in horse," Olsen said.

Crum and Bird shook hands.

"Well," Crum said. "you shoot the ball very well. You're still invited."

"Thanks sir, and I appreciate your time," Bird said. "But I'm staying in Indiana."

Crum has nothing but fond memories and respect for Bird, whom he would later coach on a USA team.

"What a pleasure to coach Larry," Crum said. "He knew so much about what was going on out there. He had all that guard training, then he played in the post as a senior. He learned to play the game as a guard—he just ended up growing a lot. Now, he's having a lot of success as a coach—he's really a good coach. He has a real good understanding of the game. Of course, he did back then, too."

CHAPTER 2

FROM HUMBLE HOOP BEGINNINGS TO UCLA

Denny Crum's basketball roots might run deep, but he was excelling in other sports before he shot his first basket.

Denny, who was born March 2, 1937, had to cope with the breakup of his parents' marriage as a youngster. Crum's mother left when he was 10, and Denny, the middle child, grew up under his father, Alwin Denzel Crum, with Denny's two sisters. Denny's father was an aircraft mechanic, who was "a math whiz"—he was incredible with figures, and he could build anything.

"My father was very competitive—no question about it," Crum said. "Probably not as outwardly as I am, but he didn't like to lose. And he was good at everything."

Denny understood that his mother and father just had not built a lasting relationship.

"I don't remember that much about Mom leaving because I was so young," Denny said. "But it didn't change my feelings for my mother—we're very close. I didn't understand it at the time, but I do now. You have to do what's best for yourself sometimes, and she just wasn't happy."

Though Crum lived in San Fernando, the area was at the time "more country than city."

"I really enjoyed playing baseball and football," Crum said. "But then a kid named Jim Buehler moved in across the street. I was going into eighth grade, and he was entering his sophomore year in high school. I was about 5-foot-8, and he was a real tall kid, about 6-foot-4. He wanted to play basketball and needed someone to practice with. Since we were becoming friends, I wanted to play basketball with him."

Denny went to his father and expressed an interest in basketball. His father thought about it and then put up a hoop.

"He put up a goal in the back half of the backyard, right there in the grass," Denny said. "It didn't take but a month and there was not a blade of grass left."

Denny's passion for basketball quickly grew to exceed that of other sports. Soon, he was shooting well into the evening.

"My Dad put a light up," Denny said. "And the court was open late, late at night."

As the grass gave way to a firmer, albeit dirt surface more conducive to dribbling a ball, the neighbors also noticed the games going into a "p.m." sort of "overtime."

"Our next door neighbors were the Kleins, and Gene and his wife, Shirley, would come to the window," Denny recalls. "The beating of the ball on the ground was loud in the still of the night."

"OK, Denny," Shirley Klein yelled from the window. "It's about time to get to bed now. You need to get some sleep."

"Yes Ma'am," Denny replied.

"I talked to Gene Klein the other day on the phone," Crum recalled. "We had the nicest, longest conversation. He said, 'Do you remember how late you used to play out there?' I said, 'It was late; it must have been 9 or 10 p.m.' He said, 'Come on Denny! Most of the time when Shirley'd poke her head out, it'd be past midnight!' I said, 'That may have been the case, but we had some great times!' We didn't just play late at night. We'd go out first thing in the morning, and on the weekends or in the summer, we'd play all day."

Crum entered his freshman year at San Fernando High School, still having a lot of talent to be tapped in baseball.

"I loved baseball—I was better at baseball," Crum said. "At least until my Dad put the goal up out back."

Back in Crum's high school days, the way for choosing teams was different.

"I went to a school that was combination junior/senior high school," Crum said. "We had the exponent system, which meant we had the 'A' team, which was the varsity, and then 'B', 'C', and 'D' teams, based on our age, height and weight. In the ninth grade, I fell into the specifics for the 'D' team because I was really small, short and thin."

But he could shoot like no one else.

"That was my strength from the beginning," Crum said. "I was into the fundamentals—really enjoyed the fundamentals, running the drills, shooting the ball from different places under different conditions."

All of his backyard practice and reliance of fundamentals paid off early—in Crum's first 'D' squad game.

"We played Eagle Rock High School," Crum said. "We won, 15-13."

Crum had 13 of his team's 15 points.

"I will always," Crum says, "remember that game."

Coach Vinnie Seekins moved Crum up to the 'B' team with another former 'D' teammate, Noble Ford, at the mid-semester mark of Crum's sophomore year.

"Coach Seekins then moved a couple of us up to the varsity after the midterms," Crum said. "Noble and I were moved up. We had good teams. We couldn't beat the teams from the city—the ones that had the 6-foot-9 kids. We had a 6-foot-2 center, and that was our biggest guy. So we weren't real big."

But Crum could play.

"I remember the first time I saw him," Seekins recalled in the late 1980s before his death. "I was down at the playground one night and saw this little kid. He stuck in my mind because he was so persistent. When he finally got on the varsity, he was super. We got the (heck) kicked out of us, but he was an exceptional team leader. He would be out there thinking right along with me. I got so attached to him that some days I would go and get him out of class, and we would go to the gym and just shoot. He was unique. He seriously considered everything we did. I could just tell he was going to be a great coach."

Crum started to live basketball.

"We played by the hour, by the day," Crum said. "We'd practice in the afternoon, go home and eat and do homework, and come back and play from 7 p.m. until 10 p.m. every night. On the weekends we'd go to the park—taking our lunch—and play until dark. I'm talking that we'd play 10 to 12 hours a day. Even during the season we'd get in that three extra hours every night after practice. That really benefited me. And then, I started to grow."

The many hours never seemed to take a toll. Rather, it just fed Crum's interest.

"I just loved it," Crum said. "The more I played, the more I wanted to play."

Crum's goal for the next level—college—was clear. He wanted to play for UCLA and its soon-to-be-legendary coach, John Wooden.

"They really did not have much of an interest in me," Crum admitted. "So I went to junior college."

That is where Crum made his mark and caught the attention of Wooden.

Crum, who was now 6-foot-2, went to Los Angeles' Pierce College. He led the state junior colleges in scoring as a freshman, with an average of 27.1 points per game. Included in that was a 47-point performance against Compton, one of the more powerful junior college teams. As a sophomore at Pierce, Crum was the League Player of the Year.

"Rex Dixon was Compton's coach," Crum recalled. "Every time down the floor, he'd yell at me, 'Shoot it, gunner! You're close enough!' So I did shoot. And I kept making it. After the game, he came up to me and shook my hand."

"That was a great game," Dixon told Crum.

"We became good friends," Crum said. "He was a good coach. He was just trying to get in my head and help his team."

Crum had more balance around him as a sophomore, and the result was that he got a look from UCLA.

"I could flat shoot it," Crum said. "That was my biggest strength. I had good quickness and a good understanding of the game. But I was not at the superstar talent level."

Crum's coach at Pierce was Collins Jones.

"He was just a spindly little kid—he was just 17 when he was a senior in high school," Jones said. "He made all-city his senior year. We were just building Pierce. He put us on the map at Pierce. We had a very good ballclub while he was there. John Wooden wanted him to come over there, so he did."

Crum will never forget being recruited by Wooden.

"When I met him personally, I was already at Pierce," Crum said. "Our college president, Dr. John Shepard, knew I wanted to go to UCLA. He asked Coach Wooden to come and watch me play. Dr. Shepard really went out of his way to help me with UCLA because he knew how badly I wanted to go there. Dr. Shepard and Coach Wooden went to the same church."

So Wooden accepted Shepard's invitation.

"He came over. I guess he liked how I played," Crum said.

Wooden agrees.

"He was like a coach in that he was very, very fundamentally sound," Wooden said.

Wooden motioned to Crum to come over and speak with him.

"He invited me to come and watch their practice at the old gym," Crum said. "I went to a couple of their games, one with my Dad, another with my girlfriend."

When Crum's sophomore season of junior college was over, his phone rang one afternoon.

"Since your season is over, Denny," Coach Wooden said, "would you like to come over and watch our practice?"

"Yes, Coach Wooden," Crum answered. "I'd like that."

Crum watched the practice, breaking down things in his mind.

"I really enjoyed watching practice," Crum said. "After practice, Coach Wooden took me and Ducky Drake, our trainer at the time, over to the old Kirkoff Hall for the team meal. Coach Wooden took me in through the back way, through the kitchen and where all the garbage cans were lined up."

They had a meal, discussed a thing or two about basketball, and then finished their sodas.

"Well?" Coach Wooden asked. "Are you coming or aren't you?"

"I guess I am," Crum replied.

So in a quick training table meal and a brief conversation, Crum had attained his goal of being recruited to UCLA.

"We were just having a normal conversation," Crum recalled. "He didn't even mention a scholarship or anything. I just thought, 'Yeah, this is what I'd love to do.' So I became a UCLA Bruin."

Crum immediately found a niche under Wooden. In Crum's first year at UCLA, as a junior (since he transferred from Pierce), he was awarded the Irv Pohlmeyer Memorial Trophy, presented annually to the outstanding first-year varsity player. In his senior year, Crum was honored with the Bruin Bench Award, which goes to the most improved player.

Crum played with some great athletes at UCLA, including future Olympic track star Rafer Johnson. The teams were decent, but did not win a national title, going 22-4 during Crum's junior year and 16-10 in his senior year of 1957-58.

"Rafer was as good as any athlete I'd ever seen," Crum said. "He was so talented physically. He could have been a tight end or a linebacker. He was my roommate on the road. At the time, we got to be pretty close. He was the student body president at UCLA. And this was back in 1957-58, and anywhere else in the country, you'd not have found an African American who could do something like that. So I was proud of him, and UCLA, for being at the front of the pack when it came to equal opportunities."

UCLA also had something else no one else would ever have: John Wooden. Crum was a solid player, but not material for the NBA.

So after graduating from UCLA, Crum served as a graduate assistant to Wooden and as the assistant freshman coach to Jerry Norman from 1959-1961.

Crum was a confident, brash, young assistant.

"He was bright, alert, very focused and so enthusiastic," Wooden said. "But in the early going he was too critical. Of course, I knew that was due to immaturity and would change with time. At first, I'd have players come to me and say, 'Coach, get that kid off our backs. He's driving us crazy.' I'd say, 'Well, he has to learn. Just remember that he wants you to be successful. It's your best interest he has at heart.' He just demanded too much of the players at first. And we had some bitter disagreements. We would argue and fuss. But after it was over, we were still friends. I think it helped both of us. We both learned from each other."

In 1961 Crum returned to Pierce as an assistant coach to Collins Jones while teaching at Pacoima Junior High School.

Three years later, in 1964, Crum took over the head coach at Pierce, a position he held until 1968.

"He got a job teaching," Jones said. "And then I got him to come be an assistant for me for a couple of years. I knew he would be a great coach. I could have retired earlier, but I held off until I knew Denny was ready to replace me. He did, and then he took over the head coaching job. But Coach Wooden wanted him back at UCLA, so he moved on."

As the head coach at Pierce, Crum was, more than ever, "Little John Wooden."

"I used Coach Wooden's basic philosophy of fundamentals, team play and conditioning," Crum said. "I learned to think about the game when I played for Coach Wooden. I learned to get mentally prepared. Heck, just about everything I know about basketball I learned from playing for Coach Wooden."

In 1968, Wooden had an opening on his staff. Wooden had won national titles in 1964 and '65, and after Texas-El Paso won in 1966, Wooden picked up titles from 1967 to 1973—seven in a row—and Wooden would pick up his final title, against Crum, in 1975.

"Denny had done such a great job for me that I decided as soon as we had a vacancy on the staff, I wanted to bring him back as a regular full-time assistant," Wooden said. "We never lost contact. And as soon as we had an opening, I asked him to come back."

Crum also stood up to Wooden when he felt strongly about something.

"Many times we didn't agree," Wooden said, "and that's one thing I liked so much about him. He would give me his opinion

25

straight up. No coach needs a 'yes' man for an assistant unless he needs someone to inflate his ego. Denny was no 'yes man.' And I think by the time he left us I had learned as much from him as he had from me."

The success was incredible for Crum as a Wooden assistant: three national titles and an 86-4 record. Wooden knew Crum was head-coaching material, and as the 1971 season wore down, he knew it was probably time to let Crum find his own team to guide.

"He was just ready," Wooden said. "And I knew by then he'd be a good head coach."

As the Bruins won another national title—Wooden's fifth in a row and seventh in eight years—by beating Villanova in 1971, Crum's career with UCLA had, as no one could have forecasted, come to an end.

When John Dromo had a heart attack on Jan. 2, 1971, it ended his coaching career at Louisville. An interim assistant, Howard Stacey—who would move on to Drake after leaving the Cards, and face Louisville several times—was not a candidate for the head job.

The head coach from Old Dominion and the freshman coach at Duke competed with Crum for the job. After the interview, there was only one candidate.

"The first time I saw him," said then Louisville athletic director and former head basketball coach Peck Hickman, "he had these long sideburns and was wearing a leisure suit. I didn't know what to think. But then we interviewed him, and he blew us all away."

"When Dad first came to Louisville in 1971, I think he just thought of it as a stop on the way to something better—it was just something on the way to UCLA," said his son Steve. Crum has two children from his first marriage, Steve and Cynthia, and one son from his second marriage, Scott, who lives with Crum in Jeffersonville, Kentucky. "Everybody just assumed he would go back to L.A."

CHAPTER 3

RECRUITING BILL WALTON

T he year before he left UCLA for Louisville, Denny Crum left the cupboard more than full for Coach John Wooden with a recruiting class that would dominate the college basketball world for years to come, and go down as one of the greatest teams in NCAA history.

"The last year I was at UCLA, I recruited several top players— Bill Walton, Jamal Wilkes (who was then known as Keith Wilkes), Greg Lee and several others," Crum said. "People were saying Wilkes couldn't play at UCLA—he was 6-foot-6 and skinny as a rail, maybe 160, 170 pounds. But we got Bill Walton, Wilkes, Lee, Hank Babcock and Vince Edwards. I recruited them all on the basis that, 'If you come to UCLA together and can play together, we'll have a good chance to win national championships. If you stay together as a group and play together, we can continue to win and you can be a part of it.'"

"Ironically, those kids I recruited to UCLA were the same ones I had to play against with my first team in Louisville," Crum said. "Of course they beat us and won the national championship. But I was glad that if we couldn't win it, Coach Wooden did. I had a close relationship with him and those kids. I was not as unhappy after that game as many people might have been."

Recruiting Bill Walton is something Crum will never forget.

"Bill Walton was the most low-key, unassuming guy I ever recruited," Crum said. "During his last year of school, I'd call every Monday night. I had found out a lot about him and that his folks graduated from Berkley. Bill also had an older brother at UCLA, Bruce, who was a 6-foot-4, 280-pound offensive tackle. There was a man named Frank Cushing in San Diego—where Bill was going to high school—and he was the one who initially called me about Bill Walton."

"When I went down to see Bill play, I could not believe how good he was," Crum said. "I mean, I was in awe—I had never seen a player dominate a game. I went back to UCLA and sat down in Coach Wooden's office to tell him about this young man named Bill Walton. To give this some context, you have to understand that Tom McMillen came out of Pennsylvania that year and was heading to Maryland. At that time, the East coast and the West coast were like foreign countries to each other. I had seen some clippings about Tom and knew he was good. But I knew Walton was so much better because he was such a complete player. Still, at that time, basketball prospects in San Diego weren't regarded as highly—or given as much attention—as other areas, especially on the East coast."

Coach Wooden sat Crum down in his office.

"You saw Walton play," Wooden said. "What did you think?"

"Coach, Bill Walton is the best high school player in the country—and the best I have ever seen," Crum answered.

Wooden got up, walked behind Crum's chair, closed the door and sat back down at his desk.

"Denny, don't ever make a comment like that in public, or people will think you are nuts," Wooden said. "There is no way people on the East coast, or even out here, are going to believe a freckle-faced, redheaded kid from San Diego is that good."

"Coach Wooden, you have to see him play," Crum said. "I will take you down there and show you him."

Crum set up a visit.

"Coach Wooden didn't really like to recruit," Crum said. "So I called Coach Wooden's wife and told her that he would be home late the next night because we were going to San Diego."

They went down to San Diego to catch Walton in action. As was Wooden's preference, he and Crum sat up in a corner of the gym so as not to be recognized, lest Wooden spend the night answering questions and signing autographs.

"Walton scored 30," Crum said. "That wasn't the amazing thing though. What was impressive was how he did it. Bill's team averaged 90 points a game and gave up only 40 a game—so they won by an average margin of 50 points a game. Bill's role was to play center. And he played the point in a 1-2-2 zone defense. They played three guards, Bill Walton and this big football player. When Bill was on defense at the top of that zone, no one got the ball at the top of the key because Bill would block the ball. Any long pass from the other team, Bill would just gobble up. The other three kids—the guards on Bill's team—would see Bill get the ball and they'd fly down the court, three on one or three on two. Bill or the football player would get the ball and just throw it to midcourt, and those three guards would get big points in transition. They'd have the ball in the basket by the time Bill reached midcourt. But he still dominated the game at both ends. So Bill didn't get many shots because they didn't run a set offense that much. Only when they took the ball out of bounds would Bill get the ball on offense. Yet Bill shot 82 percent that year."

When Walton signed with UCLA, Crum helped him find a summer job, which was within NCAA rules at the time.

"Bill was really a non-materialistic kid," Crum said. "He could care less about material things. He just wanted to have something to eat, something to read—he was a big reader—and somewhere to play basketball. Bill's brother and some of his friends had rented a house on the beach in San Diego. I asked Bill if I could help him find a summer job. He said, 'No thanks. I have enough money to get through the summer. I just want to lay around and read.' I told him that was fine, but if he changed his mind, to give me a call. Halfway through the summer my phone rang, and it was Bill."

Walton was still at the beach house.

"I'm out of money, coach," Walton said. "I guess I need a job. Just something to give me enough money to make it through the summer."

Crum called a UCLA alum in San Diego, who ran a contracting business.

"Bill had no carpentry skills, but they hired him to do cleanup work for about $3 an hour," Crum said. "The first day he worked—on a Monday—I got a call. Bill had worked hard and long, and they were pleased."

The phone rang on Friday, four days later.

"Coach Crum," the contractor said. "Bill worked Monday, Tuesday and Wednesday. We pay everyday for general labor, but he didn't show up on Thursday or today. I don't know what the problem is. He was a hard worker."

Crum looked up the number at the beach house. After six rings, Walton, who was enjoying a book and a late afternoon snack out front, answered.

"Hi Bill, Coach Crum here," Denny said. "The contractor called me and said you weren't at work today, or yesterday. Everything all right?"

"Oh yeah, it's fine," Walton answered. "Hey coach, I should have called him. You see, I only need about 60 bucks to make it through the rest of the summer. I have 72 bucks now, so I'm set."

Crum laughed.

"OK, Bill," Crum said. "Just so long as everything's all right. I'll call the guy back and tell him."

"All right, Coach," Walton said. "And thanks."

Crum still gets a smile from the memory.

"The guy would wear his thongs, his cut off jeans and carry a book—and that's all he needed," Crum said. "That's just how he was. What a good kid."

CHAPTER 4

1971-72:
EARLY SUCCESS

L ike children stuck inside the house on a bad day, the 1971-72 Cardinals were restless.

They had gone through six weeks of practice with their new coach, Denny Crum, and now they were eager to show the former UCLA assistant what they could do.

"At UCLA," Crum said, "Coach (John) Wooden took an even approach to games. He didn't believe in letting a team get too high for a game because he reasoned they would have a letdown. He always tried to avoid peaks and valleys. That way, you never lose to a team you're supposed to beat."

The 1971-72 season began in Gainesville, Fla., and Crum's first Louisville team was playing someone it was supposed to beat. Louisville was the preseason favorite to win the Missouri Valley Conference. It was ranked in every preseason top 20, as high as fifth in some polls. Florida, U of L's opener, was picked to finish last in the Southeastern Conference.

Crum knew Florida would be tough for Louisville if for no other reason than the fact that he was installing a brand-new system of play. And he was not especially pleased with the results heading into the start of the season.

"We're making too many turnovers, and our judgment on when to shoot and when to pass is not good," Crum told reporters after six weeks of practice. "But I guess it's better to improve as the season goes along than to peak too early."

On the eve of his opener as U of L's head coach, Crum said, "This is something I've looked forward to ever since I left my junior college job (at Pierce) to work as an assistant with Coach Wooden. But I know Florida will be better than in the past."

Still, no one expected Louisville to lose. After all, it had five returning starters from the 1970-71 team, including one of the nation's premier guards in 6-2 senior Jim Price. Besides Price, U of L had 6-3 Henry Bacon, 6-9 Al Vilcheck, 6-6 Ron Thomas and 6-5 Mike Lawhon. All were seniors, as was 6-foot Larry Carter, who Crum relegated to the bench when he decided to move Bacon to the backcourt and Lawhon to the starting front line. Bill Bunton, a 6-9 sophomore, was waiting in the wings for either Lawhon or Vilcheck to stumble. "We can't be a real good team unless Bunton can beat somebody out," Crum said. "But we do have experience and we do have some good players."

U of L also had Crum, who was as talented as he was outspoken. "I consider him a top head coaching prospect," said UCLA's Wooden. "Denny is an extremely confident person."

But when Crum entered the U of L locker room in Gainesville, just minutes before his first game, he was anything but confident.

"I was worried," Crum said. "I'd never seen a team act like these guys. They were jumping up and down and banging on lockers and shouting and slapping hands. They were restless to get going, and I understood that. But I thought they were a little too jazzed up."

They were.

Florida used a trapping, pressing defense and a matchup zone to beat Louisville, 70-69. The Gators led all the way, but had to hang on when they failed to make a field goal in the last eight minutes. U of L was behind 67-55 with 2:25 left in the game, but scored 14 of the game's final 17 points to nearly pull off the comeback. Tony Miller led Florida with 29 points while Ron Thomas had 21 for the Cards.

"We played a zone because we were afraid Coach Crum would use his big guards the way Coach Wooden does at UCLA," said Florida's Tommy Bartlett.

"We just weren't well enough prepared, and we made a lot of mistakes," Crum told reporters. Then he sat his new team down for a closed-door meeting.

"I told them about the peaks and valleys we tried to avoid at

UCLA," Crum recalled years later. "I told them I never wanted to see them jumping up and down and carrying on in the locker room before a game. When I was a player at UCLA, one of the things Coach Wooden taught me was how to prepare mentally for a game. So I told them I had a better way to do it."

And he did.

Crum got his first victory three nights later in Freedom Hall when U of L doubled the score on Joe Reibel's Bellarmine College team, 116-58. That was the first of 15 straight wins for a Louisville team doing things the "better" way of Wooden, via his protege´, Crum.

Besides giving Crum his first win, the game was significant for two subtle reasons.

First, John Dromo, the former U of L coach, watched the game from his front-row seat, directly across from the Louisville bench. Dromo was misty-eyed when the starting five were introduced for U of L—"Those were my kids," he said later—and the pain of not being involved with a U of L team for the first time since the 1947-48 season tugged at his heart.

Second, this was the last meeting between Bellarmine and U of L. Bellarmine was a small college in Kentucky, and Crum said he wanted to "beef up" the Louisville schedule with more attractive big-name teams. Although Crum would not say so, he may have been angered by comments Bellarmine's Reibel made after the lopsided game.

"They're not really very impressive," Reibel said. "Their zone press didn't really bother us and, they moved the ball very poorly against us. I didn't see the effort I saw last year. Last year I thought Jim Price was the best guard I saw anywhere. But not this time. I don't mean to downgrade the University of Louisville, but I just wasn't impressed with the things they were doing."

Never mind that Louisville led 53-19 at the half. Forget the Cards were just two points short of the school scoring record. So what if Price got 25 points and seven assists in 27 minutes, or that Lawhon had 18 and Bunton 14—Joe Reibel was not impressed.

"It'll take time for the kids to learn my system," Crum said.

As the Louisville players became more accustomed to Crum's system, U of L rolled over Dayton, Kansas, Alabama and SMU. The Cards headed to New York's Madison Square Garden for the Holiday Festival Tournament with a 5-1 record. And with something to prove.

"We had been to the Garden for the NIT at the end of our sophomore and junior years and lost in the first round both years," Price said. "We wanted to show the people in New York that we could play. And we wanted to win some games in New York for a change. We were tired of losing in Madison Square Garden."

The Cards applied their usual full-court pressure in the first round against Syracuse on Dec. 27 and devastated the Orangemen, 96-62 as Price scored 26 and Thomas added 18 points and 12 rebounds.

U of L jumped out to leads of 12-2 and 25-12. But with 16:45 to play, Syracuse pulled to within 11 at 61-50. Crum ordered his team to hold the ball to force Syracuse out of its zone. The move irritated Syracuse coach Roy Danforth.

"Crum must have learned that one from John Wooden," Danforth cracked afterward. "Wooden used that one in the NCAA last year and almost got beat with it. But we came out and chased them around...I'd just as soon lose by 40 as by two. Besides, I bought my wife an $8 ticket, and I wanted her to see a basketball game."

On Dec. 28 in the tourney's second round, Louisville set a school scoring record with a 126-80 rout of St. Peter's. Six players scored in double figures—Thomas 26, Price 21, Lawhon 15, Vilcheck 12, Bacon 10 and sub Ron Stallings 17 in only 10 minutes. But Crum created a furor by keeping his team in the locker room when the national anthem was played before the game.

John Condon, the Garden's public address announcer, refused to read the Louisville starting lineup and then stomped off the floor, declining to work the game. The New York media picked up the story and labeled Crum as "unpatriotic."

"We're patriotic," Crum said. "But we're also superstitious. We came out for the anthem for the Florida game and lost, and we haven't been out since then."

"We respect our coach standing up for us the way he has," Price said. "There's nothing unpatriotic about it. We don't want to cause any trouble. It's just what we normally do, and we'd like for people to respect our feelings."

Said Mike Lawhon, a part-time Sunday school teacher, "We've always had the habit of going into the dressing room and saying The Lord's Prayer in unison while the national anthem was being played."

George Shiebler, commissioner of the Eastern College Athletic Conference, the tournament sponsor, said he would "discuss the matter with Peck Hickman, the Louisville athletic director."

Crum replied, "Hickman doesn't run this show. I do."

But Hickman did soften Crum's stance on the subject, and before U of L's championship game against Fordham, Crum told reporters, "I'll come out with the American flag draped over my shoulder if that will make these people happy. This whole thing is nonsense. It's been blown way out of proportion. We have a routine we go through and that's all it is. If they insist, we'll be out for the national anthem. But we'd rather keep our routine."

U of L did appear for the anthem on Dec. 30. And then it routinely bounced Fordham, 96-82, for the tournament championship. A crowd of 12,333 saw Louisville shoot almost 60 percent as Thomas (28 points, 16 rebounds) and Price (25 points) were named the co-MVP's of the tournament.

"Louisville has great personnel, a strong bench and a great head coach," said Fordham coach Hal Wissel.

After beating Cincinnati and Dayton on the road, Louisville went to Peoria, Ill., to face Bradley in Crum's first Missouri Valley Conference game.

Bradley shot a sizzling 65.5 percent in the first half. The Braves' Sam Simmons and Louisville's Price put on a great one-on-one show in the opening minutes as Joe Stowell's team took a 44-43 lead to the locker room. Bradley increased its lead to 53-46 early in the second half and led 67-60 late in the game when Crum abandoned his usual man-to-man defense for a zone.

The Braves made only two-of-13 shots after that, and Louisville ran off 13 unanswered points for a 75-71 win.

"The zone changed the tempo in our favor, and it protected Price with those four fouls," Crum told reporters. "We were just fortunate to win."

"We took some bad shots against the zone," conceded Stowell.

Price finished with 21. But Crum praised others for Louisville's come-from-behind win. "Al Vilcheck played his finest game of the year (16 points) and Mike Lawhon (10) was just fabulous in the last 20 minutes," Crum said. "Larry Carter really helped us coming off the bench. But the big thing was we kept our poise and ran our offense even though we were behind."

Looking ahead, Crum added, "If we can beat Drake, maybe we can come back home and fill that place up."

Crum's Cards took an 11-1 record to Des Moines, Iowa, on Jan. 22, where first-year coach Howard Stacey and the Drake Bulldogs were waiting. Drake was only 4-9 under the "Gray Fox," but Stacey was eager to beat his alma mater and the team he coached after Dromo's career-ending heart attack.

"I've been watching Louisville's progress and thinking I shouldn't have worked so hard at recruiting when I was there," he said. "We're going through a rough time right now. But we'll have everybody back next year when some other people (Louisville) won't, and maybe then they'll have to do some coaching themselves."

Stacey's back-handed shot at Crum and Louisville heaped fuel on the competitive fire within the first-year Louisville coach. But Stacey had Drake ready to play.

"My players know this is a big game for me," Stacey said, "and they'll be ready."

Truth be told, Drake should have won.

Louisville led by 14 with 6:23 to play, but blew that lead as Bob

Whitley's free throw with one second left tied the score at 69. Whitley had been fouled by Lawhon taking a last-second shot. And now Whitley needed just one free throw for the win. Crum took a timeout to let Whitley think about it, and the strategy worked— Whitley missed the game-winner, and the two MVC rivals headed for overtime.

With just 15 seconds left in overtime and the score tied at 77-77, Bunton rebounded a miss by Drake's Leon Huff. Bunton fired a pass to Price who dribbled behind his back while racing up the sideline near the midcourt. The behind-the-back dribble ditched two defenders. Price then fired a 40-footer that swished through the net to give Louisville the win.

"Jim Price played his worst game of the year until overtime," Crum said. "In the overtime, he played his best game."

Before making the game-winner, Price had canned two jumpers from beyond 20 feet to bring the Cards back from a 77-73 deficit.

"What I did tonight," Price told the *Courier-Journal*, "was keep my head. Coach tells me not to complain. But I'm getting the devil knocked out of me on the court."

Price and Thomas led Louisville with 19 each while Bacon added 14.

The Cards drubbed North Texas State and St. Louis in Freedom Hall, then prepared for a Jan. 29 showdown with Bradley.

Bradley's Stowell figured his Braves could not run with U of L at Freedom Hall, so he decided to slow the game down. Before the Saturday tip-off, he conferred with referee Ray Rippelmeyer about his strategy. Crum saw the conversation, and then called Rippelmeyer over for an explanation.

"A ref can't talk to one coach without the other being there," Crum explained. "So when they got done talking, I asked Rippelmeyer for what had been said, and he told me."

"We wanted to surprise Louisville with the stall, and then the referee goes and tells Crum after I asked him not to say anything," Stowell complained.

A crowd of 10,003 napped while U of L pulled out a 52-46

yawner. Bradley had a chance to tie it late until guard Henry Thomas threw the ball out of bounds with 35 seconds to play and the Braves trailing by two.

Carter came off the bench to spark the Cards with three long bombs. But afterward he said, "I'm like an appendix. It doesn't hurt to take me out, and it doesn't hurt to leave me in."

Vilcheck added, "If I wanted to play that slow stuff, I'd have gone to Tennessee."

Crum, pleased that his team had a perfect MVC record after five games in addition to a 15-game winning streak said, "That kind of thing is lousy TV viewing."

Louisville's No. 4 ranked Cardinals braced for Memphis State's arrival on Feb. 2 and 16,758 fans turned out to see if the two teams would fight or play basketball.

"We're coming to play basketball," said Memphis State's Gene Bartow. "All those fights in the past are behind us. We are ready for this one physically and mentally."

Memphis brought a 12-4 record and talented team to Freedom Hall to battle for the conference lead. The Tigers were led by junior guard Larry Finch and an outstanding front line that included 6-7 Fred (the Chair) Horton, 6-9 Ronnie Robinson and 6-10 Don Holcomb.

Finch got 18, but the heroes for Memphis were Robinson and Horton as the Tigers ended U of L's win steak with a 77-69 victory. Robinson scored 23 points and pulled down 17 rebounds (Holcomb had 16). Horton created havoc playing the point on Memphis State's 1-3-1 zone defense. He also scored 13 points and claimed nine rebounds.

"This was one of the most important wins in Memphis State history," Bartow said. "And it was my biggest win. Crum is a class man, and Louisville is a class operation."

Lawhon led U of L with 19 and Bacon added 14. But Price was held to 10 and Vilcheck made just one-of-9 shots and scored three points.

"The season's not over," Crum told his players afterward. "That's just one loss. But I hope they're not that good all the time."

Stacey and Drake came to town on Feb. 5, and Crum shuffled his lineup at halftime to shake up the Cards. Although Thomas (21 points, 13 rebounds) and Price (20) were good as usual, the real heroes were two subs: Bunton, who had 11 points and 16 rebounds, and 6-6 Air Force veteran Ken Bradley, who had seven points, five assists and four rebounds in 19 minutes at center. Louisville won, 92-75.

"I changed the lineup at the half because the guys in there were not doing the job," Crum said, referring to Vilcheck and Lawhon. "Bradley really sparked us, and Bill Bunton did a good job."

Much had been expected of Bunton, the 6-9 sophomore, who led Male High to the state championship in 1970 and was a standout on the U of L freshman squad the previous year. But Bradley's emergence as a contributor defied explanation. He was too slow and not a very good jumper.

"Stacey (the former U of L assistant) said Bradley couldn't play in the Valley," noted Louisville assistant coach Bill Olsen.

After beating Drake, the Cards rolled over six more opponents to run their record to a gaudy 21-2. When they went to Memphis State on March 2, the Cards were 11-1 in the MVC and the Tigers were 10-2.

Much to the delight of the 11,210 Mid-South Coliseum fans, Vilcheck got in early foul trouble and played just 16 minutes. He took only one outside shot, and Memphis once again dominated Louisville inside and won 80-65. As bad as Vilcheck was, Price might have been worse. He missed 8-of-10 shots and scored a season-low four points. Carter misfired on all four shots and Bunton was errant with all three of his attempts.

Only Thomas, with 19 points and 13 rebounds, and Bacon, with 19 points and 10 rebounds, played up to par.

"Jim sprained his wrist, and that really affected his shooting," Crum said in defense of his star. "Memphis is tough, but I know we can beat them."

Although the Cards were rated No. 2 behind UCLA in the polls, they needed a win over Tulsa on March 6 to force a playoff against

Memphis for the league championship. The Cards got that win, 102-83, as 13,276 paid tribute to eight graduating seniors. Price (24 points), Bacon (22), Vilcheck (16), Lawhon (14) and Thomas (10) were all in double figures for Louisville. Vilcheck's total left him just one shy of 1,000 points for his career.

"No sweat," he told reporters. "I've got five more games to get it—the playoff with Memphis and four more in the NCAA Tournament."

The playoff against Memphis State was on March 11 at Vanderbilt University in Nashville. Both teams finished the MVC schedule with 12-2 records. Although Memphis had beaten Louisville twice, the league rule—later changed—called for a playoff to determine the MVC's representative in the NCAA Tournament.

"The conference has a bad rule because we beat them twice already," Bartow said. "It's hard to beat a good team three times."

Before the game, Vandy's Memorial Coliseum rocked with 15,581 fans that included Louisville Mayor Frank Burke and Kentucky Governor Wendell Ford. Football players from both schools engaged in shoving matches and taunts. The cheering section—evenly divided—shouted back and forth across the floor for a solid hour before the two teams came out to warm up.

In Louisville basketball history, never had a crowd been so intense or geared up for a game. The constant roar of the crowd was so loud that as the U of L team dressed in its locker room, Crum could barely hear himself think.

"You won't believe the crowd out there," an athletic department official told Crum.

"Take me out there," Crum said. "I want to see it."

Crum walked briskly through the long corridor leading to the court. And when he appeared at the end of the tunnel he stood for a long moment to soak in the atmosphere. "Amazing," Crum said. "I have never seen anything like this."

Crum could not resist. He casually strolled onto the court to the thunderous cheers of the Louisville fans. Memphis fans booed loudly as U of L fans cheered. Crum waved at the student section, and the roar became deafening. Crum then thrust his index finger in the air to signify who was No. 1, and the fans went into a higher level of frenzy.

Emotions ran so high before tip-off that officials—afraid it might get ugly—asked members of both teams to address the crowd. That took some of the steam out of the fans.

But it did nothing to cool off the Cards.

Vilcheck poured in eight early points and U of L sprinted out to an 11-6 lead. Crum called a timeout and ordered his team into a stall to bring Memphis out of its 1-3-1 zone. Memphis State refused to match-up man-to-man and Bartow later said, "I turned to my assistants and said, 'We must be pretty good because the No. 4 team in the nation is stalling against us.'"

Lawhon shot over the zone, making six baskets to loosen the Memphis defense, and U of L took a 37-35 lead at the half when Price threw in a long shot at the buzzer.

In the second half, the two teams battled nip-and-tuck to a 62-62 tie before the unlikeliest hero—Ken Bradley—led a closing fury that pushed Louisville to an 83-72 win.

"Baby Huey was the guy!" bellowed Price as he hugged Bradley.

"Everybody did it!" answered "Huey" Bradley.

"Shut up, Huey," answered Price. "You're THE guy."

Bradley, the ex-Air Force man, the 27-year-old center who looked like something right out of the funny pages, scored 13 points, grabbed nine rebounds and passed spectacularly. "Some centers look at me and figure, 'Well, he's nothing,'" Bradley said. "So I run when they walk, and I beat them down the floor even when they're faster than me."

Bradley contributed six points and three assists. But he was not the only Cardinal star. Bacon had a school record 11 assists to go with 16 points. Thomas battled the taller Memphis players on the boards and came away with 19 rebounds and 13 points. Lawhon finished with 12 and Vilcheck added 12 points and eight rebounds. Price had 15 points and hounded Memphis guard Larry Finch into 6-for-20 shooting.

"We finally beat that zone," said Crum. "This was the first time we played them with a healthy team. Thomas was sick the first time they beat us, and Jim was hurt at Memphis."

U of L's fans carried Crum off the court on their shoulders, and later his players tossed Crum in the showers.

"We can win the NCAA if we play like we did tonight," Bradley said.

"Maybe they were a little more hungry than we were," Finch said. "But we wish them all the best of luck in the NCAA."

"I think we're a better team than Louisville, but we weren't today," said a disconsolate Bartow.

After two years of frustration that ended with NIT defeats, U of L's heralded seniors were headed for the Big Time.

Louisville's first NCAA foe was a renegade outfit from Southwestern Louisiana. Although the Cards were rated No. 4 in the nation, many people thought coach Beryl Shipley's team had the talent and size to beat Louisville. Dwight (Bo) Lamar, a perimeter gunslinger, led Southwestern. But 6-9 Roy Ebron carried a 24-point average and was a behemoth on the boards.

Crum warned his team not to look past the first-round game on March 16 in Ames, Iowa. "They're all major hurdles from here," Crum told them. "You look ahead and you get beat."

Southwestern rolled to a 44-39 halftime lead, demonstrating how it was able to run up a 24-4 regular season record. But the Louisville defense tightened in the second half. Price got help off the bench from Bradley and Carter as U of L won, 88-84.

"Price did a job on Dwight," said Shipley, noting Lamar had 29 points but made just 14-of-42 shots. Thomas held Ebron to 11. For the Cards, Price had 25, Thomas 19, Vilcheck 13, Bacon 11 and Lawhon 10. Louisville made 57 percent of its shots to 37 percent for Southwestern. Price won the Regional MVP award after leading Louisville to that regional's crown with a 72-65 win over a small Kansas State squad.

The Cards zoomed to a 20-point lead as Price and Bacon throttled K-State's guard combination of Lon Kruger and Danny

Beard. The 6-2 Price again scored 25 points, and Thomas added 18 points and 14 rebounds.

"I can't wait to get back to Los Angeles," said Crum, whose team was now at 26-3. His return to L.A. for the Final Four was significant for a couple of reasons. First, he was the first "rookie" coach to lead a team to the Final Four. For another, he was returning to the town where he played as a collegian and worked as an assistant coach under John Wooden. And, as fate would have it, his opponent in the first round of the Final Four—the national semifinals—would be Wooden and UCLA.

"I don't really care who we play," Crum said. "I'm very proud of UCLA and what they've done. But we just want to win two more."

As good as Louisville was, it was no match for 19-year-old sophomore Bill Walton—recruited to UCLA by Crum—and his teammates.

UCLA had a 43-game winning streak and had won 30 consecutive NCAA Tournament games. It had the homecourt advantage playing in the Final Four at the Los Angeles Sports Arena. And it had the game's all-time top coach in John Wooden. The 1971-72 Bruins won by an average of 32.3 points during the regular season. "This is," Wooden said, "my most versatile team."

Crum, of course, knew all about that. One year earlier, Crum had been at Wooden's side as the Bruins won their fifth straight NCAA Championship in eight years. Of course, there was also the fact that Crum had recruited most of the players on UCLA's roster.

"Bill Walton was the only player I took Coach Wooden to visit personally," Crum said. "I told him he might be better than Lew Alcindor, and he didn't believe me—he wanted to see for himself."

Walton led UCLA with 33 points, 21 rebounds and five blocked shots as UCLA won 96-77. Larry Farmer, Keith (later Jamal) Wilkes, Greg Lee and Henry Bibby also helped. UCLA led only 39-31 at halftime when the Cards went cold. Lawhon missed all seven of his shots—most of them wide open jumpers after the Cards beat the UCLA press—and Thomas added just four points and three rebounds. Vilcheck managed only one rebound and six points. Had it not been for Bacon's 15 points and the outstanding performance by Price, who had 30 points and held Bibby to only two, U of L might have been beaten much worse.

"The players around Walton are better than the players we had around Lew Alcindor," Crum said. "I haven't seen anyone who can handle Walton one-on-one. This is the best UCLA team I've ever seen."

Crum was disappointed that his usually deft-shooting Cards missed so many shots.

"We broke the press often enough, but we didn't take advantage of it when we got the ball down there," Crum said. "Lawhon had a bad game. Maybe it was just Walton standing there that did it."

Vilcheck, for one, was not impressed.

"Walton was a big crybaby," Vilcheck said. "He complained the whole game. If you touch him, the refs call a foul on you."

Price was more diplomatic. "This has been the most wonderful year of my life. I just wish I had one more year. These coaches have been tremendous. They don't get enough credit."

Credit came to Price from the legend himself, John Wooden.

"Jim is a tremendous ball player," Wooden said. "I'm very impressed with him in every aspect."

While UCLA beat Florida State on March 25 for the national championship, Louisville wound up its season with a meaningless consolation loss to North Carolina as Bob McAdoo scored 30 points and grabbed 19 rebounds.

"You can plan on U of L being back in this thing again," predicted Price. "Even though all of us seniors (eight) are leaving, Coach Crum will get the people you need to win. I guarantee it."

CHAPTER 5

1974-75:
LOSING A FINAL TIME
TO A LEGEND

Junior Bridgeman was a senior when the 1974-75 season began, a three-year starter, the team's and league's Most Valuable Player. But more importantly, Bridgeman was a psychology major. Who better than Bridgeman to explain the plots and sub-plots that gave Louisville fans their most memorable—and painful—game.

Dave Kindred, the former *Louisville Courier-Journal* sportswriter, once wrote of the 74-75 Cardinals, "The University of Louisville doesn't play basketball. It makes Alfred Hitchcock movies. Nothing happens in the beginning. Just some nice scenery and lilting music. But you keep watching because pretty soon a body will turn up in the bathtub."

"Looking back," Bridgeman would say more than a decade later, "I don't think we were challenged (by other teams) enough to stay sharp. There's an old saying in the NBA that the Boston Celtics somehow, some way, will find a way to beat you. And that's the way we were at Louisville that year. We didn't have to play well to win. We could play lousy for 30 or 35 minutes but execute well enough in the end to beat you."

Of course, there were reasons—tons of them—why Crum's fourth and most talented Louisville team did not always play well.

"We were held together with band-aids," said the team's resident psychologist.

At the very least, Louisville had 12 players—maybe more—who could start for most major college teams. In fact, 11 of the team's 12 best players did start for U of L at one time or another during their careers.

"On all good teams with a lot of talent, you'll always have guys who don't get to play as much as they think they should," Bridgeman said. "We had guys sitting on the bench who felt they were better than the guys playing—and maybe they were."

There were five seniors. Besides the 6-5 Bridgeman, U of L had 6-5 Allen Murphy, 6-1 Terry Howard, 6-8 Ike Whitfield and 6-8 Bill Bunton, who was back at center after a year to work on his grades.

Bridgeman, who was so good that after 12 NBA seasons the Milwaukee Bucks retired his jersey, started at guard but played defensive forward. Early in his college career he buried opponents by taking smaller guards underneath for easy turnaround jumpers. By the end of his senior season, he was a terrific perimeter shooter. As good as Bridgeman was, he never thought of himself as the team's best player—he believed Murphy, his roommate for four years, was the best.

"Murph was as good as anybody I ever played with, and that includes the NBA," Bridgeman said.

Murphy was an outstanding shooter but an even better defensive player. As a forward on offense, he was a model of consistency, averaging 16 points for three consecutive years. Going into the 1974-75 season, he had scored in double figures in 41 straight games. Defensively, he drew the opponents' toughest guard.

When Bridgeman was a junior, the Missouri Valley Conference named him its Most Valuable Player. "Allen told me I won the award, and the first thing I said was, 'Oh really, how come you didn't get it?' I mean, when a guy is your leading scorer every year and when he does all the things Allen does," Bridgeman said, "you have to think he deserves an MVP award."

None of the other three seniors were in the running for MVP awards, although Bunton may have deserved one for his rebounding and defense. He was too unselfish and easygoing to get caught up in scoring points. But he enjoyed winning, and more importantly, he genuinely cared about his teammates.

Whitfield wanted to play more than he had as a junior when he transferred from Compton Junior College in Los Angeles. But he knew that with Bunton back his time would be limited. Gradually, he accepted his role and in the end produced mightily when Crum called his number. "Being a senior, with all the talent we do have," Whitfield said, "it's hard for me to play. A lot of players on this team are coming back for two or three more years, and I can understand playing them for experience. If I was a coach, I probably would do the same thing."

Howard had been a starter for two years. When Crum decided to go with younger, quicker guards, Howard considered quitting the team. In seasons past, he had enjoyed giving the ball to his more talented teammates; his thoughts of quitting now, therefore, were not motivated by a sense of selfishness. But this was his senior year, his last opportunity to win a national championship, and he wanted desperately to play an important part in the team's success. Crum's decision to bench Howard was difficult for the coach, who had stuck with his sometimes-erratic guard for two years while absorbing severe criticism for it.

"You can't say that just one thing sets Denny apart from other coaches," said Louisville assistant coach Jerry Jones. "But one of his real strengths as a coach is that he doesn't let personalities influence his basketball decisions. How much he likes a person never influences how much that person is going to play. That's a unique ability that most coaches don't have. Believe me, that's a very, very hard thing to do."

Crum liked Terry Howard. But as much as it hurt Crum to put his senior on the bench, the decision wounded Howard even more. For a while, the sensitive guard walked the brink between self-pity and self-sacrifice. But when he finally decided to bury his pride for the good of the team, he won both the respect and the admiration of his teammates. In the end, of course, Crum found a way to use Howard's talents for handling the ball and shooting free throws.

The team's only junior, 6-5 Tony Kinnaird of Jeffersonville, Ind., had played a key role in a couple of games during the previous season. But Crum suggested—and Kinnaird agreed—that it would be best for him to sit out this year as a redshirt.

Of the sophomores, 6-5 Wesley Cox was the most celebrated. Cox had become the starting center the previous year and won the Missouri Valley Conference's Newcomer of the Year award. If either Murphy or Bridgeman slipped, Cox would be the team's best player and a genuine All-American candidate.

But there were four other sophomores who could play, and play well. Phil Bond, a 6-2 guard who missed the '73-'74 season with mononucleosis, was back and challenging for a starting job. His main competition was 6-4 Danny Brown, who lacked Bond's quickness and speed but provided better outside shooting and was a brilliant passer in the open court. "Everyone wants to be a starter," Brown said. "It's a matter of pride. You're not practicing to sit on the bench."

Billy Harmon, a 6-4 teammate of Brown's at Jennings County High in North Vernon, Ind., turned down Crum's request to redshirt. He thought he could contribute. Stanley Bunton, a slender 6-7 forward, knew his minutes would be limited, but he wanted to play on the same team with his brother, Bill.

"(Bill) Bunton and Harmon didn't want to redshirt, and we never force anybody to redshirt who doesn't want to," Crum said.

The least publicized of the team's freshmen was David Smith, a 6-7 forward from tiny Milltown, Ind., High School. Smith spent most of the season playing with the junior varsity team. But newcomers Rick Wilson (6-4) and Ricky Gallon (6-11) contributed to the varsity almost immediately.

Wilson was a rock solid left-hander who could play guard or forward. He came to Louisville from Atherton High School where he was lightly recruited, turning down Wichita State and a late rush from Kentucky to play for his hometown university.

Gallon was only 16 years old when he was a senior in Tampa, Fla., where he had been recruited by every major college in the nation. Dana Kirk, the assistant coach who signed him, called Gallon "the greatest thing to come out of Florida since the orange."

Crum said he would not trade Gallon—a gazelle with a soft-shooting touch—for either of Kentucky's prized freshmen, 6-10 Rick

Robey and 6-10 Mike Phillips. Gallon had enormous potential. But he was severely lacking in maturity, as Crum and the players would soon discover.

For all of their talent, Louisville's '74-'75 Cardinals were picked by *Sports Illustrated* as the nation's No. 1 team. For three years Bridgeman and Murphy wondered out loud if their U of L teams would ever get the recognition they deserved. For three years they labored in the shadows of Kentucky and the highly publicized Wildcat players, especially Jimmy Dan Conner, Kevin Grevey and Mike Flynn. Bridgeman and Murphy knew they were better than the UK players, who seemed to be getting more coverage. Crum knew they were better, too. He told reporters Murphy "would eat any of UK's guys alive."

"We had finally arrived," Bridgeman said. "With *Sports Illustrated* picking us No. 1, the pro scouts began coming to practice every day. They were at all the games, and we suddenly began to get all kinds of media attention. That part of it was great from Oct. 15.

"But other parts of it were not great," Bridgeman said. "We had a lot of guys who wanted to play, which I understand."

Later in the season, Crum would tell a reporter, "No substitute is ever happy with the amount of time he's playing. If he's averaging 10 minutes a game, he wants 15. If he's averaging 15, he wants 20. I wouldn't want anybody who didn't feel that way."

For the time being, however, Bridgeman and Murphy ignored the unsettled atmosphere that surrounded their team. After all, they were seniors and their starting positions were secure.

Murphy's nickname was "Ink Man" because he had a habit of showing up on the sports page more often than others. One reason for that was Crum, who viewed Murphy as the prototype player for his Louisville program—quick feet and hands, fast and agile, a good shooter and a great jumper.

Murphy came to U of L from Birmingham, Ala. Bill Olsen, the assistant coach who signed him, liked Murphy as a player but loved him like a son. In a day when U of L's entrance exams were very stiff, some questioned whether Murphy could handle college classes. But

Olsen knew Murphy. He knew Murphy had a deep-rooted desire to learn and grow and to lift himself out of the Birmingham ghetto. Olsen put his neck on the line for Murphy. He convinced the admissions office that Murphy desired an opportunity to at least try. And when Murphy earned his degree in the mid-'70s, Olsen's faith in the "Ink Man" was vindicated.

"When he was a freshman," recalled Olsen, "Allen had the toughest English teacher at U of L, Mrs. Meta Riley Emberger. Mrs. Emberger took a lot of pride in developing her students and was willing to devote whatever extra time necessary to help them achieve success in her class. Allen was a willing student but not thoroughly prepared coming from high school. He failed English under Mrs. Emberger at his first attempt. He could have asked for an easier English section, but he felt he was learning for the first time in his life and appreciated the help. He loved that teacher, and she loved him. He worked hard under her guidance and eventually passed."

Olsen believed all along that Murphy would pass.

"Allen Murphy," Olsen said, "cared about doing the right things in life. A lot of players would have taken the easy way out. But not Allen. To Allen, the most important thing was that he learned, not that he made an A, B, C or whatever."

"Murph was shy when he first came to U of L," recalled Bridgeman. "He wasn't real good at expressing himself. But he always went to class and worked hard to improve. By his sophomore year, it was amazing how far he had come along. We had a great time together. One of the luckiest things that happened to me was having Murph as a roommate. The reporters loved him because he was funny and great to interview."

The reporters also loved Bridgeman, who answered questions introspectively as one would expect from a psychology major.

If academics made Murphy a risky recruit, they made Bridgeman a college admission officer's dream. He had been vice president of the student council and the senior class at Washington High School in East Chicago, Ind. He was president of the school band, a member of the National Honor Society and a National Merit Scholarship semifinalist. He graduated in the top 10 percent of his class.

Those weren't the only differences between Murphy and Bridgeman. Murphy was from the Deep South; Bridgeman from the frigid north, off the mean streets of East Chicago. Murphy honed his basketball talent in Birmingham's asphalt rough-and-tumble playgrounds. Bridgeman was too busy for the playgrounds—he spent most of his free time singing for the church choir.

For all their differences, there was a common bond that tied Murphy and Bridgeman together: They knew what it meant to be poor. Murphy had grown up in a small shanty in the belly of Birmingham. Bridgeman was raised in a tiny, three-room house in East Chicago, a sooty slum that was known for its steel mills, one of which happened to employ Ulysses Bridgeman, Sr.

When *Sports Illustrated* said Louisville was the nation's best team in November 1974, Murphy and Bridgeman piled into Junior's $400 Galaxy 500—"It was actually a double-zero," Bridgeman said. "The '5' was always falling off"—and to celebrate they headed to the pair's favorite restaurant, which was "wherever we had a two-for-one coupon," Bridgeman said.

"Me and Murphy were a little cocky," said Bridgeman, who was pictured with his roommate in the *Sports Illustrated* feature. "We knew we had the players. The talent was there. But we also knew it was now or never."

Louisville's season opener at Houston was the toughest in Crum's four seasons—and his teams had lost the previous three. Houston featured 6-9 Lewis Dunbar, 6-11 Maurice Presley and 6-2 Otis Birdsong. "I don't think a loss would hurt us," Crum said. "We've lost our opener every year, and it hasn't hurt us. But we don't intend to lose."

Crum knew his fourth Louisville team was something special. In a conversation with reporters before the season began, someone asked Crum if U of L could win the national championship. "Yes, sir," said the coach. "I'm not being a pop-off. I'm just being honest."

Crum decided to start Brown in the backcourt with Bridgeman for the Dec. 2 opener. "Danny doesn't turn the ball over as much as the others," Crum said. "And his outside shooting is better." Bunton was back in the middle after his one-year absence, and U of L had, perhaps, the two best forwards in Cox and Murphy.

In its first game, Louisville was ragged as usual, making only 40 percent of its shots. Houston's leaping front line blocked an amazing 15 shots. But a three-point play by Bridgeman with 21 seconds to go put the Cards in front, 89-87 and two free throws by Bunton gave Louisville a 91-87 victory.

"That's only our third loss here in five years," said Houston Coach Guy Lewis. "We have nothing to be ashamed of. We were beaten by a great team."

Crum used 10 players, and several turned in sterling performances. Bridgeman had 18 points and eight rebounds. Murphy ran his streak to 42 consecutive games in double figures with 20. Gallon played 19 minutes and collected eight points and eight rebounds. But Brown played tentatively and made just one-of-five shots while Bond, who replaced him during the first half, connected on four-of-seven shots and finished with nine points.

If the Cards had an outstanding player, it was Cox, who finished with 21 points and 16 rebounds and drew raves from Houston's Guy Lewis. "My gosh," Lewis said, "is Cox good or what? He's great!"

Because there was so much competition for playing time and because everyone wanted to impress Crum, Louisville was not a well-oiled machine in his second game, a 76-65 win at Dayton. Gallon, in his second college game, came off the bench to play 19 minutes, score 10 points and grab 11 rebounds. When Dayton pulled to within three at 56-53 with 10:15 left to play, Gallon responded with eight straight points to put Louisville in front.

"Ricky just dominated 'em offensively and defensively," said U of L assistant coach Dana Kirk, who considered the 6-11 freshman his personal project. "He turned it around."

"I love to shoot," said Gallon. "The guys were giving it to me, and I put it up. I wish all I could play was offense. I really do."

At times, that's all he did play. But Dayton's Don Donoher was impressed. "He's already arrived," he said. "I can't imagine what he's going to be like over the next four years."

Crum was less enthused.

"We just didn't play together. Everybody was going one-on-one," Crum said. "This is still a team game. You can't be helter-skelter and take 20-foot shots. I told them at halftime I would play the players who hustled. I didn't care if we won or lost. If you get outhustled, that's something to be ashamed of."

When Louisville won 84-75 at Florida State on Dec. 14 for its third consecutive victory, Crum decided Bond should start ahead of Brown in the backcourt. That decision gave Louisville its first-ever all-black starting unit, and Crum bristled when someone mentioned it to him.

"So what," Crum snapped. "I don't care if a guy is red, black, white or green. Color isn't important, at least not to me. If people in Louisville are worried about that, then they hired the wrong coach."

If Crum was defensive about starting five black players, he wasn't the only coach who had to deal with the changing colors of college basketball. At Washington State, coach George Raveling faced a similar situation. Raveling, an African American, received a complaint from his athletic director. "He said I should recruit more white players to keep the folks in Pullman happy. So I signed Rufus White and Willie White."

Brown responded to his demotion by coming off the bench to score 12 points on six-of-eight shooting. "It looks like Danny plays better coming off the bench," Crum said. "I think he's more relaxed that way."

But Bond was equal to the challenge in U of L's next game, a 90-75 romp past Clemson in Freedom Hall. The 6-2 sophomore scored a team-high 16 points, making seven-of-12 field goal attempts. If players were battling for starting jobs, the Bond vs. Brown confrontation was clearly one of the team's most interesting early-season skirmishes.

Crum found out just how good his fourth-ranked Cardinals were on Dec. 21 when they traveled to Milwaukee to play Al McGuire's sixth-ranked Marquette Warriors.

"There was no way Louisville would be coming here if I were doing the scheduling," said McGuire's assistant Hank Raymonds. "When Denny Crum calls up, asking for a game with us in Milwaukee, you know he's got to be loaded. I'd prefer playing a softie."

McGuire used the occasion to unveil the team's new uniforms, designed by fashionable forward, Bo Ellis. Besides the 6-9 Ellis, Marquette had a load of talent that included lightning quick guards Lloyd Walton and Butch Lee and a stylish 6-6 forward, Earl Tatum.

Marquette's starting lineup was one of the nation's best, but McGuire's bench was no match for Crum, who used his full deck of Cards.

"We won because we have 10 or 11 guys who can play and still do the job," Bridgeman said after U of L's stunning 80-69 victory.

Neither team got much done in the first half when the officials whistled 27 fouls. With Bridgeman scoring 12 of the Cards' first 25 points in the second half, the Cards raced out to a whopping 56-38 lead. During that run McGuire took his team out of its customary 2-1-2 zone defense and, as Murphy said afterward, "We picked them apart."

Bridgeman led of U of L with 22 points and 10 rebounds, playing in the same arena he would later star in as a member of the NBA's Milwaukee Bucks.

"I'm proud of you guys," Crum told his players in the locker room. "Really proud. I think we can play lots better. We made a ton of mistakes. But I'm really proud."

"I voted them No. 1 last week, and I'll vote them No. 1 again," said McGuire, who was gracious in defeat—which was only Marquette's fourth loss in its last 111 home games. "If we played 10 times, we might win one. They're dynamite. They seem destined to be a team to do something great this year if they stay together."

That was a very big "if."

The band-aid, as Bridgeman called it, was starting to come

loose. By the time the Cardinals hosted their own Holiday Classic in Louisville in December, many of the bruised egos were painfully exposed.

One of those suffering was Wesley Cox, an enormous success in the first few games but struggling in the team's most recent two wins. To be fair, Cox was playing on a sprained ankle, and he had a chronic asthma problem that affected his endurance. But when Louisville beat Western Kentucky 107-81 on Dec. 26, it was Cox's wounded psyche that most hampered his performance.

Cox had a boat-load of talent, but even more pride. He wanted the team to win and had always been a team player. But he also thought that with his considerable talent, he could lead the team. On a team as immensely talented as this one, however, no one else thought the road to victory ran directly through Wesley Cox. Neither did Crum, although he doubted that Louisville could win a national championship without its most gifted star.

So the rumors were rampant after U of L's win over Western that Cox was going to transfer. Cox had played only seven minutes against Western. Late in the first half, Crum stood in front of the Louisville bench and admonished his star. "Pass the ball, Wesley!" Crum shouted.

"Take me out!" Wesley shouted back.

But only 38 seconds remained in the half and Crum waited until halftime to bench his sophomore forward.

When Cox was asked by reporters in the locker room after the game why he only played in the first half, he pointed at Crum and said, "You'll have to ask him."

"Wes sprained his ankle Monday, and he was having a rough time getting up and down the court," Crum answered.

Not that Whitfield, Cox's replacement in the second half, did any better—he missed all seven of his shots.

Louisville's ho-hum 79-61 win over Florida State in the Holiday Classic final on Dec. 28 marked Cox's fourth straight sub-par performance. In 24 minutes he managed only 2-of-6 shooting for four points and had four rebounds.

But there were enough other stars to fill the void. Bond had 11 points, Bridgeman missed only one shot and scored 18, Bunton had six points but a game-high 15 rebounds—and Murphy scored 20 to walk away with the tournament's MVP award. And then there was freshman guard Rick Wilson, who handed out four assists, scored all eight of his points when it mattered—and did all that in 15 minutes, causing some fans to wonder why he wasn't starting.

"Rick Wilson is not developing," said Phil Bond when asked about his young team's improvement. "He's always been tough. He's just showing what he can do."

Crum was pleased with MVP Murphy and all-tournament guard Bridgeman, but he chastised the press for leaving Bunton off the all-tournament team.

"I don't know who voted," Crum said, "but if you guys did, you did a lousy job. Bunton deserved to be there. When somebody like Bill doesn't make it, it's not right."

Sports Illustrated covered the tournament, and in the photo of the Louisville bench the faces of the players appeared to show everything from boredom to disgust.

"I remember the Holiday Tournament," Bridgeman would later reflect. "We looked at the competition and figured we were going to beat these teams no matter what we did. A couple of guys hadn't gotten to play as much as they wanted, and they were beginning to realize they weren't going to play. And they were upset. Because of that, we began to slip some."

Billy Harmon, a high-spirited sophomore, played well in the Holiday Tournament. He came off the bench twice to spark the Cards and ignite rallies. "Billy gives our team a lift when he's in there," Crum said. "He makes us run. He gets a lot of loose balls and he hustles."

"Coach wanted me to redshirt, but I didn't want to, especially not this year," said Harmon. "I felt I could help this team. I'm pleased with the amount of playing time I've played. I always want more time. But as long as he gives me a chance, I feel maybe I'll get to play more. We're 7-0, so you can't complain."

Maybe not, but the rumbles of discontentment were still being felt. And Cox continued to slump.

On Jan. 4, a capacity crowd of 16,233 filled Freedom Hall to see Louisville win its MVC opener, 82-80 against Bradley in a game the Cards should have lost.

Bradley led 70-68 with 10 seconds left and freshman Roger Phegley on the line for a one-and-one chance. He had missed only one of eight previous free throws in the game.

Crum called a timeout just before Phegley was given the ball to shoot. When the two teams lined up for the free throw after the timeout, Crum asked for another. Whether the two timeouts affected Phegley is not known, but the young Bradley star missed when he finally had the opportunity. Bridgeman rebounded, passed to Bond and Crum called another timeout with six seconds to play.

He designed a play to get Murphy an open jumper, but the usually reliable senior missed from 20 feet out. Ricky Gallon tipped the ball in at the buzzer to send the game into overtime.

"Long Tall Shorty was right on time," quipped Bunton in regard to Gallon.

"That was only Ricky's second rebound basket all year," said Crum, who added that he put the 6-11 freshman in the game for just that possibility.

"I like to make moves," Crum said. "Strategy—that's the part of the game I like the best."

"One thing about Denny Crum," Bridgeman recalled, "he always had the ability to take control of a game. He always projected that confidence. And after a while, we expected him to make the right decisions. Even when we felt nervous and thought it was time to panic, Denny always gave you the feeling that it's not time to panic. His strength was his ability to come up with a 'need play' at crunch time."

U of L scored the first seven points in overtime and then relaxed in the closing seconds as Bradley fought back to lose by only two. Bridgeman had 25 points and 10 rebounds and Bunton added 17. Cox played 27 minutes before fouling out, finishing with four points.

After beating Cincinnati 82-74 in a non-conference game, the Cardinals took their No. 3 ranking and 9-0 record to Amarillo for a Jan. 9 MVC game with lowly West Texas State. Once again, Louisville should have been beaten. With 2:55 left to play, West Texas led 51-47. But Cox, who scored only three baskets, put in a rebound shot to cut the deficit to two. Bunton followed that by blocking a shot by William Dise, but at the other end of the court missed the front end of a one-and-one free throw opportunity.

The Texans tried to run the clock down, but Murphy swiped a pass and fed Cox, who passed to Bridgeman for a layup that tied the game with 59 seconds left. West Texas ran the clock and spread the floor again. With six seconds left, freshman Maurice Cheeks drove the lane and lofted a 10-footer, but Bunton blocked the shot, slapping the ball to midcourt. Bond picked it up and scored the game-winning layup as time expired.

"I had to block that guy's shot," Bunton said. "He was open. He never saw me coming. But I saw him."

"I thought there was about 15 seconds left," Bond said. "I had no idea time was running out. I was just trying to beat my man down the floor. The only reason I even hurried was because I didn't want him to catch me."

There was no joy in the Louisville locker room afterward. Players stared blankly at one another. Clearly, this was a 10-0 team with a No. 3 ranking that was, despite the impressive numbers, going nowhere.

"We were totally awful," Bridgeman remembered. "But we found a way to win."

On the morning of Friday, Jan. 10, the players gathered at the Amarillo airport for a flight to El Paso and a 30-mile bus ride for Las Cruces, N.M. On the way they stopped to change planes in Dallas, and everyone agreed that a team meeting was in order. A photographer from WHAS in Louisville, making the trip with the team, got wind of the proposed meeting and approached Bridgeman about the problems.

"This team is still not together," Bridgeman said, thinking he was off the record. "I want to make sure we get together before we fall apart. We could very easily be 0-2 in the conference. And that's unbelievable."

The WHAS photographer called his station in Louisville and reported the news to the sports department. The Associated Press picked up on the story after hearing about it on WHAS radio, and then sent a brief story—quoting Bridgeman—across its national wire service.

Behind closed doors in Las Cruces, N.M., and with only players and managers Steve Mouser and Chris Wood present, the team discussed its problems.

Right off, of course, there were complaints about playing time. Phil Bond had moved ahead of Danny Brown and Terry Howard, both of whom thought they should be playing more, if not starting. Ike Whitfield knew he could play better than Wesley Cox had been playing. Some thought too much time and attention was going to Ricky Gallon when it was Bill Bunton who really held everyone together. Rick Wilson and Billy Harmon played hard and gave the team a lift. They believed they had earned the right for more minutes. Cox thought the others were ignoring his talent. He was worried that everyone was too concerned with individual statistics and not concerned enough with winning. Cox wanted to win. But he also wanted a larger hand in the winning.

Complaints about the coach surfaced, too.

Denny Crum has never been like other coaches. He never put much stock in scouting opponents, believing it was better to spend time perfecting his own team's talents. "Let the other teams worry about stopping us," he said. "If we spend time worrying about them, that just takes away from the time we could be spending to improve ourselves."

Crum differed from other coaches in the way he handled players and established team rules, too.

"We have two rules," Crum said. "Go to class and be on time. We don't have a curfew, and we don't have rules about drinking and smoking. We police each other. Our players know what is expected of them and how they should represent themselves, our team and the university."

In the early '70s, this was revolutionary stuff for a coach. More traditional coaches were taskmasters who ruled with an iron fist. The public—and players—expected that.

"I think I'm fair with the players," Crum said. "I don't treat them all equally because you can't. They're not all equal. They get what they earn. I treat them as adults. I don't expect them to do anything I wouldn't. Part of an education is learning to make decisions and accepting the consequences. If I tried to control their every moment, I'd be doing them a disservice."

At the time, of course, Crum was both young and single. He was handsome and enjoyed being a bachelor.

Some of the players talked in the meeting about the team's lack of discipline. They blamed Crum and his lax rules. They questioned his ability to provide necessary discipline and order to the team.

"Some of the guys were reaching," Bridgeman recalled. "They were reaching out for excuses because they weren't playing well. Players don't usually want to blame themselves. That's human nature. So some of them blamed Denny's lifestyle."

Eventually, the conversation in the players' meeting turned to the media. Everybody was upset that the media reported on the team's problems. No one knew exactly who to blame, but everyone agreed not to talk to the press. That was the first thing everyone agreed on in the meeting, and it was a starting point for bringing the players together.

"The media thing was good because it was a rallying point for all the guys," Bridgeman said. "It was one of those 'Us against them' things, and it brought us all together. But the real problem was playing time for everybody. Some of the guys not playing much blamed the starters for not playing hard all the time. Because of that, we weren't beating teams the way we should have been, and it meant fewer minutes for the guys on the bench."

"So we all agreed that the guys not getting to play were going to subdue their egos for the good of the team. And those of us who were starting were going to play as hard as we could. We were going to go out against New Mexico State and play as hard as we could from the start. And when we got tired, we were going to let Coach Crum know so that he could take us out and play somebody else."

And that's what happened.

New Mexico State was 9-2 and ranked in the top 20. It was a pivotal MVC game matching two of the league's best teams. The Cards broke away from a 12-12 tie, outscoring New Mexico State 25-8 to take a 37-20 lead. For all practical cases, the game was over. In the end, Murphy had 22 points, Bridgeman had 16, Bunton had 14 rebounds and Cox—playing 24 minutes—returned to his usually great self and scored 15, only the second time in a month that he reached double figures. Louisville won, 82-69.

Aside from their worries about playing time, the U of L team was, at times, as close-knit as any that ever wore the Cardinal red. It's unlikely that any group had more fun together from that point on. Cox had a quick wit and a bag full of corny jokes that kept players laughing. Bond and Stanley Bunton were playful pranksters, and Howard and Harmon were especially mischievous. Home-spun humor flowed from the lips of Bill Bunton. The young players had enormous respect for the seniors. And the seniors were amazed— even awestruck—by the talents of the young players.

In addition to their playing abilities, the '74-'75 Cardinals were a team full of good students. Bond was the school's first Academic All-American. Bond, Bridgeman, Cox and Harmon were all named to the league's All-Academic team at the end of the season.

"All that talk about troubles on the team makes me laugh," said Bill Bunton. "All the guys on this team pull for each other. We're close on and off the court. If we weren't, we wouldn't be undefeated right now."

But one day after beating New Mexico State, the team's new-found unity suffered another serious blow.

As the players boarded their commercial flight for the return trip to Louisville, someone noticed that Cox, Stanley Bunton, Harmon and Brown were all missing. The team flew home without them.

"They said they didn't get a wakeup call at the hotel, and nobody noticed they were missing until we got on the plane," Bridgeman recalled. "They spent the whole day at the airport trying to get tickets to Louisville. They didn't have any money, and they had to convince the airlines to put them on a flight. We just had this big unity meeting to pull everybody together. And when they showed up at practice on Monday, they were blaming the other guys for leaving them behind. They wanted to know what happened to the team unity."

Back in Freedom Hall, Drake had a chance to beat U of L, but Ken Harris missed a short baseline jumper with two seconds left, and the game went into overtime tied at 45-45. The Cards woke up and scored the first eight points of overtime, and won the game 55-53.

Louisville ran its streak to 13 by beating St. Louis, but lost for the first time on Jan. 25 when Bradley forced 31 turnovers and outscored the second-ranked Cardinals 12-2 in the closing minutes for a 65-69 victory.

"This was our season for us," said Bradley guard Tom Les.

"I hope this makes us play better and stop having those close games," said Bill Bunton.

The Cards did play better, but not great, in beating New Mexico State and North Texas at home and Wichita State on the road. In that game, on Feb. 6, Murphy's string of consecutive games in double figures ended at 57 games. He made just 3-of-11 shots and scored six points.

"At least I don't have to think about that streak anymore," Murphy said.

Whitfield came off the bench to "play like a million dollars," said Wichita State coach Harry Miller as U of L won, 62-57.

Two nights later on Feb. 8, Murphy slumped to an all-time career low, scoring just three points in a shocking 82-77 loss at Tulsa. Murphy made only one-of-nine shots and found himself in an uncustomary seat on the bench. "I took him out because he wasn't playing well," Crum said. "He was passing the ball to the other team."

The loss dropped U of L to 16-2 but more importantly, 7-2 in the conference. Other than Bridgeman, who scored 32—16 in the final 10 minutes—U of L was awful. "They played harder than we did," Crum said. "We got outhustled. Every game is a crusade for our opponents."

Ken (Grasshopper) Smith led Tulsa's crusade with 26 points and 11 rebounds.

Some observers wondered if Louisville lost because its usually unflappable coach lost his cool six minutes into the game. That's when Crum leaped from the U of L bench and charged into the Fairgrounds Pavilion stands to challenge a heckling fan. Crum had to be restrained by athletic department officials from both schools.

"I think fans should yell for their home team," said Crum, still red-faced after the game. "But when a fan gets personal, that's bush league."

Whether the incident disturbed Crum's concentration enough to affect the outcome of the game will never be known. But Louisville did play like a headless team for most of the first 30 minutes.

If Dave Kindred thought this team was an Alfred Hitchcock thriller, he was only partly correct. In reality, this team had turned into a long-running soap opera. The drama took a different twist on Monday, Feb. 10, when Crum went to the hospital with kidney stones that refused to pass. By Monday night, the doctors were ready to perform surgery. But the pain subsided and surgery was postponed.

Crum remained in the hospital as the team prepared for its most crucial game of the season, Drake, on Thursday, Feb. 13, at sold-out Veteran's Auditorium in Des Moines. Assistant coaches Bill Olsen, Dana Kirk and Jerry Jones put the team through its paces and even added a few new wrinkles, including a change in the fast break or "early" offense and a few low post options for Bill Bunton.

The Cardinals flew to Drake without Crum, who remained hospitalized. But Crum flew to Des Moines on the day of the game with his personal physician, Nat Zimmerman.

"The pressure is on," said Murphy. "It's time for us to be killing somebody or be killed."

"Yeah," added Bridgeman, "it's time to get intense. We have to do what we have to do."

Crum wondered if his team could rise to the occasion. "This team seems to have a lack of respect for its opponents," Crum said.

"They play with no emotion," noted Bradley coach Joe Stowell.

"We might not be very expressive," answered Bridgeman, "but just because we don't slap each other on the back and run or jump around, don't think we don't play without emotion."

A Drake victory would throw the MVC race into a three-way tie with Drake, Louisville and New Mexico State.

With Bunton enjoying a newfound success with the changes in the offense, Louisville raced to a 14-2 lead. Bunton scored 10 of the 14 points. Drake wasn't ready to die, however, and when Crum inserted Gallon to take Bunton's place, the Bulldogs rallied. Midway through the half, Drake's Larry Haralson scored over Gallon to cut the lead to 20-18. And that's when the day-time drama took another turn.

Walking the ball up the floor after Haralson's basket, Bridgeman passed in front of the U of L bench. With one hand he dribbled and with the other he pointed down the floor at Gallon. "Get him outa here!" Bridgeman shouted at Crum.

Crum respected Bridgeman, not just only for his immense talents, but also his intelligence and leadership. He might have been stunned by Bridgeman's uncharacteristic outburst, but he respected the senior guard's wishes. He grabbed Bunton and hurried him to the scorer's table.

"That," Bridgeman would later recall, "was a momentary attack of lunacy on my part!"

Whatever it was, it worked. Bunton blocked three straight shots, and U of L steadied. Drake refused to fold, charged mostly by a crowd of 12,500. Drake was also charged by the belief that it could win after the overtime affair earlier in the year in Louisville.

But a Bunton tip-in with 8:16 left to play pushed Louisville's lead to 10, 64-54. The Cards followed that with nine unanswered points for a 19-point lead, holding on for an 86-66 victory. Murphy was spectacular, scoring 26 points. But Bunton was just as valuable, scoring 14 points and a team-high nine rebounds. Bond and Cox were also in double figures and Brown, coming off the bench, added eight. Gallon finished with six points but saw little time after Bridgeman's request.

"When Ricky Gallon came to U of L, he was heralded as the best center ever and was going to break all of Wes Unseld's records," Bridgeman recalled. "Boy, that was a pipe dream. Everybody expected too much out of him that first year, and that was so unfair. He was a great guy. Talent? He had as much as anybody. He could run, jump and shoot. But when he came to Louisville, he had just turned 17, and most of us were 18 or 19 when we were freshmen. He felt so out of place with us, and we didn't make it any easier for him. We called him 'The Big Kid' and he took it all to heart. He was being asked to grow up and grow up right now, and it was unfair for us to expect that of him.

"But," added Bridgeman, "when you look back to that season and to that game at Drake, Ricky was in way above his head. Denny handled him the right way. But Ricky didn't put out—he didn't practice hard, and guys resented that. It built up and up all year. In practice all week before the Drake game, Bill Bunton had played great, and we had given him some opportunities to score. And in the game, it was working. When I yelled at Denny, it was just an emotional outburst at the moment—just a culmination of what everybody on the team was feeling. All any of the guys wanted from Ricky was just the effort. The rest of us played 100 times harder than Ricky. And we knew it was going to take that kind of effort to beat Drake at Drake. We just didn't believe Ricky was old enough or mature enough at that time to give us the effort that Bill could."

Beginning with the lopsided win at Drake, Louisville won 11 games in a row, a streak that did not end until the one that would end their season in the NCAA tourney.

But the victories did not always come easy for the Cards, who continued to play up and down. Just three days after beating Drake, for example, the No. 6 ranked Cards played then lowly St. Louis in a rare Sunday evening game.

When the two teams went into the locker room at halftime, 12,752 Freedom Hall fans serenaded the Cards with a loud chorus of boos as St. Louis led, 41-26.

"The boos were justified," Bridgeman said. "I would have booed, too. We were terrible."

Crum asked his players if any of them wanted to play. "The first five hands that went up started the second half," Crum said.

Bridgeman and Murphy were not among the starters. But the lineup change did not help. The hungry Billikens were ready to close the casket with 13:23 left and building a 23-point lead, 59-36.

"Hey, coach," called out Murphy, "that's enough."

"Are you ready to play?" Crum asked Murphy.

He was, and so was Bridgeman. Crum put the pair back in the game, and they led an incredible rally. Using a full-court press, Louisville forced St. Louis into 11 consecutive turnovers. The Cards forged ahead and finally won the game by seven points. In the final 13 minutes, Louisville went on a 39-9 run for a 75-68 victory.

On Feb. 20, Louisville came up with an 85-76 win over Wichita State. Murphy and Bridgeman combined for 39 points. But Cox was at his spectacular best, scoring 32 points while setting a record with 15-of-16 shooting from the field. He made his first 11 shots, and all but one came from beyond 12 feet.

"I wasn't trying to prove anything," Cox said. "I was just open."

"That performance was even greater than Bill Walton's 21-of-22 in the NCAA Final," said Wichita State coach Harry Miller. "Walton made most of his baskets from in close. Cox scored from everywhere."

Bob Elmore, Wichita State's 6-10 shot blocker, prevented Cox from making all 16 shots when he slapped away his 12th attempt. "That wasn't a shot—I was trying to pass the ball," Cox said. "If I had been shooting, Elmore would never have blocked it."

The Cards improved to 20-2 and gained a measure of revenge with a 104-79 triumph over Tulsa on Feb. 22.

"Louisville comes to play every game," said Tulsa coach Ken Hayes. "I'm tired of hearing they don't take all games seriously. They've got chemistry just like every other team, and nobody plays in top shape all the time."

Tulsa's Ken (Grasshopper) Smith, who buried the Cards earlier in the season, was held to 7-of-19 shooting by Murphy. "The Hopper wasn't hopping tonight, was he?" noted Bridgeman.

Cox had 21, Murphy 16, Bridgeman 16, Bond 14 and Wilson came off the bench to add 10.

"They're just a sensational team," said Tulsa's Hayes.

And he was right. At long last, through all of their struggles and differences and problems, the Cardinals had finally become a team. And not just any team—a sensational team. When the regular season came to an end on March 6, the Cardinals had the MVC Championship wrapped up and a berth waiting for them in the NCAA Midwest Regional. They put the finishing touch on a weird and wacky season by beating Dayton, 83-67 in the finale, in which Crum started five seniors. Cox was in street clothes on the bench, trying to recover from a painful hamstring pull that made him doubtful for the NCAA Tournament.

In an emotional pre-game farewell against Dayton, the five seniors were honored by a crowd of 14,109 and the U of L athletic department. Of course, the longest and loudest ovations were for Bridgeman and Murphy, undoubtedly two of the best players in Cardinal basketball history.

Although Whitfield stole the show by producing 14 points and five rebounds in a rare start—"Ike plays that well in practice all the time," Crum said—Murphy and Bridgeman combined for 30 points and 18 rebounds in their last home game. When Crum removed his seniors from the game, he saved the roomies for last. It was fitting that Crum removed Bridgeman and Murphy from the game at the same time. For three seasons they had been inseparable friends. They came in together to build on U of L's growing basketball tradition, and they deserved to go out together.

Even Dayton coach Don Donoher acknowledged the moment.

"You kind of sit and wish you were going through that again," said Donoher, who had pulled his team off the floor so Bridgeman and Murphy would be alone in the adulation. "They deserved that ovation. Those two guys gave these fans some great basketball."

"That moment," Bridgeman recalled, "you don't want it to end. When we came (to Louisville), me and Murphy didn't really have a sense of U of L basketball history. I'd followed the Big Ten, and Murphy grew up in SEC country. The rivalries with Memphis State and Bradley and Drake and Cincinnati and Dayton were all new to us. But as each year went by, you grew, and you became more and more involved in it. And you began to realize the magnitude. On the other hand, you're glad you made it through. It was a relief. There was so much pressure to win every game in the conference. There was pressure to beat a Memphis State on a Thursday night and then you had to go back to the dorm and study all night for a mid-term exam on Friday morning.

"But that final moment, when you realize it's all over, it's something you hold on to forever. College was such a great family feeling. It was the best four years of my life."

If Louisville rarely played up to snuff in winning 24 of its 26 regular season games, the Cards were ready to tap their remaining potential in the NCAA Tournament.

"We reached our potential less that season than the two previous years," Bridgeman recalled. "But that was the first time we felt the pressure of having to play up to our potential."

Louisville looked like a team wilting under the pressure in the tournament opener on March 15. Playing a quick, aggressive Rutgers team (at Tulsa's Oral Roberts University), U of L fell behind 39-31 in the closing minutes of the first half. They rallied, but still trailed 46-44 at the intermission.

"We got on them at halftime for dilly-dallying around," Crum said. "We were just getting outhustled."

A 12-2 burst late in the game and some exceptional outside shooting by Bridgeman—he was 15-of-18—carried the Cards to a 91-78 win.

"That first half put a scare in my heart," Murphy said. "This is my last go-around. And I didn't want it to end here."

"If we don't get this one," admitted Bridgeman, who scored a career-high 36 points and grabbed 11 rebounds, "they don't get any bigger."

Murphy had 16 points, while Bunton had 13 and 11 rebounds. But part of U of L's problem was Cox, who was heavily bandaged and slowed by his injured hamstring. He scored six points and picked off seven rebounds in a game he probably should not have played.

One of Louisville's heroes was Howard, who had been called on all season to direct U of L's four-corner offense. When Louisville fans saw Crum call on his heady senior guard, they knew Howard would put the game on ice by freezing the ball and hitting the important free throws.

Against Rutgers, Howard did his thing in the closing minutes and was perfect at the free throw line, 4-for-4.

"That makes 24-for-24 at the foul line," a reporter told Howard after the win in reference to Howard's perfect mark that season.

"Don't tell me that," Howard said, hoping to avoid a jinx.

"It was just one of those games," Bridgeman said. "Last year, we lost to Oral Roberts on this floor, and I had a miserable game. In my mental preparation for this game, I just wanted to make sure that didn't happen again."

The Cards moved to the familiar surrounds of Las Cruces, N.M., to face a familiar rival, Cincinnati, in the tournament's second round.

Bridgeman was also as spectacular in the second game of the tourney, canning his first six jumpers over the Cincinnati zone as U of L rolled up a stunning 42-25 halftime lead. The Bearcats returned to their normal man-to-man pressure in the final 20 minutes, but it was too late to change the outcome. With Bridgeman getting 20, Gallon 16, Murphy 13 and Bond 10, Louisville romped into the Midwest final, 78-63.

"It was a coaching error," Cincinnati's Gale Catlett confessed after the game. "We should not have been in a zone defense at the beginning. It would have made a different game had we been man-to-man against them."

"It surprised me," Bond said. "Of all the teams we play, Cincinnati gives us more trouble man-to-man than any other."

Crum was especially pleased with Gallon's performance. The 6-11 freshman had the 16 points and six rebounds in 17 minutes. "He just turned 18 on March 12," Crum said. "There's a pressure on a kid 99 percent younger than everybody else in the tournament."

Whitfield also filled in admirably for the ailing Cox, scoring eight points in the first half.

Crum was asked before the Maryland-Notre Dame game if he had a preference for the Midwest Final. "I'd like to play the worst one," Crum said. "But the worst one usually doesn't win. So we'll play who we get."

In this case, the worst may have won as Maryland got 24 points from John Lucas in an 83-71 win.

"Although we didn't know it at the time," said Bridgeman, "we had too much talent for Maryland. I talked to John Lucas about that game when we played together in the NBA. He told me they were intimidated, that they had never seen a team in the ACC with talent like we had. 'You had so many guys who could run and jump,' he told me. 'We couldn't play with you guys.'"

That was simply the truth.

Although Bridgeman picked up his third foul in the opening 15 minutes and Murphy would foul out with 8:36 left in the game, Louisville stormed into the Final Four with a 96-82 victory.

At long last, the Cardinals were being challenged. And they were responding with royal performances. Louisville sprinted ahead of Maryland early and maintained a lead for most of the first 30 minutes. The Cards led 71-55 midway through the final period. But behind Lucas, Maryland rallied to cut the margin to four, 82-78, with 4:20 left to play.

Bunton scored on a follow shot and Bridgeman came up with his fourth steal. Crum sent Howard and Brown into the lineup to join Bond, and the slick Cardinal guards closed the door on a

Maryland rally. Bond beat his man down the middle and dished off to Gallon, who laid it in for an 86-78 lead. First Bond, and then Howard—who was now 28-of-28—made free throws, and Louisville was headed for the Final Four in San Diego.

"Nobody said anything before the game," said Murphy, who scored 20. "But you could tell how intense everyone was by the quiet. We were all concentrating on the game."

"Those were all the marbles down there," said Bunton who scored 13 points and 12 rebounds. "This was it for the seniors."

"Wes is nowhere near healthy," said Crum, talking about his ailing 6-5 sophomore, Cox, who nonetheless scored 15 points and grabbed nine rebounds. "But he made up his mind to play."

Bond, who led U of L with 23 points, picked up the tournament's MVP award, too.

"We played scared," said Maryland guard Moe Howard. "They're the best team we played all year. We shut down Bridgeman and Murphy, then Cox, Bunton and Bond killed us."

"I never felt this is a one-man team and today proved it," Bridgeman said. "One-man teams get beat. This is not a two-man team, either. We're a 12-man team. Everyone did a great job today."

Cox and the two Bunton brothers had more than one reason to celebrate that March 22 victory. Back home in Louisville, their alma mater, Male High, won the state championship for coach Wade Houston, who would later join Crum's staff. A couple of talented juniors, Darrell Griffith and Bobby Turner, led the Male High charge.

But the Cards quickly turned their attention to the Final Four.

Joining Louisville in the Final Four were West champion UCLA, Mideast champ Kentucky (which upset No. 1 Indiana in the regional final) and East champ Syracuse. UCLA was 26-3, Kentucky 25-4, Syracuse 23-7 and Louisville 27-2. Strangely, the Cards' win over Maryland dropped them in the polls. UCLA replaced Indiana as No. 1 and Kentucky moved up to second, IU slipped to third and Louisville slipped from third to fourth.

Crum said the polls were meaningless. But he ripped the media for leaving Bridgeman off the Associated Press All-American squad.

"You guys who voted for that team are going to look pretty silly when Bridgeman goes in the first round of the pro draft—and he wasn't even an All-American," Crum bristled to reporters.

As the Cards prepared for the semifinal game with UCLA, basketball fans across the nation buzzed with anticipation. The NCAA championship offered a variety of strange, intriguing plots.

For one thing, Crum was going up against his former coach and mentor, John Wooden. It was their second meeting in the finals in four years. UCLA beat the Cards 96-77 in 1972, Crum's first season at Louisville.

For another thing, there was the possibility that Kentucky, which to that point had refused to schedule Louisville, would finally have to meet Crum and the Cards.

"Nobody on our team mentioned Kentucky," Crum said. "But I hope we get to play them—because that would mean we are playing for the national championship."

Well, not exactly. If both teams lost in the semifinals, they could be playing in a meaningless consolation game.

"I know there's a rivalry between us," Bond said. "But it feels good to see Kentucky here. It's nice having two Kentucky teams in the Final Four."

"There was a lot of pressure in the NCAA Tournament," Bridgeman remembered. "But it was different than the pressure you feel during the season. The season got to be such a grind. But now you had people pumping you up everywhere you went. Everybody was excited and patting you on the back and getting you ready to play—it was great fun."

Bridgeman wondered if he was perhaps destiny's darling in 1975. "Two of my teammates in high school, Tim Stoddard and Pete Trgovich, had played on NCAA champions in 1973 and 1974. Pete won it with UCLA in '73, and Tim won it with North Carolina State in '74. Even though Pete was back again with UCLA, I felt like 1975 was my team."

Jerry Lucas, the great Ohio State center who led the Buckeyes to the NCAA title in 1960, agreed with Bridgeman. As the four teams went through one-hour workouts in the San Diego Sports Arena on March 28, one day before the semifinals, Lucas watched.

"I really like Louisville's team," Lucas said. "They have great athletes. That's the team I'm picking to win it all."

Lucas was in San Diego to work NBA's telecast of the Final Four with veteran announcer Curt Gowdy and color commentator Billy Packer.

"I'll never forget the day before the game with UCLA," Bridgeman recalled. "Everybody was so pumped up. It was just a great feeling to be there." The Cards were not in awe of UCLA. A year earlier, the Bruins' incredible string of seven consecutive national championships had been broken by North Carolina State.

"We're not playing dead because it's UCLA," said Bill Bunton.

What Bunton and other U of L players did not—and could not—realize at the time, however, was that UCLA was a team on a mission. Dave Meyers, UCLA's superlative senior, told a friend in later years that the Bruins were determined to give Wooden another title because they knew he could retire soon.

Bunton knew all about UCLA. He was a sophomore on the 1972 team that had received its comeuppance from the Bruins and Bill Walton. The 1975 Bruins who met Louisville on March 29 in San Diego featured the 6-8 Dave Meyers and 6-7 Marques Johnson at forward. Ralph Drollinger, a 7-2 center, shared time in the pivot with 6-10 Richard Washington. Andre McCarter and Pete Trgovich anchored UCLA's backcourt although Jim Spillane played some, too.

"It was strange," Bridgeman said. "There was no look of confidence in their eyes, and I'm sure there was none in our eyes, either. We were like two boxers staring at each other before the big fight."

Ten minutes into the game, Louisville had a 27-18 lead that could have been even bigger had Bridgeman—soaring high above the rim for two alley-oop passes—not missed on both attempts.

In 1975 NCAA rules did not allow players to dunk. In 1967, college rule makers voted the dunk out of the game, immediately after Lew Alcindor's (later Kareem Abdul-Jabbar) sophomore season at UCLA. Coaches who voted for the rule change argued that the dunk was too easy for big men and threatened to turn college basketball into a game only taller players could play. But there was an ulterior motive behind the ban on dunking. As long as Alcindor could stand close to the basket and catch lob passes, UCLA was assured of winning most every game. The real purpose of taking out the dunk, therefore, might have been to handcuff a powerful UCLA program.

Against UCLA in the 1975 semifinals, the Cardinals began to be plagued by turnovers as the first half wore down. Gradually, the Bruins closed within four points, 37-33 at halftime.

The two teams slugged it out, toe-to-toe, basket-to-basket, in the final 20 minutes. UCLA never led by more than two points at any time in the game. On the other hand, Louisville's largest lead was just six in the second half.

The Cards held that six-point lead, 59-53, late in the game when Meyers and Washington sparked a rally for UCLA. But with 1:06 left to play, Bond was fouled and went to the line for Louisville. He dropped in both free throws and Louisville's lead was 65-61.

"We had the game won," Bond said. "And suddenly, we were in overtime."

Meyers drove into the lane but Bunton—helping out as he had all season—blocked the 6-8 forward's shot. Meyers got his own rebound and shot again. And again, Bunton rose to block it. But Washington came up with the loose ball. And with 48 seconds left, he put up an off-balance shot in the lane. Bunton swiped at the ball, but caught Washington's arm. Washington hit both free throws to close the margin, to 65-63. Wooden ordered UCLA into a zone press and Cox, inbounding the ball, fired cross-court in the direction of Bunton. But Marques Johnson stole the pass and fed Jim Spillane, who missed. But Johnson was there for a tip-in to tie the game, 65-65.

Cox again threw the ball inbounds, this time to Howard—who was put in the game to run the four-corner offense. Howard passed cross-court to Bunton. Johnson tipped the ball off of Bunton's hands and out of bounds, giving the Bruins the ball with 34 seconds left. After UCLA had a shot blocked by Bunton, Bridgeman's 12-footer missed everything. Bunton was in position to catch the ball and put it in, but he just couldn't get a handle on it, and time expired in regulation with the two teams tied at 65-65.

"The ball had a funny spin on it," Bunton said. "It just spun out of my hands."

In the memorable overtime, Murphy put U of L ahead with a soft, 14-footer. Spillane tied it at 67-67 with a 15-footer. Murphy countered for Louisville, scoring on a lay-up and drawing a foul from UCLA's Andre McCarter. His free throw gave U of L a 70-67 lead.

Washington answered for UCLA with a turnaround 10-footer to cut the margin to 70-69. But two free throws by Murphy put U of L up 72-69. Marques Johnson again answered the call with a follow-up off a rebound to cut the margin to one, 72-71. But Cox, still heavily bandaged around the sore hamstring, tipped in a basket to put Louisville ahead, 74-71, with 1:18 left. However, Cox fouled Meyers at the other end and the UCLA All-American made both free throws to narrow the gap to one, 74-73.

Crum called a timeout and ordered his team into the four-corner to use the clock. The Cards were 5-0 in overtime games over the past four seasons. And if UCLA chose to foul, that could benefit the Cards, since the 1974-75 U of L team led the nation in free-throw shooting at 76 percent. And, of course, Howard was 28-of-28.

"Don't foul Howard!" Wooden told his team as they broke from the huddle.

So what happened? UCLA's McCarter went out and fouled Howard.

With 20 seconds remaining in overtime, Howard shot his 29th free throw of the season. "I thought it was in when I let it go," Howard said.

But it missed, and the Bruins hurried across midcourt before calling their final timeout. Crum sent the Cards back out in a 2-3 zone, and Washington found a seam on the baseline, 12 feet from the basket. Bunton saw the pass coming and reached out just enough to tip the ball, but it wasn't enough. Washington turned and scored, lifting UCLA to the win, 75-74.

Louisville used its last timeout to set up a long shot for Murphy, but he fumbled the inbounds pass near midcourt, and his 40-foot prayer went unanswered.

Washington led the Bruins with 26 points. Murphy was the game's leading scorer with 33 while Bridgeman had 12 points and 15 rebounds. Cox had 16 rebounds to go with 14 points, but struggled from the free throw line, making just 4-of-11 attempts.

Terry Howard sat in the Louisville locker room, his head buried in a towel, sobbing, as did others. The Bunton brothers leaned on each other for support while Murphy banged his fists in frustration on the walls and lockers with tears running down his cheeks.

"Of all the losses in high school, college and 12 years in the NBA," Bridgeman said, "that was the worst I've ever known. I'll never forget everybody's reactions in that locker room. It was not a loss. It was a death. I'd roomed with Murphy for three years, and yet I was totally unprepared for his reaction. I'll never forget that locker room."

Denny Crum worried about Howard.

"I feel sorry for Terry—but I don't want anybody putting the blame on him. He's a kid who has had to sacrifice a lot after starting for two years. And he has worked his butt off for this team."

Some in the media did blame Howard, infuriating Crum.

"We wouldn't have been where we were if it weren't for Terry— he won a lot of games for us," Crum said. "He had a great, great career. And he's had to take a lot of heat over the years. I have a world of respect for Terry Howard. We didn't lose that game because he missed a free throw. We had a lot of guys miss free throws. And give UCLA some credit. They played well."

"It was a great, great game," remembered Bridgeman. "Most things in life grow bigger as we grow older. But from a fan's standpoint, it was a great game."

"Usually, we have to play against a lot of factors besides basketball talent," said UCLA's Dave Meyers. "Players talk at you, cuss at you. Here were two teams not saying a word, doing everything they could to win a basketball game. Playing hard, playing clean. That's what it's all about. It was a great game. It was like looking in a mirror and seeing yourself."

"I know how the kids feel, and I'm disheartened for them," Crum told reporters in the post-game press conference. "But I can't feel disappointed with the way we played. I couldn't be prouder of a bunch of guys. We tried and we lost to a great team with a great tradition. The scoreboard may have said we lost, but this team has been, and always will be, a winner."

At the other end of the building outside the UCLA locker room, Wooden began to speak.

"Before I answer questions about the game," Wooden said. "I would like to announce that Monday night's championship game will be my last at UCLA."

A lot of things were going to change. But other things would remain the same. One thing was certain: The 1974-75 season for the University of Louisville basketball team was over. But the soap opera was taking another twist. Or maybe Kindred's analogy was best; and where would Crum's body turn up the following year?

CHAPTER 6

1979-80: FIRST NATIONAL CHAMPIONSHIP

S urely, Darrell Griffith knew the ropes by now. He's been knocked through them enough.

Oh sure, Griffith was the second coming of Dr. J., Julius Erving. His own amazing leaping ability and monstrous dunks had earned him the nickname, Dr. Dunkenstein.

And he had an impressive portfolio that included scoring averages of 12.8, 18.6 and 18.5 in three seasons as the University of Louisville's most spectacular player. He was named to *The Sporting News* All-America team as a junior and earned second-team All-America in a UPI poll that same year.

But when the 1979-80 season began, nobody was taking Griffith—or the University of Louisville—seriously.

"I have the best player in the country," said DePaul coach Ray Meyer, speaking of enigmatic Mark Aguirre. "That Griffith boy is just too individualistic."

Even UCLA coach Larry Brown referred to Griffith as, "Griffin, or whatever."

In 1976, when Griffith announced his decision to attend the University of Louisville, he promised that he would bring "several NCAA Championships."

"I'll settle for just one," said Griffith's father, Monroe.

But for three years, Griffith failed to deliver on his promise. And with each passing season, Louisville fans sank deeper into despair.

The Cardinals hit bottom on March 15, 1979 when Arkansas and its great guard, Sidney Moncrief, eliminated U of L from the NCAA's Midwest Regional, 73-62, in Cincinnati.

One U of L fan took out an ad in a local weekly newspaper, calling for fans to vote on whether Crum should be replaced as the head coach. "Teams reflect their coach," said the man, "and Crum's teams just don't seem to care."

Arkansas did such an outstanding defensive job on Griffith that Crum was forced to remove his flustered star from the game. When U of L rallied in the second half, Griffith had to sit and watch as Tony Branch and Roger Burkman provided the leadership that was supposed to have come from Griffith.

Even Crum wondered about Griffith. "He had great games and scored points, but he'd do a lot of other things that would hurt you," Crum told the *Louisville Courier-Journal's* Billy Reed.

"In other words," wrote Reed, "for every gravity-defying, rim-rattling slam, there would be a sloppy pass, a bad shot, a lost man on defense. Nothing Crum did to help Griffith seemed to work. Crum even had a university psychologist, Dr. Stanley Frager, try a form of hypnosis on him."

Humbled, but undaunted, Griffith pushed himself in the summer before the '79-'80 season, spending lonely nights in the school's Crawford Gym dribbling around chairs and shooting over a 10-foot-high volleyball net.

Griffith was as easy-going and as pleasant as his coach. But like Crum he took pride in his—and his team's—performance. If the rumors and newspaper ads stung Crum, he was tight-lipped about it. Griffith, on the other hand, acknowledged his failures.

"I worked harder than I ever have," he told reporters before his senior season. "This is my last year, and when you read in the papers what certain people say about your game, especially the experts, you'd be foolish not to work on it. I can see improvement through hard work, and I hope it carries over."

If Griffith was ready to deliver on his promise of a national championship, one question remained: Who, if anybody, would be there to help?

The Cardinals did not look like a team that would contend for the NCAA crown.

Three starters returned from the frustrating 1979 season: Griffith and Branch, the guards, and center Carlton (Scooter) McCray.

The 6-foot Branch had neither the size nor the scoring punch Crum was looking for in a starter. And early in the team's third game, McCray was lost for the season to a knee injury.

But Crum told reporters in preseason that, "We have enough potential to be one of my best teams."

The Cardinals were a blend of youthful enthusiasm and determined experience. Griffith and Branch—the only seniors—could, and would, provide the experience. Both were excellent students, hard workers, and classy individuals.

For enthusiasm, Crum had four precocious sophomores—6-6 forward Derek Smith, 6-8 forward-center Wiley Brown, 6-4 guard Jerry Eaves, and 6-5 swingman David "Poncho" Wright, who was academically ineligible as a freshman. Scooter, of course, was a sophomore, too, but the early knee injury kept him from playing.

The Cards also had 6-5 junior Roger Burkman, a defensive whiz who wrapped himself around opponents tighter than an Ace bandage. "He's not afraid to go into the pack for bone," one coach said, describing Burkman's helter-skelter, devil-may-care play. By season's end, no less an authority than Al McGuire called Burkman "Instant Defense—the best sixth man in college basketball."

Like most Hoosiers, Burkman grew up dreaming of playing for Bobby Knight and Indiana. But Knight never called Burkman. Gene Bartow—then the UCLA coach—did call. But Burkman wasn't home to talk to the Bruin coach, so he wound up at Louisville.

The Cards had others who contributed in less publicized ways. Greg Deuser, a heady sophomore guard, could handle the ball, shoot from outside and keep the team loose with his dry wit.

Marty "Mountain Man" Pulliam was a 6-9 sophomore and crowd favorite. He was also a favorite with his teammates. Pulliam, like Deuser, a straight-A student, loved professional wrestling and kept the team laughing with tag-team matches whenever the Cards caught cabin fever on long road trips.

Daryl Cleveland, a 6-7 junior, was disappointed that he had not improved enough to contribute more, but he rooted long and loud from the bench, encouraging his teammates' every move.

What about freshmen? Well, the Cards had walk-on Steve Clark and a chubby kid named Rodney McCray.

"Rodney was really a disappointment in preseason practices," said then-assistant coach Bill Olsen. "He wasn't working very hard. He was like a lot of young players who see that they aren't going to get an opportunity to start, and then let up."

If Griffith was Dunkenstein, then Rodney McCray was Dr. Jekyll-Mr. Hyde. When Scooter went out with the knee injury, Rodney replaced his older brother and—in the end—became the glue that held U of L together.

"I saw a lot of potential in Rodney in high school," said then-assistant coach Wade Houston, who signed both McCrays. "But when he came here, he had a noncompetitive attitude. He figured he wasn't going to play right away, so what the heck. Why not take it easy?"

Most experts figured Louisville was a team with a flashy talent in Griffith, but was too young to compete for an NCAA championship. What they didn't figure was the genuine friendship that developed among the players and managers.

"Team chemistry is a funny thing," Crum said. "It's either there or it isn't. The kids either get along and give to each other and care for each other, or they don't. It's not something you coach."

Two things happened before the U of L team ever won a game that may have turned the 1979-80 Cardinals into a "team of destiny," as Al McGuire called them.

One thing was the humiliating loss to Arkansas at the end of the '79 season. Crum had always accepted defeat better than most coaches. "Losing is nothing to be afraid of," he told his players more than once. "But getting outhustled is something to be ashamed of. There's no excuse for losing because another team outhustled you." In the late '70s, especially in that loss to Arkansas, Crum wondered if his teams were being outhustled or simply being beaten by better opponents. He found the answer in the final game of the 1978-79 season. Arkansas enjoyed a 17-point lead when Crum sent his Cardinals—minus Griffith—into a suffocating zone press that produced a 22-4 run and near victory. He had toyed with the zone press throughout his U of L years, even during the '78-79 season. But the comeback against Arkansas convinced him of its value. The Louisville coach determined then that his teams might lose again— but with the press, at least they would not be outhustled.

"We won the 1980 national championship on March 15, 1979," said one U of L coach. "That's when the press was born. And that's when Denny decided to sink or swim with it the next year."

"I really thought we played hard in 1979," Crum said, deflecting the criticism. "I wasn't that disappointed. But I did remember Coach Wooden saying the byproducts of the press were more important than the press itself. Those are the things a press can give a team, even if it never gets a steal."

So Crum entered the 1979-80 season poised to quiet the critics. And the muffler would be a 2-2-1 zone press he had learned from Wooden at UCLA.

"We had pressed some on and off before that season," Crum said. "I just felt like we had the quickness and intelligence to press in '80. If anything, our press got better when we substituted—Roger, Poncho and Tony were all good at it."

Secondly was an unreported incident that established Griffith as the leader U of L's young players desperately needed.

In a preseason practice, a U of L player took a poke at Tony Branch. It was the kind of thing that happens from time to time at every level of basketball when the competition becomes heated. The uncalled slaps and hacks erupt into pushes, shoves, verbal wars and sometimes punches. But this was different. This time the victim was Branch, recognized by his coaches and teammates as something of a saint on a team full of nice kids. Swinging at Tony Branch, in other words, was just unthought of.

Griffith reacted swiftly and strongly. Coming to the rescue, he took one mighty swing at Branch's offender. "Don't ever do that to Tony again!" Griffith barked.

Heads turned. Balls stopped bouncing. Was this the easygoing, oft-smiling, always-friendly Doctor of Dunk?

It was.

Perhaps Griffith was working off his own frustrations, having grown tired of listening to critics. They pummeled him time and again after the 1979 season, leaving him hurt and stunned by their disparaging words.

Perhaps Griffith was only doing what came naturally for a young man who genuinely cherished friendship and believed in loyalty; he was protecting a buddy.

Perhaps he was showing everyone that he was a changed man, a more competitive and determined athlete than the one teammates had seen in the past.

Or perhaps Griffith was aware that he had painted himself into a corner with his promise of a national championship. And now that he was an empty-handed senior and down to his final round, he did what any great champion would do: He came out fighting.

Whatever his reason, Griffith made it clear that he was "The Man." If U of L was going anywhere in 1980, the others had better fall in line behind him.

And they did.

"Every practice was a war," said Burkman, "bodies flying, guys going all out every day. It was unbelievable."

It was also a style that captured the hearts of U of L fans when it carried over to the Freedom Hall floor.

"Enthusiasm is what it's all about," said Rob Hickerson, a mortgage broker and self-appointed cheerleader in Section 141. Using body language to spell "Cards" and his coat or shirt to whip up the crowd, Hickerson led the cheers for the Cards that season. "If this team goes in a slump," he said, "we just don't sit. We get 'em rocking and rolling again."

Rocking and rolling again. Just like practice in the Crawford gym. "The games," said Burkman, "were easy compared to the battles we had in practice."

U of L opened the season Dec. 1 with an inauspicious 75-73 win over visiting South Alabama. The Cards lost a 14-point lead and trailed 71-69 with 3:30 left to play. But a long jumper by Griffith helped avoid a disaster.

Four nights later, the Cards were better during an 87-63 win over Tennessee-Chattanooga. Poncho Wright told a reporter, "We're going to the Nap—you can write that down," which meant U of L was going to IndiaNAPolis, site of the 1980 NCAA Final Four. Indy, or "Naptown," was also the hometown of Wright and Burkman. Ironically, it was where Wright and his Marshall High School team ended Burkman's high school career in 1977 when Marshall beat Burkman's Franklin Central in the post-season tourney.

Saturday, Dec. 8, was the day that one McCray, Scooter—went down with the season-ending knee injury. Scooter would not come back until the 1980-81 season. But U of L clawed and fought for its life that night, beating Tennessee, 77-75 in Knoxville, its second two-point win in three games.

Crum's lineup included two 6-4 guards, Griffith and sophomore Jerry Eaves, two sophomore forwards in 6-6 Derek Smith and 6-8 Wiley Brown, and now a freshman center, 6-7 Rodney McCray. Branch was relegated to a ball-handling role as a reserve. Burkman was the defensive stopper. Wright gave the Cards hot and cold outside shooting and perhaps the team's best athletic talent. He could jump, he could run, and when the 2-2-1 press was rocking and rolling, he could create havoc.

Griffith scored 32 against Tennessee, and at least one defender, Bert Bertelkamp, was impressed. "It kind of demoralizes you," he said. "You're right on him, right in his face, and he still puts it in. He just outjumps you and shoots it."

"Tonight we made believers out of a lot of people," said Griffith. "We proved that just because we're young, that doesn't mean we can't win."

Crum, though, wondered if his youngsters would be able to win 15 games. As the Courier's Reed wrote, "The season seemed to be over almost before it had started."

Well, not quite.

After winning at Tennessee, U of L returned home to win its own Holiday Classic, beating Western Kentucky, 96-74, in the final.

Five players scored in double figures, led by Griffith's 20. But Smith had 17 points and 14 rebounds, and the young Rodney McCray had 17 points to go with eight rebounds. Eaves had 19 points.

A sellout-crowd of 16,613 turned out on Dec. 19 to see Louisville chop down second-ranked Ohio State, 75-65. OSU was led by 6-11 Herb Williams and 6-8 Clark Kellogg. But they were no match for the revenge-minded Cards, who suffered a humiliating loss, 85-69, in Columbus to OSU the previous year.

"That hurt my pride," Griffith said. "When this season's schedule came out, the first thing I did was look to see when we played Ohio State. We had to settle up with them."

U of L's smaller but more aggressive front line out-rebounded the Buckeyes, with Smith and McCray getting nine each.

Louisville withstood a late Ohio State rally and rode the press to victory. Late in the game Griffith made a steal and fed Burkman for a layup and a 63-57 lead. Then Burkman stole the ball and fed Griffith for another bucket, and it was over.

"Take that, y'all," Griffith said.

"I'm not saying we're No. 1," Wright told the *Courier-Journal.* "But tonight there weren't many in the country that could play with us."

The first loss came on the road to Hawaii. U of L stopped to play Utah on Dec. 22. The Utes won, 71-69, despite 12-for-13 shooting and 25 points from Smith and 23 more from Griffith.

From Utah, the 6-1 Cards went to Hawaii for the Rainbow Classic in Honolulu. There was no pot of gold waiting for the Cards at the end of this rainbow.

Louisville was lethargic in beating pass-happy Princeton, 64-53, on Dec. 28. If Griffith had not scored 21, Louisville might not have won.

The Cards lost in the tourney's second round, falling to Illinois, 77-64, although Griffith had 28 points and 10 rebounds. Rodney McCray continued to come into his own with 13 rebounds.

In the tourney's consolation game, U of L won a boring 65-58 decision over Nebraska.

Both Wiley Brown and Derek Smith struggled throughout the tourney. They were both unhappy about being so far from home—both came from rural Georgia—over the Christmas holidays. Their lack of desire to play basketball during the holidays showed just how young the team really was—and how badly it needed Griffith to stay afloat.

There was one bright spot on the trip to the islands. Rodney McCray proved he could do the job.

Back home in friendly and familiar Freedom Hall, the entire U of L team came to play, winning three straight—Tulsa, Kansas State and St. Louis.

Wright's long-range bombs helped to break open the 78-58 win over Tulsa. But again it was Griffith grabbing the spotlight, scoring 21 points and breaking Charlie Tyra's 23-year-old scoring record. Tyra had scored 1,728 points in four seasons.

Brown broke out of his slump—he was 2-for-17 during the three games in Hawaii—with 21 points as the Cards, and Griffith with 27 points and six assists, beat K-State 85-73. Branch went almost unnoticed in that win, failing to take a shot from the floor in a bit part as a reserve.

"It's always difficult for me to sit on the bench," Branch told the *Courier-Journal.* "It's something I have to constantly work on. After last year, when I was a starter, this is awful difficult."

But Branch and Kansas State would meet again in the NCAA Tournament, and in that game the heady guard would leave the Wildcats with something to remember him by.

Eaves turned his ankle in the win over Kansas State, then sat out as U of L opened the Metro Conference schedule with a 94-65 win over St. Louis. Branch, making his first start of the season, hit four-of-five shots and finished with nine points, making the most of the opportunity. Burkman, who rarely shot, scored 19 points, including an incredible 13-of-14 free throws.

Branch started again as Eaves sat out Louisville's 69-48 win at Memphis State on Jan. 12, with Smith's 22 points and Griffith's 20 paving the way.

On Tuesday, Jan. 22, Crum got his 200th coaching victory—no coach in the history of the game won 200 games faster than Crum— as Louisville beat old rival Marquette 76-63 in Freedom Hall. Griffith paced the way with 23 points. Wright filled it up from the outside with 15. Burkman continued to make teams pay from the line, making 9-of-11 free throws, and finished with those 9 points. Rodney McCray was his usual quiet, consistent self. He scored 12 points, picked up 10 rebounds and was as unspectacular as he was flawless. Never had Louisville seen a player who did great things with the flair of a Griffith. And never had Louisville seen a player who accomplished so much in such a quiet, unassuming manner as Rodney McCray.

Still, the hour belonged to Crum.

"He's a Cool Hand Luke gambler," former U of L coach John Dromo said after watching the win over Marquette. "Denny always plays the percentages, never loses control of a game, never pushes the panic button. He's the best in the country at conversing during timeouts. He might get beat, but he never beats himself."

Crum's team was now 14-2 and ranked No. 7 in the polls. The Cards were playing as well as anyone could remember, and the 2-2-1 zone press was making life miserable for opponents—and easy for Crum.

"It's beautiful to see everybody pulling in the same direction," Crum said. "I've had no acid stomach this year. No headaches. No tension neckaches. These guys are fun to be around. They haven't given us one single problem all year. They all go to class, do what we ask them to do, and they're having fun."

Having fun was all Crum ever really asked of his players.

"The win-at-all-costs philosophy is a bunch of bull," Crum once told the *Courier-Journal.* "I like to see my players have fun. That's what life is all about, having fun without hurting somebody. There's nobody that likes to win more than I do. But you've got to be realistic. What price is victory? It's not the end of the world if you lose. Life goes on, and you have to live with it."

Wins over St. Louis (99-74; Griffith 28, Wright 15, Brown 14),

Florida State (79-73, Griffith 27, Brown 13, McCray 11) and Tulane (64-60; Deuser came off the bench to help direct the Cards, who fell behind 37-30 at the half) left U of L with a 17-2 record going into the Jan. 25 showdown with Lou Carnesecca's St. John's team in Jamaica, N.Y.

St. John's was 17-1 and making its first national TV appearance of the season. Al McGuire, the great Marquette coach and a graduate of St. John's, was handling the color commentary for NBC.

The star of the show, though, was Griffith—of course. He did an amazing high-wire act, scoring 23 points in just 27 minutes, including four baskets on four different but spectacular dunks as U of L won 76-71. When Griffith caught an alley-oop pass from Eaves that was short and off target, he stayed in the air long enough to complete a reverse alley-oop stuff that left a St. John's fan on the row wondering, "Is that legal? Can he do that?"

"He's a much-improved player," Carnesseca told reporters after the game. "He has more poise, and his shot selection is so much better. He helps them just with his presence on the floor."

The Cards left New York to continue their assault on the Metro Conference teams.

On Feb. 4, the day after beating St. Johns, Louisville buried Memphis State 88-60 as Griffith scored 31, and Smith added 17 points and 12 rebounds in Freedom Hall.

Louisville beat visiting Cincinnati 88-73 on Feb. 6, giving Crum his ninth 20-win season in as many years. Smith had a team-high 26 points and took down 10 rebounds, and as good as Griffith was, some were starting to wonder if the sophomore from Hogansville, Ga., was perhaps the team's best all-around player.

Burkman, relishing his role as the team's sixth man and throwing on the full court zone press, provided the spark that ignited U of L against Cincy. In the first half, he knocked the ball loose from a Bearcat guard, and Griffith picked it up and scored. A perfectly timed behind-the-back pass from Griffith to Brown on the baseline resulted in a stuff. Cincy called time out. The zone press forced another turnover by Cincinnati, and Burkman—who was second on the team assists but sixth in playing time—fed Eaves for a three-point play that broke Cincinnati's back.

"Every game," Crum said, "the press seems to take its toll on the team we're playing. With our inexperience and size, we don't have the strength to play a great half-court defense. But the press allows us to string the other teams out and take away disadvantages we have. It's been a positive thing for us. Our kids enjoy it, and they do a good job with it."

Next for the Cards was a grueling road trip that took them to Providence, Virginia Tech, West Virginia and Cincinnati—four games in eight days. The worst part of the trip came after beating West Virginia. First, their charter flight was canceled by a snowstorm. Then, their charter bus broke down twice. After 25 hours on the road, they caught a few winks and showed their true grit in a 61-57 win over Cincinnati.

On Feb. 18, after a rare day off, Louisville beat Virginia Tech 77-72 in the regular season finale at Freedom Hall. Six Cards scored nine or more points, with Griffith's 23 leading them.

The record was now 25-2, the win streak was up to a school-record 18, and Louisville—unranked by most polls at the start of the season—was ranked third in the nation.

Sooner or later, of course, the bubble had to burst. It happened on Feb. 21 when the Cards were demolished 77-60 by Jeff Ruland (30 points, 21 rebounds) and Iona College in Madison Square Garden.

The margin of victory for Coach Jim Valvano's Iona team made some people wonder if Louisville was as good as it had appeared.

Griffith's 29 points and a combined 44 points from Smith, McCray and Brown helped U of L end the regular season at 28-3 with an 83-75 win at Florida State. Back in Freedom Hall for the Metro Conference Tournament, U of L beat Memphis State 84-65 (Smith 24, Griffith 20, Wright 14) then downed Florida State 81-72 (Griffith 30, Wright 16, Eaves 11) for the championship. That win completed a perfect 14-0 season for the Cards in the Metro and earned them a berth in the NCAA's Midwest Regional in Lincoln, Neb., where Kansas State would be the first-round opponent.

No less an authority than Al McGuire said winning the NCAA Tournament takes two things: "First you need luck," he said after his Marquette team won in 1977. "And secondly, you need to be on a roll going into the tournament, to get some confidence and momentum going."

Louisville knew Kansas State. It had beaten the Wildcats by 12 earlier in the year in Freedom Hall. It knew Jack Hartman's team had a rugged rebounder in Ed Nealy, who was built in the mold of Iona's Jeff Ruland. And it had one of the nation's underrated stars in Rolando Blackman.

With Nealy getting a game-high 11 rebounds and banging U of L's small front line around under the boards, K-State hung tough for 40 minutes. Louisville shot well—over 55 percent for the game—but it could not shake the Big Eight champion. The U of L guards were below par, too. Griffith scored 18 points, but needed 20 shots to get them and played with foul problems before picking up his fifth in overtime. Eaves took only three shots and missed them all.

On the plus side, Smith had 20 points and Wright came off the bench to make 4-of-6 shots for 10 more points.

But the game went into overtime when the Cards made too many turnovers and Blackman made a rebound basket with two seconds to go in regulation.

U of L—with its star, Griffith, having fouled out—seemed headed for an early exit in the NCAA tourney. Enter Tony Branch, U of L's "other" senior and its forgotten man.

Branch's playing time fell from 672 minutes as a junior to 92 as a senior. Crum decided Branch, Eaves and Burkman were "all about equal" after preseason scrimmages, and chose the younger Eaves to be the team's starter and Burkman to be its first sub.

"When all things are equal," Crum said, "always go with the younger player because he will usually develop more than a senior."

But Crum hated putting Branch on the bench. "There's nobody who likes or respects Tony more than I do," Crum said. "I got a lot of criticism for starting Eaves in front of him because everybody loved Tony. But I felt it would be best for our team."

If Branch was anything, he was a team player. Griffith, his roommate on the road, helped him with his constant encouragement. So when it came down to last-shot time in overtime against Kansas State, there was Branch—not Griffith—at the top of the key and the overtime clock ticking down, "Three, two..."

Branch wanted to pass the ball to somebody else, somebody inside, somebody—anybody—closer to the basket.

"Coach Crum called a 1-4 offense, a last-second pattern that we had practiced all week," Burkman said. "The difference was we had Tony in the game instead of Darrell."

So when nothing developed, Branch did the only thing left that he could do: He shot the basketball.

It hit the rim, bounced high, banked off the glass and...

"It took," Branch said, "forever."

Griffith rose from his seat on the bench. Perhaps he was thinking back to that day in practice—that day he jumped between Branch and his attacker. Branch hoped and prayed the ball would fall through.

"Nobody deserves it more than Tony," Griffith said he thought to himself as the ball was in the air.

The ball fell through the net, and Louisville won, 71-69.

"It couldn't have happened to a nicer guy," said Crum.

"Roomie, oh Roomie!" shouted Griffith, who embraced Branch. "This is MY roommate!" Griffith shouted like a proud father.

The win sent U of L to Houston for a March 14 meeting with Texas A&M.

The Aggies controlled the tempo, especially in the second half, when U of L could not buy a basket. McCray was 0-for-4 and missed four free throws. Smith was 2-for-6. Griffith scored 24 points, but needed 24 shots to get them, his second-straight struggle from the field.

When the game went into overtime, again, at 53-53, U of L was again dangerously close to elimination. But this time there was one difference: Griffith was around to play the entire five-minute overtime.

He got eight points in the extra session as the Cards, finally appearing to wake up from a two-game slumber, outscored A&M 13-2 to win going away, 66-55.

Griffith made a free throw to give the Cards a 54-53 lead. When his second foul shot missed, Burkman put the ball back in the hoop for a 56-53 lead. Griffith got eight of his 24 in the final five minutes to lead the Cards.

At that point, U of L had both luck and momentum on its side. Now, it was on a roll. And next up was LSU, an enormously talented team led by Louisville native and long-time Griffith buddy Rudy Macklin.

Griffith said he and Macklin were "real close friends. Every time he comes home, I'm the first one he calls."

LSU got to the Midwest Region Final with a 68-63 win over Missouri. Griffith watched the game from the stands after leading the Cards past Texas A&M. He cheered for Macklin and LSU throughout.

"If you can keep Griffith from scoring the way he wants to and take the rest of them inside, they can be beat," said A&M's Vernon Smith after his team's loss. "They can't beat a team with a good inside game."

If LSU had anything, it was an inside game. Besides the 6-6 Macklin, the Tigers boasted 6-8 DeWayne Scales and 6-8 Greg Cook.

A crowd of 15,400 filled Houston's Summit Arena on Sunday, March 16, to see the boyhood pals, Griffith and Macklin, battle for the right to go to the Final Four in Indianapolis. And what they saw was stunning.

Griffith was on the bench early with three fouls, but U of L was leading 21-13 thanks to some heads-up play from Branch and Brown. Suddenly, though, LSU erupted for a 16-0 run and led 29-21. Branch steadied the Cards in the closing minutes of the half, and at intermission Louisville was back on top by a slim 31-29 margin.

"We had played poorly and still had the lead," recalled Burkman. "At halftime, we decided to go back out there and bury them if we could."

They could. And they did.

Eaves hit two long jumpers, Griffith added a 20-footer of his own and Brown scored on a spectacular follow shot. McCray kept it going with a turnaround 15-footer, and suddenly Louisville was in the driver's seat. As the *Courier-Journal's* Mike Sullivan described it, "..the game was being played in the fast lane, and LSU was hanging onto the hood ornament—which turned out, to its horror, to be a little red bird."

LSU crumpled under an avalanche of dunks and fast break layups. For many of U of L's players and coaches there would be other wins on other days, but none as satisfying as this one.

Louisville won because it refused to crack when Griffith went out. It won because Brown played over his head when others were struggling. It won with the bench giving the starters a lift. And it won because everyone did his job on defense, especially Smith, who held Macklin to seven shots and nine points in a physical bruising man-to-man war.

As much as Griffith liked Macklin, Smith disliked him. At least that's what some who knew Smith well said. "Rudy's a nice guy, but there's something that kept us from being friends," Smith told the *Courier-Journal.* "I guess it goes back to summer pickup games at U of L. We're the same type of players, and we went after it so hard. He beat up on me pretty good during the summer, and I was determined to show him."

Smith had 13 points and 10 rebounds. McCray added 12 points and 10 rebounds. But Griffith had 17 points in only 18 minutes and Brown made 8-of-10 shots for 16 points.

"There's something about this team—I've said it all year, but I can't put my finger on it," said Crum. "Here we are, 31-3, and I still can't believe it. They love each other. They play hard and they play together. They refuse to quit. Adversity doesn't bother them."

On Saturday, March 22, Louisville met Iowa for the right to play UCLA in the championship game. UCLA had upset Joe Barry Carroll and Purdue in the semifinal game, 67-62, before U of L hooked up with Iowa.

Griffith, having finally gotten over the hump by making it to the Final Four, played loose and spectacular. The Cards gave an indication of their confidence and loose spirit the day before when, in a one-hour workout before the media and fans, they put on an awesome display of dunking. One after another the U of L players slammed and jammed, leaving mouths open and eyes wide on press row. And now, with so much on the line against Iowa, the Cards were sure of themselves.

The game against Iowa promised to be more difficult than any so far. The Hawkeyes played tenacious defense and featured a guard, Ronnie Lester, that Iowa coach Lute Olson thought was better than Griffith. If LSU had more firepower than Iowa, it had also been more predictable.

"The LSU players were one-dimensional," said one U of L assistant. "Every player did one thing, and one thing only. They each had one basic move on offense, and we knew that if we could take that away, we could force them to start taking a lot of bad shots. Iowa is tougher."

But not as tough as Griffith, who put on a phenomenal show by scoring 34 points on 14-of-21 shooting, usually with an Iowa player draped on his chest. McCray added 14 points and nine rebounds— not bad for a freshman making his first appearance in the Final Four—and U of L pulled away from a 34-29 halftime lead to win 80-72. The Cards shot almost 60 percent, compared to 43.7 for Iowa.

The Hawkeyes lost Lester to a knee injury in the first half after he scored 10 points. But Eaves, for one, thought the Big 10 team was better when he went out.

When Griffith left to a thundering ovation in the final seconds, he went to the Iowa bench to shake hands with all the Hawkeyes and their head coach. "I know how their team felt, coming this far and losing," Griffith said, perhaps remembering his own disappointment of the last three years. "I just wanted to congratulate them for a great game."

Iowa's Bob Hansen provided America with the tournament's best quote after the game when he told reporters, "I've guarded other players who could leap as high as Griffith. But all of them came down."

For the third time in his nine seasons at Louisville, Crum was back in the Final Four. And for the third time, he was playing his alma mater, UCLA. Would he ever escape the shadows of John Wooden and Westwood?

The difference this time, though, was that Wooden would watch from the stands and Larry Brown, the new UCLA coach—and third since Wooden's retirement five years earlier—would be on the sidelines.

Still, UCLA was counting heavily on its mystique. After all, this was a school that won 10 national championships from 1964 through Wooden's final season in 1975.

"We're very proud to be from UCLA," said Bruin forward Kiki Vandeweghe. "I don't know what it will mean to them. But it means something to us."

No UCLA team had ever lost an NCAA Championship game before. And while this team was young—freshmen Rod Foster and Michael Holton joined sophomore Mike Sanders and seniors Vandeweghe and James Wilkes in the lineup—it righted itself after a terrible 8-6 start to take a 22-9 record into the final.

Eaves, for one, wasn't impressed. "UCLA's never beaten me," he said. "I've never played them."

On Sunday, the day before the final, Griffith and his teammates were guests on a TV special for a Louisville station. Griffith used the opportunity to say hello to an old friend, Jerry Stringer, a friend he grew up with, who was battling cancer.

"It's like it's in the third quarter, and he's losing," said Griffith. "Hey Jerry—tomorrow night's for you."

Wooden watched nervously in the stands as much of the media attention centered around him. He was noncommittal in interviews, but several years later admitted, "Yes, I was pulling for Louisville privately. I wanted to see Denny win that championship that eluded him. And besides, I pull for people, and not necessarily schools."

The Cards won the 42nd NCAA Championship and the first in

U of L school history on March 24. They beat UCLA 59-54 by scoring the final nine points of the game. At last, Darrell Griffith had done what he'd set out to do four years earlier.

It didn't come easily for Griffith or Louisville. The Cards trailed through most of the first half and made only 11 of 31 shots for a miserable 35 percent, and missed four of their nine free throws.

But no one remembers those stats. What they remember most about the 1980 final is this:

At breakfast that morning, Wiley Brown left his artificial thumb on the table. Brown had lost most of his thumb in a childhood accident, and for this season he was playing with a specially made prosthesis. When he remembered he had left the artificial thumb on the breakfast table, it was several hours before a student manager finally retrieved it from a dumpster. In the final, Brown had eight points, seven rebounds, three assists, one blocked shot, one steal—and both thumbs.

At halftime, Crum abandoned his typical, low-key talk to reprimand his players for "choking."

"He really chewed us out," Smith said.

"He called us a bunch of chokers," said Burkman.

"Yes, I told them they were choking," said Crum. "They weren't, really—both teams were just responding to the pressure. Just before the second half started, I apologized to them. You don't want to hurt people you care so much about. I told them that I didn't mean it and that I love them—that they ought to go out and have fun."

At the four-minute mark, UCLA led, 54-50, when Vandeweghe stole the ball and headed by himself—he thought—to the basket to put the final nails in Louisville's coffin. But Eaves hustled back, cut him off and forced him to alter his shot, which he missed, and Brown grabbed the rebound.

Eaves hit a 16-footer. Eaves scored on a driving layup. Griffith pulled up from 18 feet, elevated and scored. Louisville had the lead 56-54 and UCLA took a timeout. The Cards had 13-of-21 for 62 percent when the Bruins came back for the final 2:17. The Cards got three more points while UCLA did not score again. For the most part, the young Bruins spent the final two minutes taking poor shots and throwing the ball away against U of L's swarming press.

But perhaps the thing U of L fans remember the best about the final was a lob pass that led Griffith to a field goal when Louisville was teetering on the brink of disaster.

The Bruins led 50-45 with 6:28 left in the game after a layup by Sanders. As the clock ticked down, U of L looked confused and perhaps even beaten. That's when Griffith—who had been held scoreless for 10 minutes—took the lob from Brown, and while twisting in the air, somehow double-pumped and kissed the ball off the glass before being fouled by UCLA's Michael Holton. Griffith's free throw cut the Bruin lead to 50-48, putting new hope into his team while keeping the old promise he'd made alive. Although he led both teams with 23 points and was the only Cardinal in double figures, it was more than fitting that Griffith's basket at 2:21 put U of L ahead, 56-54, in what turned out to be the winning shot.

"Griffith is tremendous," said UCLA's Larry Brown. "Just his presence makes them so tough. We were trying to guard the greatest player in the country."

The win was especially sweet for Crum, for a number of reasons. Besides giving him his first national title after two previous trips to the Final Four, it also came against his alma mater—the same team that knocked his 1972 and 1975 Louisville teams out of the tournament.

"It's a tremendous thrill to win it," Crum said.

Griffith, who was named the tourney's Most Valuable Player, later received the John Wooden Award as the nation's best player. Griffith was ecstatic with the win.

"This is a great feeling," he said. "This is what I wanted since I came here."

Smith and Brown paraded around the court holding up a mock newspaper with a headline reading, "WILEY AND DEREK WIN NCAA!" All year, Brown and Smith spoke to one another in a funny language known as "pig Latin." They often confused opponents by calling plays using their special code. "Sometimes, I didn't know what they were talking about myself," laughed Griffith.

Every player made a contribution in the championship game, either by his presence on the court or his encouragement from the bench. Not since Louisville's 1956 NIT championship had there been a Cardinal team so closely knit. The threads of genuine love, respect and friendship tied them all together, forever, in U of L history.

Their accomplishment did not go without celebration back home in Louisville. In fact, when the team rolled into Louisville by charter bus early Tuesday morning, they were greeted by a mob gone out of control. Fans stormed the bus, climbed on top of it and did everything possible to reach out and touch their conquering heroes.

A crowd of 20,000 packed into Freedom Hall Tuesday night to celebrate the championship. Crum got the loudest ovation when he said, "At least for this year, and maybe for evermore, we ARE the University of Kentucky."

One by one the players were introduced, and the fans roared. Griffith, of course, got the longest and loudest ovation of any player. But there were still those who felt Smith was the team's real unsung hero. And many others, some of them the most knowledgeable coaches in America, believed it was the freshman center, Rodney McCray, who before the season started was not even expected to be a contributor.

Griffith thought they were all important.

When he received the Metro Conference Player of the Year award at the end of the season, he said, "I want to share this honor with all my teammates because without them we wouldn't have enjoyed a successful season, and I wouldn't be under consideration for such prestigious honors. The secret of our success has been our togetherness and with this in mind, I want to accept this award for the entire team."

The glorious season came to an end on Thursday, April 3. The Cardinals went to Washington, D.C., to visit with President Carter who, like Smith and Brown, was a native of Georgia. And Brown—uproariously hilarious and the team's clown prince—had a poem ready. "Even though you, President Carter, are the best man in the land, now you'll get to shake the No. 1 Cards' hands." The meeting with Carter lasted 10 relaxed minutes. He praised the team for its tenacious play and called it "steady under pressure."

Smith, Brown and Daryl Cleveland, the three Georgia players—presented Carter with an autographed basketball and T-shirt that proclaimed U of L the national champions. Crum gave the president an NCAA Championship watch that Carter promised to wear.

As he went down the line shaking hands with the players and officials from the U of L team, he paused in front of Griffith. "It is Dr. Dunkenstein, right?" asked the President.

Griffith nodded, and smiled.

And for a brief moment, on a cool spring day in the nation's capitol, two men who knew what it meant to be cornered against the ropes, acknowledged each other's greatness.

CHAPTER 7

1985-86: A SECOND NATIONAL CHAMPIONSHIP

Denny Crum, who survived a coin toss to the head (a quarter thrown during a game against rival Kentucky) and barbs to his ego, arrived at the opening practice of the 1985-86 season with a sparkle in his eyes, gum in his mouth and a smile on his lips.

For years, Crum has been an object of wrath to University of Kentucky fans, including the one who zinged him upside the head with the 25-cent missile. As Dave Kindred wrote, "The only thing Kentucky fans want to hear a Louisville coach say is 'Goodbye.'"

For years, Crum has been widely recognized as the best X's and O's coach never to win a coach of the year award from his peers. He pretends not to notice.

"That stuff is not important," Crum said. "All an award and a quarter will buy you is a half-a-cup of coffee. I don't know how you win one of those awards because I've never won any. If they don't respect you when you do what I've done, what must you do to get it? I guess I could schedule 30 wins a year and win a lot of awards. But I'd rather be in the Final Four."

And now you know why Denny Crum had a sparkle in his eyes and a smile on his lips. The 1985-86 University of Louisville basketball team, he would tell you, had the stuff national champions are made of.

It had two great senior guards in 6-4 Jeff Hall and 6-5 Milt Wagner. Funny how things turned out. Wagner was scheduled to graduate a season earlier. But a broken foot in the team's second game cost Milt the entire season. His absence put added pressure on Hall, forcing him to improve his ball-handling skills and defense. Without Wagner to carry the load, Hall became a more complete player. The 85-86 Cardinals had two complementary forwards in 6-7 senior Billy Thompson and 6-7 sophomore Herbert Cook. Thompson was the consummate passer Crum needed at forward. Thompson was also a strong physical force in the paint. Crook, on the other hand, was a willowy forward who specialized in scoring and rebounding his teammates' missed shots. Turned sideways, Herbert Crook would disappear. He was that thin. When the wide bodies tried to screen Crook off the glass, he turned and vanished. He reappeared again—in a hold pattern—with outstretched arms waiting somewhere above the rim.

Crum had freshman Pervis Ellison in the middle. He was 6-9 going on 7-1. He was there because Barry Sumpter, the starter a year before, was academically ineligible. Rodney McCray was also a freshman starter at center back in 1979-80, so it really was funny the way things turned out.

Crum smiled a lot because his team had experienced depth, too. Chris West, a junior guard, started occasionally in '84-'85. Mark McSwain, a 6-7, 210-pound muscle, could play forward or center. A part-time starter as a sophomore, McSwain had the largest hands in college basketball. If Atlas carried the world on his shoulders, then McSwain at least could palm it. Mike Abram, a sophomore, had played well as a starter in the NIT a year ago. He was 6-4 and he could run and jump.

For youthful exuberance, Crum could call on 6-7 freshman Tony Kimbro, the best high school player in Kentucky a year earlier and a kid with windmills for arms. He could play guard or forward, which made him valuable. But 6-1 redshirt freshman Kevin Walls could score—44 points a game at Camden High, home of Billy Thompson and Milt Wagner—and he had quickness. Kenny Payne, a 6-7 freshman, brought a long range jumper from Mississippi.

Robbie Valentine, Will Olliges, David Robinson, Avery Marshall and Keith Williams provided enthusiasm and bench support.

When Crum surveyed his team, he smiled at what he saw. When he surveyed the schedule, he smiled again. "It's tough," Crum said. "But you can't be a great team at the end of the year if you play patsies in December."

The question Crum heard most often was, "How can you keep everybody happy?"

Crum had two answers. "First of all," he said, "those things have a way of working themselves out. And secondly, you get what you earn on this team. I'm not going to lose games playing guys who don't deserve to play. If you play and you don't get the job done, somebody else will take your place. They know that. They don't always like it. But they accept it."

But Crum's players weren't the only ones forced to accept things they did not like. Early in the season Crum, a fierce competitor, had to accept some losses he thought his team could have won. To his credit, Crum remained patient. "Championships are won in March and April," he reminded critics.

The season began in Cincinnati's Riverfront Coliseum on Nov. 29. The Cards whipped a good Miami of Ohio team 81-65 in the opening round of the Big Apple NIT. Two nights later the Cards beat Tulsa 80-74 and losing coach J.D. Barnett was impressed. "They ought to be in the Western Division of the NBA," Barnett said.

From Cincinnati, the Cards took their show to Madison Square Garden for the Big Apple semifinals. Crum's team lost 83-78 to Kansas, then fell to St. John's, 86-79 in the consolation game on Dec. 1. Both Kansas and St. John's were ranked in the top 20 and figured to be contenders for the NCAA Championship in March.

"I knew after that tournament that we had as good a chance as anybody to win it all," Crum said later. "Even though we lost, we hadn't played that badly. Milt was coming off a year of not playing, and it took him time to get back into the flow. I think he shot 25 or 30 percent in the first four games. We made a lot of stupid mistakes in the end of both of those games or we would have won. I figured if those were two of the best teams in the country—and they were— then we should be as good as anybody by the end of the year."

The Cards returned home on Dec. 7 to beat Purdue in convincing fashion, 77-58, then ripped Iowa and Western Kentucky. On Dec. 18, Indiana came to town bent on avenging last year's loss in Bloomington.

The game featured two of the best shooting guards in the nation—Wagner and IU's Steve Alford.

Neither team gained much of an upper hand, but Alford riddled Louisville's defense for 11-of-16 shooting and 27 points. "I'd tell them to hound Alford, and we allowed him to bring the ball all the way down," Crum said. "I must have told them 27 times to double-team Alford. Next time it will be 28."

Alford scored 10 of IU's final 14 points. But Wagner—who wound up hitting 7-of-12 shots and eight free throws for 22 points—scored Louisville's last 10 points in a pulsating 65-63 victory before 19,493 fans.

"Wagner made the difference in the game," said IU coach Bobby Knight. "He hit the free throws down the stretch."

"We played fairly well," Crum said. "Better—and a little smarter."

Crum's suicidal schedule next took the Cards to Lexington for a Dec. 28 showdown against Kentucky and first-year coach Eddie Sutton.

The 13th ranked Wildcats trailed only once in the second half, but never led by more than seven. Wagner pulled Louisville to within 61-58 on a layup with 2:24 to play. But Richard Madison got two points on a goaltending call against Pervis Ellison and Roger Harden's two free throws with 41 seconds left provided a 65-58 lead. The Cats went on to a 69-64 win.

Winston Bennett paced Kentucky with 23 points while Wagner missed only four shots and led Louisville with 19. Herbert Crook added 14 and Ellison—playing against UK All-American Kenny Walker—had 13 points, eight rebounds, four blocked shots and three assists.

"If I had to choose a freshman right now and say, 'I want to coach that guy the next three years,' it'd be Ellison," said Sutton. "But I hope he goes hardship (to the NBA)."

Louisville lost at the foul line, where UK made 19-of-25 attempts to only 6-of-7 for the Cards.

"That's a lot better than the last time we were up here," Crum said. "It was 34 to five then, so we've gained on them. I didn't have a whistle. I wish I had because there were a lot of them I would have called differently. But I'm prejudiced."

The real problem was Kentucky's 20 to five advantage in offensive rebounds. "Every ball seemed to bounce in the right spot for them," Crum said. "But good hustle will create that for you. They went to the boards hard, and we obviously did a lousy job of screening off. Any time you get 20 offensive rebounds to your opponent's five, you've got a heck of an edge."

By March, Sutton thought that Louisville might have the edge.

"They have the type of squad, if they continued to improve—and I have to believe they will—they may very well be in Dallas (for the Final Four)," Sutton said.

Crum's squad returned to the friendlier confines of Freedom Hall on Jan. 4 and pounded Wyoming 94-62 as Thompson scored 30 points on 13-of-14 shooting.

"Thompson was great," said Wyoming's Jim Brandenburg. "But to tell you the truth, they looked like a bunch of clones out there. Every one of them looked like they might have a Superman insignia under their uniform."

Louisville's "Supermen" followed up with an 86-55 rout of Eastern Kentucky. But Mark McSwain left early to change clothes. And he wasn't leaving early to stop a speeding locomotive, either.

McSwain told reporters he wanted to get whirlpool treatment for an ankle injury when he ran from the court with 12 minutes left in the game. But later, he admitted Crum ordered him to the locker room for refusing to enter the game.

McSwain eventually apologized to the team and returned with Crum's blessing. But his brief fling with selfishness would not be the last one for this team.

On Jan. 9, Louisville took an 8-3 record to Memphis for the Metro Conference opener. The Tigers were coming off a Final Four appearance but were missing 6-10 Keith Lee, who had completed his eligibility the previous spring. Still, Dana Kirk had plenty of talent and—some suspected—a team with better chemistry than the one Lee had dominated. For proof, Memphis had a 13-0 record and the nation's No. 6 ranking, not to mention four starters back from the Final Four squad.

If that wasn't enough to intimidate U of L, there was always the Mid-South Coliseum of whackos—one of whom threw an open pocket knife on the court during Memphis' 66-59 victory a year before.

"It's no picnic," Crum said, describing the atmosphere.

For all the things Memphis had going for it, Louisville should have won. Although the Tigers held off U of L to take a 73-71 win, Crum thought the better team was Louisville.

"We beat ourselves," Crum said. "We had an opportunity to win if we'd just hit our free throws. And we didn't. It's our own fault. We gave it away at the free throw line."

U of L made only 9-of-17 free throws but outscored Memphis 62-50 from the field. The Tigers got 20 points from 7-foot William Bedford and 15 from point guard Andre Turner.

Crook's 14 led U of L, but Tony Kimbro came off the bench to add 13.

Memphis took a 73-69 lead with 1:07 left in the game when Vincent Askew sank two free throws. But Kimbro pulled U of L to within two with 55 seconds left on a 14-footer. Turner missed a 10-footer with seven seconds to play and Memphis leading 73-71. That gave Louisville a final shot at a tie, but Jeff Hall's 20-footer bounced off the rim.

Crum was testy with reporters after the game, particularly when they raised questions about the 2-for-7 shooting of U of L's leading scorer, Billy Thompson.

"What about him?" snapped Crum. "I've seen him play better. But I've said before that we haven't had all of our starters play good on the same night yet. Memphis is a great team. They ought to be. They've got four starters back from a Final Four team. That's pretty good, isn't it? We've lost four games to teams in the top 20, and all on the road."

Louisville improved to 10-4 in its next two starts, beating Southern Mississippi and Florida State on the road. Wagner canned

13 straight field goals at one point against the Seminoles in a 27-point effort. On Jan. 18, they faced powerful Syracuse of the Big East Conference in Freedom Hall.

With a national television audience and a sellout crowd looking on, U of L raced out to a huge early lead, then held off a mild Syracuse rally to win 83-73. The loss dropped the fourth-ranked Orangemen to 13-2 and furthered Wagner's claim that he was 100 percent recovered from the foot injury that sidelined him last year.

"One thing about Milt," said Syracuse guard Pearl Washington, "when he gets his points, they're honest. Just jumpers. Pure jumpers. For my money, he's the best shooter in the country."

Wagner finished with 24 points, hitting the first seven shots of the game. But he wasn't the whole show. He combined with his backcourt buddy, Jeff Hall, for 40 points—14-of-18 field goals and 12-of-13 free throws.

"Emotionally, this was a big game for us," Hall said. "We had to prove something to ourselves—that we could get together and beat a good team. We'd had trouble beating a top-10 team, and that was kind of disappointing."

"They're a top-five team," Washington said of Louisville. "They're as good as any team in the Big East."

But after an 84-82 loss to Cincinnati at Freedom Hall in its next start, U of L fans wondered if the Cards were as good as ANYBODY in the Metro.

"We were thinking about the past, about Syracuse, and if you live in the past, you die in the present," Crum said. "They were out there dinking around in warmups, laughing and throwing behind-the-back passes. We earned a defeat, and we got what we earned."

What the Cards got was 35 points by Cincy's Roger McClendon, including 24 in the second half when the Bearcats rallied from a six-point deficit.

Seventh-ranked Kansas improved its record to 19-2 with a second win over U of L, this one coming on Jan. 25 in Lawrence. Three turnovers—two by Thompson and one by Wagner—in the final minutes allowed Kansas to escape with a 71-69 victory.

That loss dropped U of L's record to 11-6 and had Jerry Jones, the long-time assistant coach, muttering.

"I guarantee you at that point I wouldn't have given you a plug nickel for our chances of making it to the Final Four," Jones later told the *Courier-Journal*. "We hadn't really beaten anybody good other than Syracuse, and we'd given three or four games away. If you can't beat good teams on the road, how are you going to win the NCAA Tournament?"

But Crum told reporters after the game, "I'm proud of my team. They played another top-10 team on the road and almost won. We're getting better."

"So close," said Mark McSwain, "and yet so far."

By now, members of the media were open in their criticism of Thompson's play. His 1-for-5 shooting and six turnovers against Kansas intensified the criticism.

U of L fans, watching the Kansas loss on TV, agreed with the media. For three years they had waited for the nation's best high school player to blossom into a college All-American. They were tired of waiting.

It all came to a boil in U of L's next start on Jan. 28, a 72-60 win over LaSalle. Thompson had 12 points and 10 rebounds, but he was also the target of boos when he entered and left the game.

He had scored in double figures just twice in the last six games, and there was the mysterious performance at Kansas.

After beating LaSalle, Crum launched into a passionate defense of his senior forward. When asked about the boos, the U of L coach said, "That shows stupidity. He's trying as hard as anybody I've ever coached. He's doing everything right, but he just doesn't happen to be playing well right now. Even great players have slumps. And I'd rather he do it now than at the end of the year."

"He needs encouragement and support. Sometimes salesmen go out and sell three pots and pans after selling 60 the week before."

Thompson had heard the boos, and they stung.

"Yeah, it bothers me," Thompson said. "I've been here four years and have led the team. And now they start booing me all of a sudden. I've just got to keep my faith in God and in my family and friends. They've been helping me through this and keeping me right."

Crum also defended his team's 12-6 record.

"I told everyone at the start of this year that this team would have its ups and downs and probably wouldn't have a great record, but that we had the potential to be an outstanding team by the end of the year. I still feel that way. We're not bad right now. Tell me who else has played five top-10 teams on the road."

There was another controversy brewing after the win over LaSalle. Kevin Walls, disenchanted with his playing time, did not show up for the game. In fact, he staged a four-day walkout from practice and contacted his high school coach, Clarence Turner, who said a lot of unkind things about Crum and the U of L program.

Crum refused to sling mud back at the Camden coach. He brushed aside Turner's criticisms. And when Walls decided to return to the team, Crum welcomed the freshman guard back to the family. Well, it was actually assistant coach Jerry Jones who welcomed Walls back to the fold. Crum was in bed with the flu, which is where he was on Saturday, Feb. 1, when UCLA came to town.

Thanks to sports information director Kenny Klein's behind the scene maneuvers, Crum was linked to the U of L bench by way of a special telephone hookup. As he watched the nationally televised game from his bed, he relayed plays by telephone to U of L trainer Jerry May, who passed the information along to the assistant coaches—Jerry Jones, Wade Houston and Bobby Dotson.

"He didn't trust us," said Dotson, joking.

Using the "Dial-a-play" format, U of L blasted UCLA, 91-72. The Cards won because Wagner did some long-distance calling of his own, making 9-of-14 shots while scoring 20 points and getting seven assists. Thompson's stardom was on the rise, too. The 6-7 senior had 16 points, eight rebounds and six assists.

UCLA coach Walt Hazzard should have called "Dial a prayer" in the second half when U of L broke away from a 41-38 lead to put the game out of reach.

"I don't like being beat by a coach who isn't even here," deadpanned Hazzard.

"His voice was kind of weak at times," May said of Crum. "But he would get pretty upset, just like he does when he's here on the sidelines."

The Cards squeaked past South Carolina 74-72 and romped past Virginia Tech 103-68 before traveling to Raleigh, N.C. to meet North Carolina State in yet another national TV game.

For this one, the U of L coach was all there. But his players were not. "We looked a little tired," Crum said after the Wolfpack rode Chris Washburn's 27 points to a 76-64 win. "We always seemed to be a step away from where we needed to be—a half-step slow. And the combination of them being alert and playing well was too much for us."

One of U of L's players was alert—Billy Thompson, who scored 21 points, missed just two shots, and pulled down nine rebounds. Mark McSwain played only nine minutes in the first half before leaving with a strained knee ligament that would sideline him for a few games.

"I was surprised at how soft Louisville's defense was," said N.C. State's Ernie Myers. "I expected pressure like Duke's man-to-man, but it was easier."

It was impossible to know at the time, but that would be Louisville's last loss of the season. In Louisville's final nine regular season games—five of which were on the road—Louisville finally played the way Crum thought it could and would. Two of those nine wins were especially satisfying for Crum and the Cards.

On Feb. 13 at Riverfront Coliseum, U of L beat Cincinnati—an 84-82 winner at Freedom Hall—with astonishing ease. The final score was 74-58. In the first four minutes, Cincinnati missed all seven of its field goal attempts and lost the ball on a turnover. By the time play stopped for a TV timeout, U of L led 20-6 and the Bearcats never recovered.

Crum enjoyed watching his players gain a measure of revenge, but he didn't enjoy the Cincinnati fans.

"I got hit in the head two or three times by ice being thrown at our bench," complained Crum. "I'd said that was kind of bush league. They were screaming obscenities and throwing things the whole game. They put their students behind the bench. They have a few beers and get carried away, and I don't like it."

Crum felt much more secure on March 2 when his Cardinals hosted Memphis State in the regular season and Metro Conference finale at Freedom Hall. So did Billy Thompson—and this time, no boos.

The game matched the two best teams in the Metro—perhaps the two best teams in the nation. Memphis State was ranked No. 7 at 25-3, while U of L, which had won 13 of its last 14 games, including nine in a row, was 24-7 and ranked 13th. A record crowd at Freedom Hall of 19,582 turned out for what promised to be a classic.

They weren't disappointed.

Louisville had trouble getting the ball inside to Pervis Ellison and Herb Crook in the first half, and the Tigers led, 41-37, at the break. Memphis opened an eight-point lead early in the second. But the Cards surged back behind Thompson and Ellison. But a shot by Vincent Askew counted when Thompson was whistled for goaltending with 52 seconds left to play. That gave Memphis a 69-68 lead.

Wagner then missed on an 18-footer with 23 seconds left and Ellison's follow shot was blocked by 7-foot William Bedford. After two timeouts by Memphis with 14 seconds left, Memphis State's Andre Turner, the leading free throw shooter in the conference, was fouled by Crook with eight seconds left.

"Andre is blue-chip stock—I thought the milking contest was over," said Memphis State coach Dana Kirk.

Crum used a timeout to give Turner a chance to think. Meanwhile, Billy Thompson did some quick thinking for U of L.

"What do you want me to do if he misses and I get the rebound?" he asked Crum. "You want another timeout?"

"Just get the ball," Crum said, "to Milt."

That turned out to be an important issue.

As Turner toed the line, U of L's Jeff Hall considered the options.

"He's the best free throw shooter in the league," Hall said. "It was looking dim for us—very dim."

But Turner's free throw took two bounces off the rim and Thompson grabbed the rebound. Seven seconds were left in the game as Wagner took the pass from Thompson. The 6-5 senior drove the ball down the right side to a spot deep along the baseline. He turned and fired an off-balance 18-footer over State's Dwight Boyd. But Turner, trying hard to make up for his missed free throw, caught up with Wagner as he was shooting and reached for the ball from behind. One second remained when Turner was called for a foul.

"We were very fortunate," said Hall. "I don't know why they fouled him. Even if he got off the shot, it's very unlikely that he would have hit it. The percentages weren't good. In that situation, you're just praying somebody will foul you."

One second remained. Memphis State led by one, 69-68.

As he eyed the basket, Wagner parted his lips. The tip of his tongue curled out the left side of his mouth. This was a delicious moment for the "Ice Man," and he wanted to taste every sweet second.

Wagner never heard the noise of the crowd, although he felt their presence, their warmth, breathing softly on the back of his neck—they all loved the "Ice Man." This was his moment, the very reason he was put here at this time.

At crunch time, the ball in Wagner's hand was as good as money in the bank. Everyday at practice, Wagner would shoot and call out the same word, "Money!"

Time to cash in.

Of course, Wagner had been here before. Three years ago, in the final game of the 82-83 season, Wagner penetrated against the same Andre Turner, forcing the point guard off-balance as Wagner stopped and sank a 16-footer to give U of L a dramatic 64-62 victory in overtime.

Only a week ago, Wagner beat South Carolina with two free throws and only two seconds left to play for the 65-63 win. Against

Western Kentucky early in the year, Wagner's two free throws with 11 seconds left provided the winning margin in a 73-70 triumph. Against Indiana, which fell 65-63, Wagner contributed three free throws in the final 10 seconds and scored the final 10 points for the Cards. In another game with South Carolina, his 18-footer with 24 seconds to play pushed U of L ahead, 74-71. The Cards won 74-72.

"I've only seen one player with as much confidence as Milt," Hall said, "and that was Darrell Griffith. Milt wants the ball at the end."

Milt Wagner always wants the ball.

"The 'Ice Man' never lets things worry him," said Milton Wagner, Sr., an elementary school janitor who calls himself "Ice Cube."

"He's experienced greater pressure than that just walking out the door in the morning," said Louisville assistant coach Wade Houston. "So making two free throws isn't going to bother Milt Wagner."

So Wagner calmly sank the tying free throw, knotting the score at 69-69. He turned to the roaring fans and waved both hands above his head, smiling from ear-to-ear, then returned to the foul line and sank the other.

That gave Louisville the 70-69 win—it also brought the Metro Conference title to U of L.

"I've said before there's no one I'd rather have at the free throw line under pressure than Milt," Crum said. "That's why they call him 'Ice'—he's always been able to come through in those situations for us."

Wagner finished with 18 points, tying Ellison for the team scoring honors. But Thompson did the most damage, scoring 16 on 8-of-10 shooting and adding six rebounds and three assists.

"We will be back to clean up next week," promised Memphis State center William Bedford, referring to the Metro post-season tourney.

But it was Wagner who mopped up Memphis in the tournament final. After beating Cincinnati 86-65 in the semifinal round on March 8, U of L blistered Memphis State 88-79 before 19,611 fans—another Freedom Hall attendance record.

Wagner led the way with 31 points and Ellison, the tourney's MVP, added 21 points, 13 rebounds, four blocked shots, three steals and three assists.

Louisville led only 40-36 at halftime, but a 15-1 run to start the second half settled the issue.

"Milt won it for us," said Ellison. "I think he was the MVP. He made every big shot for us. He's a big reason why we've come on this year. Milt is our leader."

"We are capable of being a Final Four team," Wagner said. "We've got us a true center for the first time."

Crum's Cards now sported a record of 26-7 after winning 11 straight and 15 of their last 16, earning an automatic spot in the NCAA Tournament. The NCAA Tournament Committee gave the Cards the No. 2 seed in the West regional behind top-seeded St. John's.

"It doesn't look easy," Crum said. "But there aren't any easy draws anymore. You either keep up or you go home and start watching. We're going to try to play for a while. I think we are ready for the tournament."

In the opening round of the West Regional in Utah, Louisville was sluggish but deep and talented enough to whip Drexel, 93-73. The game produced two memorable performances and one memorable quote.

The outstanding player was Thompson, who hit 9-of-12 shots from the field, all six of his free throw attempts, and 24 points to go along with 10 rebounds. The award for outstanding supporting role would have gone to McSwain, who thought seriously about quitting the team only two short months earlier, but came off the bench to score 15 points and grab eight rebounds in only 19 minutes of playing time.

The memorable quote came from Wagner. Did he know anything about the first-round opponent before the pairings? "Drexel," Wagner said, "is one of those academic schools, I think."

Bradley, an old Missouri Valley Conference rival of U of L before the Cards joined the Metro, beat Texas-El Paso 83-65 to earn a shot at the Cardinals in the round of 32.

"Louisville is one of those TV teams," said Bradley guard Jim Les. "And those are the kind of teams we want to play."

If Bradley's players were yearning for recognition, they blew their opportunity against Louisville on March 15. The Cardinals came out sluggish. At the half, Louisville's lead was only four points, 35-31.

But Kimbro turned in a solid 23-minute relief performance with eight points, four assists and some solid defense. McSwain logged 20 minutes off the bench and came up with a rally-killing steal. And with Thompson (14 points), Ellison (16) and Wagner (16) sharing the scoring load, Louisville pulled away to win 82-68.

"I thought we looked tired for some reason," said Bradley coach Dick Versace. "I think we could have beaten Louisville if our energy level had been a little higher."

"The big difference," said Crum, "was our depth. Our bench was deeper, and they got fatigued at this altitude and couldn't keep up. Tony has had a great second half of the season. He's come off the bench and lifted us in a lot of ways. He's made a lot of clutch plays at both ends. He's an excellent defensive player."

With Drexel and Bradley out of the way, Louisville could focus on North Carolina.

"North Carolina is good, but we're good, too," said Wagner. "It'll be two great coaches and two great teams."

Funny how things turned out.

U of L met Carolina at The Summit in Houston—the same place Crum's Cards won the Midwest Regional in 1980. For 13 straight weeks the Tar Heels—now 28-5—were rated No. 1. But a late tailspin caused by injuries resulted in four losses in the last five regular season games. Still, Carolina had not lost to a team outside the Atlantic Coast Conference.

"They were No. 1 all year until they had those injuries," Crum said. "Now that they're back and healthy, why wouldn't they be the same team they were before? They look like No. 1 to me."

In fact, the Tar Heels were rated No. 8 going into their game with Louisville. But Gene Bartow, the Alabama-Birmingham coach, wasn't fooled. "I'm a little in awe of them," Bartow said of UNC after

UAB lost to the Tar Heels 77-59 in the second round of the regional in Utah. "They're just a great all-around basketball team. Until a month ago, they were everybody's No. 1 team in the country, and now they're healthy again."

Much of the pre-game hype centered around the center, 7-foot Brad Daugherty for North Carolina and 6-9 Pervis Ellison for Louisville. Someone asked Crum if he thought that would be a good match-up.

"I'm sure Dean (Smith) thinks so," Crum said. "I'd like to line up every week against a freshman. I think that's a distinct advantage they have."

Daugherty said he wasn't too familiar with Ellison, who was named Freshman of the Year by both the *Basketball Times* and *Basketball Weekly*.

"I really don't know much about him," Daugherty said. "From what I understand he's having a good year and coming along. But I really haven't had a chance to watch him play that much."

Crum told reporters he wasn't concerned about North Carolina's heralded bench strength. The Tar Heels started three guards—6-4 Steve Hale, 6-3 Kenny Smith and 6-2 Jeff Lebo—to go with 6-10 Joe Wolf and the 7-foot Daugherty. But much of the team's success resulted from contributions made by 6-11 Warren Martin, 6-9 Dave Popson and 6-5 Curtis Hunter.

"They have as much depth as anybody, or more," Crum said. "We're just going to have to outplay the ones they've got in there with the ones we've got in there."

And that's what Louisville did.

With Crum masterfully exploiting mismatches—especially on the front line, where Billy Thompson and Herbert Crook performed doggedly—Louisville sent the Tar Heels packing, 94-79.

Carolina had a problem covering Thompson with the 6-4 Steve Hale. When Dean Smith substituted the larger Warren Martin for Hale, Crook outquicked the slow-footed big man.

"Louisville had a great game," said Smith. "They were tremendous—better than I'd seen on tape. I think we got their best shot."

For the longest time, Carolina hung tough. Jeff Lebo's 25-footer beat the buzzer at halftime and tied the score at 43. But Louisville exploded out of the blocks to start the second half, outscoring North Carolina 16-4 in the first 4:41 to open a 59-47 lead and force Smith to spend a timeout.

"Louisville's intensity was so great at that time that they were getting every loose ball," said Carolina's Joe Wolf. "We turned the ball over too many times, and they got a few fast breaks and dunks."

But Crum told his team during the timeout to be prepared for a Carolina rally. It came after Thompson's 12-footer put U of L ahead, 69-57.

"When you play against good teams, you expect them to do that," said Jeff Hall. "Coach Crum told us they'd make a run at us, and that's exactly what they did."

The Heels ran off 18 of the game's next 22 points, and with 4:31 to play, UNC was back in the lead, 75-73.

"I thought we were in the driver's seat," Dean Smith said. "They were looking shaky."

But a rebound basket for Thompson tied the score and started a string of eight straight points by U of L that resulted in an 81-75 lead with 1:58 left.

"Our guys have all the confidence in the world," said Milt Wagner. "North Carolina came back on us, but we did a great job of coming right back on them when we needed to."

Carolina sliced the U of L lead to four at 81-77 with 1:33 left to play, but it was no contest after that. Crook, who made 9-of-10 free throws, led a parade of Louisville players to the foul line to bury the boys from Tobacco Road. The Cards pushed Carolina out of the tournament by scoring 21 of the game's final 25 points.

"It got away from us at the end," Smith said. "But we were gambling, trying to do anything we could. I thought this was a championship-caliber game—very intense."

"At crunch time, we did things right," Crum said, perhaps reflecting back to early in the season when Louisville gave away several opportunities for wins. "We've made a lot of progress, and now we're making a lot fewer mistakes when the going gets tough and everything is on the line."

Although U of L got its usual balanced scoring—with all five starters in double figures—none stood out any more than bookend forwards Thompson and Crook. Thompson had 24 points, nine rebounds, five assists and two blocked shots. Crook finished with 20 points and tied Thompson for the lead in rebounds with nine.

As for the match in the middle, Daugherty played well with 19 points and 15 rebounds. Ellison supported his teammates with 15 points and six rebounds.

The win raised U of L's record to 29-7 and gave Crum his first victory over Smith in five tries.

"This is the only one that's important," Crum said. "It's the only one that allows us to play again this year."

Louisville's opponent in the West Regional Final would be Auburn, a 70-63 winner over Nevada-Las Vegas. The Tigers finished third in the Southeastern Conference, but like Louisville—now on a 14-game winning streak—Auburn was one of the hottest teams in the country. Earlier in the tournament Auburn and coach Sonny Smith eliminated the West Regional's top seed, St. John's, 81-65.

The best and most ferocious Tiger was Chuck Person, an overlooked 6-6 forward. He made none of the season's All-American lists but would go on to become the NBA Rookie of the Year in 1986-87. Person was a muscular, broad-shouldered senior who could shoot the lights out from anywhere on the floor. He averaged 21.4 points and nearly eight rebounds.

The entire Auburn team was loaded with wide-bodied, high-jumping athletes. "They've got a great player in Person and a lot of really fine players around him," Crum said.

But Auburn's Sonny Smith was in trouble, and he knew it.

As U of L blew the wheels off North Carolina in the final minutes of their game, Sonny Smith watched impassively. When the game ended, he turned to an assistant coach and said matter-of-factly, "The wrong team won. I KNOW we would have beaten North Carolina. But Louisville . . . I just don't think we can beat that team."

He was right.

The West Regional final on March 22 belonged to Louisville.

But U of L had to rely on an uncustomary zone defense and a stroke of genius from Ellison before putting the Tigers away, 84-76.

First, the zone. Before his Bradley team played Louisville, Dick Versace said he watched a game in which the Cards briefly played a zone.

"It was funny," he said. "They had no idea what to do."

But Sonny Smith wasn't laughing when Crum sent his players into a 1-1-3 zone with about 10 minutes to play and Auburn ahead 65-54. For the first 30 minutes, the game had been played up-and-down, back-and-forth, and Auburn's tremendous athletes seemed to be equal—if not superior—to Louisville's own stars.

But the zone—a defense Crum abhors—provided the impetus that lifted U of L to its eight-point win and sent the Cards to Dallas for the sixth Final Four in Crum's 15 seasons as coach.

"We were just trying to change the tempo, and hopefully, they'd make a few mistakes," Crum said of the defensive switch. "We're not a great zone team; we hardly ever practice it."

"You learn that in high school," said Wagner, who teamed with Hall to provide 30 points and 11 assists to lead the U of L attack. "We don't like to play zones, but it doesn't take that much to know what spots to cover."

All day Crum's assistants had urged him to employ a zone against the strong and quick Auburn team. But Crum steadfastly refused until the final 10 minutes.

Certainly, Crum has come a long way as a coach. A man remembered a spring day in Houston in 1971 when Crum engaged his boss—John Wooden—in a spirited debate on the Bruins' bench. The argument between UCLA's legend and his brash young assistant was the same one Crum was now having with his assistants on that day in Houston. Crum wanted UCLA to go to a zone.

"Don't blow the national championship just because you're stubborn," Crum allegedly told Wooden.

But Wooden didn't win 10 national championships because of his assistant coaches alone. Wooden waited patiently until—just at the right time—the legend ordered his team into a zone that turned the game in UCLA's favor and gave the Bruins another national championship.

"Timing has so much to do with it," Crum said after Louisville's win over Auburn. "There are always some real key spots. You don't want to do something out of anxiety or worry. You have to be under control and be able to make the right decision at the right time. I didn't want to rush into something and give them enough time to adjust."

The change to a zone upset Auburn's rhythm so much that the Tigers managed only three baskets over a nine-minute span as Louisville grabbed the lead and gradually pulled away. Auburn made only 43.3 percent of its shots in the second half after hitting a sizzling 62.5 percent in the first half.

"I thought the zone changed the tempo and won the game for them," Auburn's Smith said. "We didn't react to it. It was a tempo-killer for us. They played great inside defense. We could get free to run two or three plays and had to go totally away from them."

Ellison, who by then was 18 going on 30 in basketball years, made a heads-up play that took Auburn out of the game. U of L was clinging to a 73-70 lead with two minutes to play when Auburn forward Jeff Moore got the ball in the lane and tried a 10-footer over Ellison. The 6-9 freshman swatted the shot to Jeff Hall in the backcourt, and Hall raced the other way for an unmolested layup and a 75-70 lead with 1:53 left to play.

"I don't think Moore even saw me," said Ellison. "Once he turned, I tried to tap the ball to Jeff."

"We kind of had eye contact, and I could see Pervis was going up to block the shot," Hall said. "He just tapped it out to me. That's one of Pervis' biggest assets—when he blocks a shot, he doesn't try to put it five rows up in the stands. He finesses it enough to keep it in play so somebody else can go to the races."

"We played about as well as we can play," said Coach Smith, who got 23 points from Person, who took 24 shots. "Louisville is just a great team with good coaching and super players. They deserved to win."

The jubilant Cardinals had five players in double figures once again. And Crook, the unsung forward, was the leader with 20 points and a game-high 11 rebounds. Thompson was again spectacular, chipping in 13 points with seven rebounds and four assists. Ellison finished with 15 points and 10 rebounds. Wagner had 16 points and nine assists. Hall knocked in 7-of-12 shots for 14 points.

With a 15-game win streak and 19 wins in its last 20 games, Louisville rolled into Dallas for its fourth Final Four appearance of the decade. "The reason his peers had not voted Denny Crum their Coach of the Year this season is simple," wrote one reporter for the *Dallas Star.* "He's college basketball's Coach of the Decade."

Before U of L met LSU—a 59-57 upset winner over Kentucky in the Mideast Regional Final—in the Reunion Arena on March 29, Rick Bozich of the *Louisville Times* made a revealing observation.

"They call this the Final Four," wrote Bozich. "That's an appropriate place to find Crum's team because in the Final Four minutes—crunch time—of their four tournament games the Cardinals, suddenly indomitable, have pounded past four tired and confused teams. Remember the numbers: In sweeping over Drexel, Bradley, North Carolina and Auburn, Louisville has outscored its NCAA opponents 66-26 over the final four minutes. Against Carolina and Auburn, two powerful Final Four-caliber teams, the final lights-out runs were 21-4 and 15-6."

"We pushed them as hard as we can push a team," said Auburn's Sonny Smith. "We threw everything we had at them. And they took it all and were ready for more."

Now it was LSU coach Dale Brown's turn to throw something at Louisville. His Cinderella team had used a blend of chemistry and Brown's "freak defense" to reach the Final Four. After a 14-0 start, the Tigers were crippled by the loss of leading scorer Nikita Wilson to grade problems and then by an outbreak of chicken pox that weakened John Williams, leading to three losses in five days.

"We had to get down a little before we started to pull together," said guard Derrick Taylor, explaining his team's 26-11 record.

Louisville fans remembered John Williams as the forward Crum and his assistants coveted in the summer of 1984. He was hailed as the nation's best high school player and reportedly had narrowed his choices to Louisville, UNLV and LSU before signing with LSU.

Herbert Crook remembered John Williams, too. Crook's signing from Eastern High School was no big deal, according to critics. No big press conference. No glowing predictions of success for the local kid. Crook was a nice player, but he was not THE recruit—no John Williams.

Williams was an outstanding sophomore, to be sure. He was the best player on a very talented LSU team. But Crook had developed faster than anyone at U of L had hoped. He improved so much over the summer between his freshman and sophomore seasons that he easily beat out McSwain for a starting job. He had been a key player throughout the season. But in the West Regional he was very nearly the best performer on a team of great performers.

Crook was the perfect mix of grit and guile that Crum's team needed to make a run for the national championship. No one knows what would have happened had Williams chosen U of L over LSU. Perhaps he would have done marvelous things for the Cardinals, or maybe the team's chemistry would not have been the same. Perhaps Crook would have been reduced to a role player.

As Crum said before, "These things have a way of working themselves out."

So on Saturday, March 29, in Dallas, Louisville (30-7) and LSU (26-11) were in one semifinal while No. 1 Duke (36-2) met No. 2 Kansas (35-3) in the other.

"I'm on a mission," announced Milt Wagner. "I've already been to the Final Four two times. This is my third trip. Just getting here isn't enough for me. My mission is not complete. This time, I want to go out in style. I want to win this one."

So why was Denny Crum chewing out Wagner at halftime in Dallas on March 29? Perhaps it was because LSU owned a 44-36 lead after Wagner played what Crum considered "mission impossible" basketball. The 6-5 senior guard missed four shots in a row, had four turnovers and was twice pulled from the game.

"I told him at halftime that he was supposed to be one of our leaders," Crum said, "but he didn't play like a leader."

"He motivated me," said Wagner, who went out in the second half and hit five of his first six shots and played 20 minutes without an error.

Of course, the Cards made other adjustments in the second half, most notably ganging up around the bullish 6-8 Williams. That meant conceding jumpers to the Tiger guard, but they were firing blanks. In basketball, if you can't hit the outside jumper, life is going to be tough.

Louisville used a 13-0 run in the second half to assume control and ran away with an 88-77 win. During Louisville's big run, LSU missed 11 straight shots.

"They double-and triple-teamed John (Williams), and when he kicked it back out, we couldn't hit the jumpers," said Derrick Taylor.

The Cards were as brilliant in the final 20 minutes as they were dull in the first 20. By the time it ended, five players again scored in double figures, topped by 22 points each from senior forward Billy Thompson (10-of-11 shooting from the field) and senior guard Milt Wagner, who added a career-high 10 assists.

Crook had 16 points and nine rebounds (Williams had 14 points and nine rebounds for LSU). Ellison had 11 points and 13 rebounds while Hall had 14 points.

The U of L players combined for 26 assists. They out-rebounded LSU 44-35. They shot 64 percent in the second half to LSU's 35 percent, and it all added up to Louisville's 16th straight victory and its 20th in the last 21 games.

"At halftime," said assistant coach Jerry Jones, "he told them they looked like they never had been coached."

But Wagner responded to Crum's criticism, and Thompson was marvelous, adding 10 rebounds in the second half while holding Williams to only one basket in the second half. In five NCAA Tournament games, the star-crossed Thompson had ascended to new—and long-awaited—heights.

Coaches and players alike will tell you the NCAA Tournament really is a separate season. Under the glare of the TV lights and before a large national TV audience, every winning basket is magnified, just as is every turnover.

It was during this separate and wonderful season in March 1986 when the pieces of the basketball puzzle fell into place for Billy Thompson.

"It's been messed up for four years," Thompson told Rick Bozich. "My freshman year had some rough spots. My sophomore year I got hurt. My junior year Milt got hurt. But I knew that eventually it would all come together."

The question that begged an answer was obvious. Could Thompson lead U of L to a national championship and, in the process, erase the painful memories of past seasons and games—games where he was booed by his own fans?

"When people say I'm not coming to form like they expected," Thompson said, "I ask myself, 'What am I doing on the court? Am I not giving 100 percent? What is it that you want?' If I have to score 40 points, I don't think I'm going to score 40 points at Louisville. If I went to another school, I'd probably have to score 40 points because no one else would be able to score 10 or 15. But it's not that way here."

Thompson accepted the criticism, but his coach did not.

"I don't think anybody could have played as well as people thought Billy should have played when he came to Louisville," Crum said. "It was hard for him initially because there was so much attention. Undue pressure was placed on him, but he's handled it well. He's as complete a player as I've ever coached."

For proof, Crum pointed out that Thompson was the team leader in scoring and field goal percentage; he was second in assists, rebounds and blocked shots. But when Thompson came to U of L from Camden High, he moved from the hot-seat to the hot-house. Because Al McGuire called him America's best high school player and because others said he would be even better than Julius Erving, the kid with the soft jump shot and telescoping arms never had a chance.

He was born in Camden and lived in the city until he was 11. His family moved to Stratford. Unlike many U of L players, Thompson came from an upper-middle class family. His father, Curnell, was program officer for the federal government's Housing and Urban Development; his mother, Hazel, was a librarian; an older brother, Tommy, was a model and actor in New York City; a cousin, Lola Falana, a well-known entertainer.

Every year the All-America teams ignored him. Even the Metro-Conference all-tournament team snubbed him this season. And even now—after five outstanding NCAA Tournament games—Thompson was taking a back seat to Johnny Dawkins, Danny Manning and John Williams.

Going into his senior year, Thompson said his biggest thrill was playing against the U.S.S.R. in the 1985 World University Games. Now, finally, he was on the threshold of something greater. He was on the verge of winning the most important prize in college basketball, the price Louisville fans unfairly believed he would win once a year, not once in a career.

"The boos and the disappointments are all in the past," Thompson said on the eve of the NCAA Final. "I don't look back. I look at today and tomorrow."

Crum put Thompson and his teammates through their final practice on Sunday, March 30. It was a brief, one-hour workout— nothing more than a tune-up for Monday night's showdown with Duke, which had beaten Kansas in the other semifinal game.

As practice came to a close and players began leaving the court, Crum had an idea. "Hold up, fellas," said the coach. "Let's go over one thing before we leave."

"I was sitting in the stands and all the media were sitting around me watching this practice," remembered John Dromo, the former U of L head coach. "Denny got all the guys together as an afterthought, really. And then he walked them through an option in his offense that he thought he might use against Duke. It turned out that the option he showed them was the very one he went to in the last three minutes that got Ellison and Wagner baskets to win the game."

"Everybody was there watching—all the media experts—and nobody noticed. Nobody realized what was happening."

John Dromo realized it, of course. He had been a coach too many years not to notice. He left Reunion Arena surprised. "It amazed me that he could add something that late in the season—it only took him five minutes—and then to have those kids execute it perfectly the next night. I've always said that Denny Crum is the best at communicating to his players what he wants them to do. He explains those things so clearly that they almost never get it wrong."

Crum once said, "I'm always looking for a small edge. That's all you need. When we get down to the end of a game I always feel we have an edge because our kids are in good condition. Our schedule has given us the confidence to play against the best. The kids have confidence in my ability to make the right decision, and they've been drilled enough to know what to do."

At 9:12 p.m. EST on March 31, 1986, No. 7 ranked Louisville went looking for "the edge" against top-ranked Duke.

For all but the final two minutes and some change, Louisville's quest for a second national title was a nervous, uphill schedule.

On a couple of occasions, U of L led by a couple of baskets. But for most of the night, the Cardinals trailed. The Cards eased into the lead with 17:13 to play, 42-41, but Duke quickly regained the advantage and U of L went back to its struggles.

With eight minutes left in the game, Duke's All-American guard, Johnny Dawkins, already had 22 points. Almost single-handedly he kept the Cards at bay. Crum searched for an answer. He tried Milt Wagner at first, but that didn't work. He called on Tony Kimbro and Kevin Walls, two quick freshmen. Dawkins still cruised. Herbert Crook, the forward, got the assignment next but Dawkins continued to score. With eight minutes left in the game and Duke leading 58-55, Crum tried man-to-man defense and gave the assignment to Jeff Hall, not as quick as the other Cards who had tried to guard Dawkins.

"It was a combination of defenses," Crum said. "I told Jeff to stay between Dawkins and the ball wherever Dawkins went."

Had Crum lost his marbles?

Dawkins was a blur. He had rockets on his feet. Running from end line to end line, Dawkins would probably beat Hall by 20 feet. When Hall came to U of L from Westwood, Kentucky, (population 5,000), the mountain folks in eastern Kentucky were stunned.

"Honey," said Jeff's mother, Martha Hall, "this part of Kentucky is all UK."

For the longest time, Jeff Hall was all UK, too.

"Jeffrey was a UK fan," Martha said. "Now, don't get me wrong, he loves Louisville and Louisville is his home, but like any kid growing up in this part of the state, he liked Kentucky."

"I never heard a lot about Louisville until they started recruiting me," Hall remembered. "Then I began paying attention to them, looking at their box scores. When I came for my visit here, I just fell in love with the place."

Hall had been recruited by Morehead State and Marshall in nearby Huntington, West Virginia. Kentucky made a late rush when the Wildcats heard Hall was leaning toward Louisville. But by then, it was too late. His mind was made up.

"I had Jeff talk to Wade Houston and Wade did a great job with him," remembered Bobby Dotson, the U of L assistant coach. "Wade told him he had an opportunity to be a hero here. And he was right."

Hall was already a hero in Westwood and surrounding towns. He had averaged 28.5 points for Fairview High and, as a senior, was named to the Kentucky All-Star team after earning a spot on the All-State team. When he signed the scholarship papers with U of L, Westwood woke up to the wonderful world of Denny Crum and the Cardinals.

Brian Unrue, who grew up across the street from Hall, said, "We all got to be good friends with Coach Dotson. Most of the people who went to (high) school with Jeff started liking Louisville."

"I'll give you an example of how things have changed," Hall said. "When I was growing up, you wouldn't see anything Louisville. Now, you see license plates on cars and things like that. It makes you feel good to be a part of that."

Crum's eyes lit up the first time he saw Hall shoot a basketball. "Probably the best shooter we've ever had here," said Crum.

In four seasons, he improved the other parts of his game, too. Wagner's injury in Hall's junior year put more pressure on the 6-4 Hall to handle the ball and direct the offense. He worked hard—as hard as any player Crum had ever coached—and he made remarkable strides.

But Hall didn't have quick feet. He never had blazing speed. He was appreciated for his shooting touch. He surprised people with his jumping ability, but he was never quick.

When Hall was a freshman playing in the Final Four, Crum gave the mountain boy a crack at the big time. Wagner needed a break. "Play good defense and don't force anything," Crum told him as he sent him into the game against Houston. "If you're open, shoot. But just concentrate on playing good defense."

Hall nodded and checked in. His man, 5-9 Alvin Franklin, was quick on quick. Twice he blew past Hall, once scoring on a jumper and then passing to Clyde Drexler for a layup. When Franklin beat Hall a third time, Crum had no choice. He wanted Hall to have a taste of the Final Four. He knew Hall would fit into his plans somewhere down the line. The experience against Houston would be helpful to him as well as the team, but Jeff Hall was just too slow to stay with Alvin Franklin, and Crum had to yank him.

"Coach," Hall said returning to the bench, shaking his head, "I'm sorry. I couldn't stay with him. He was too quick for me."

Of course, Crum knew that before Hall went in. "I know," Crum told Hall, "you did your best. That's all you can do."

Now, four years later, here was Jeff Hall being asked to shut down Johnny Dawkins, the quickest player in college basketball.

"I just tried to face guard him and deny him the ball," Hall said. "He's awfully hard to stop once he gets the ball. So I just tried to stay right with him."

Hall bounced off picks and screens like a pinball. But he stayed low—and determined—and he dogged Johnny Dawkins every step of the way.

Getting a feel for the history and tradition: Not long after being named Louisville's coach, Denny Crum holds the game ball from the University of Louisville's 76-61 win over the University of Kentucky in the 1959 NCAA Tournament.

Denny as a baby in 1937.

Denny captured in a suit and tie already at age two.

Smiling Denny at 4 years old.

Denny, 4, playing ball with his
sisters, Juanita and Pauline.

Five-year-old Denny enjoying his two puppies,
Princess and Dutchess.

Crum coaching an NCAA
Tournament game in 1982.

Denny at 4 years old.

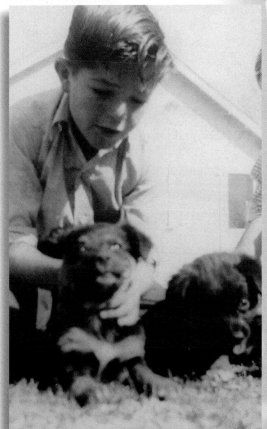

Game at Freedom Hall in 1999.

Denny, his younger sister, Pauline, and his father, Alwin Denzel Crum in 1940.

Denny with his two sisters and their grandmother, Rachael Crum.

Pauline and Denny and their two puppies.

Denny and his childhood best friend, Don Woods, during their trip to the Northern California Redwoods in 1952.

Pauline and Denny (1940).

Denny and his sisters.

Denny, Aunt Marie, Pauline, Uncle ~~rlie~~, and Grandfather Crum in 1949.

Coach Crum focused on the game (1998).

Denny and his father (1970).

Denny and his cousin, Leona Sharp, in 196[

Denny as the coach of a Pan Am team in 1987.

...shing on Lake Ponderay with son Scott, ...en age 2.

Denny with one of his players, Kip Stone, in 1991.

Coach Crum appearing on a commercial for Dairymen Assocation in 1981.

Denny and Scott at Disneyland in 1986.

Denny fishing with friends on a house boat in Vene.
Left to right: Howard Patterson, Doug Wearren, Jc
Rogers, Russ Brown, and Denny.

Charity golf tournament with John
Dorkin, CEO for WDRB TV.

Denny and Robbie Shaw
after their 1986 NCAA
Championship.

Bone fishing with a guide in Venezuela in 1991.

Smallmouth fishing at Lake Erie in 1994.

Denny, Mike Conliffe, Bob Shaw, Steve Crum, an unidentified golfer, and Daryl Elser at the Wildwood Country Club charity scramble for a cerebral palsy school.

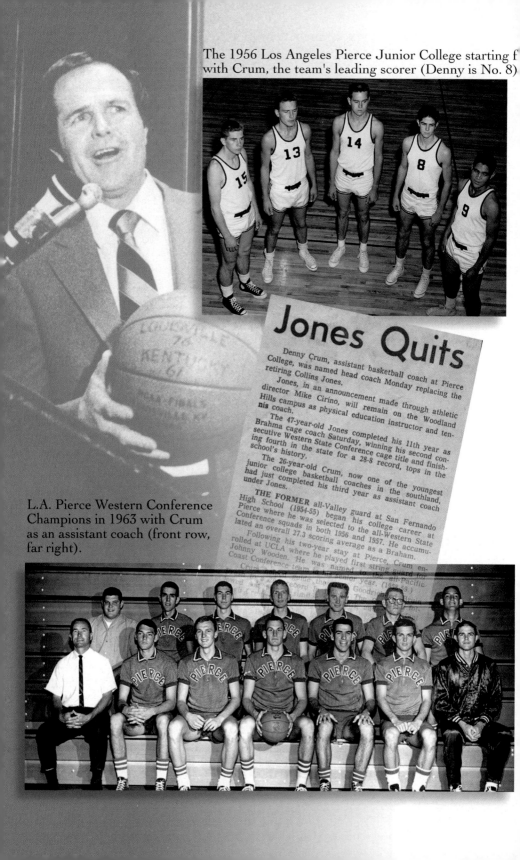

The 1956 Los Angeles Pierce Junior College starting f
with Crum, the team's leading scorer (Denny is No. 8)

Jones Quits

Denny Crum, assistant basketball coach at Pierce College, was named head coach Monday replacing the retiring Collins Jones.

Jones, in an announcement made through athletic director Mike Cirino, will remain on the Woodland Hills campus as physical education instructor and tennis coach.

The 47-year-old Jones completed his 11th year as Brahma cage coach Saturday, winning his second consecutive Western State Conference cage title and finishing fourth in the state for a 28-8 record, tops in the school's history.

The 26-year-old Crum, now one of the youngest junior college basketball coaches in the southland, had just completed his third year as assistant coach under Jones.

THE FORMER all-Valley guard at San Fernando High School (1954-55) began his college career at Pierce where he was selected to the all-Western State Conference squads in both 1956 and 1957. He accumulated an overall 27.3 scoring average as a Brahma.

Following his two-year stay at Pierce, Crum enrolled at UCLA where he played first string guard for Johnny Wooden. He was named to the all-Pacific Coast Conference team in the junior year, (1958-59.)

L.A. Pierce Western Conference
Champions in 1963 with Crum
as an assistant coach (front row,
far right).

Crum Named Basketball Coach

Jones Resigns After Guiding Team to Title

By Joe Marek
Sports Editor

Denny Crum, former assistant basketball coach, has been named to succeed Collins Jones as the head coach of the Pierce basketball squad.

Jones, who guided the Brahmas to their most successful season ever this year, resigned last Monday, stating, "I've really enjoyed my tenure as head coach at Pierce. However, because of conflicting interests, and because I've been in the coaching business for a long time, I decided to step down." Jones will continue as a regular P.E. instructor and coach of the tennis team.

Crum, who for the past three seasons has been as assistant to Jones, said, "I'm very grateful for the opportunity to become the head coach of the basketball team. I hope to continue the winning tradition that the coach has established at

11 seasons as head coach at Pierce, Jones compiled a record of 130-124. His won-lost mark for conference games was 52-35.

A familiar face on the Pierce

DENNY CRUM

WINGTON HERALD-LEADER, FRIDAY, FEBRUARY 11, 19

Coach Crum: greatness was always a goal

By Gene McLean
Herald-Leader staff writer

Years and many, many rubber basketballs ago, there was a bunch of high school kids who hung out together at the city park in San Fernando, Calif.

One day, between arguments, kidding, and an occasional pickup game, the Valley Boys noticed a sign hanging on the chain link fence. "Spring Summer Basketball League. Begins this year. Get your team ready."

The kids knew about the league.

But there remained one question. Who was going to be the high school coach...

Rupp had 14, Smith 13 and Tarkanian 12.

Crum's overall record now is 283-77 for a winning percentage of .786. That ranks him second in the nation among active coaches (behind Tarkanian) and fifth among the winningest major college coaches of all time (behind Clair Bee, Rupp, Wooden and Tarkanian).

Also ... is the seventh ... one ... NCAA tournament winning. ... active ... coach.

Down on the farm, Denny Crum and his 19-month-old son Scotty gaze at the pond on their Jefferson County pond.

Denny Crum's teams in NCAA and NIT action

1972 — Lost to UCLA 96-77 in NCAA semifinals in Los Angeles.

1973 — Lost to Notre Dame in the second round of the NIT.

1974 — Lost to Oral Roberts 96-93 in the Midwest Regional semifinals.

1975 — Lost to UCLA 75-74 in OT in semifinals in San Diego.

1976 — Lost in first round of NIT to Providence.

1977 — Lost 87-79 to UCLA in first round of West Regional in Idaho.

1978 — Lost to DePaul 90-89 in two OTs in Midwest Regional semifinal.

1979 — Lost to Arkansas 73-62 in Midwest Regional semifinals.

1980 — Beat Iowa 80-72 in semifinal and beat UCLA for the title.

1981 — Lost to Arkansas 74-73 in second round of Midwest Regional.

1982 — Lost to Georgetown 54-46 in Final Four semifinals.

... and his record at Louisville

Year	Won - Lost	Year	Won - Lost
1971-72	26 - 5	1977-78	20 - 7
1972-73	23 - 7	1978-79	24 - 8
1973-74	21 - 7	1979-80	33 - 3
1974-75	28 - 3	1980-81	21 - 9
1975-76	20 - 8	1981-82	23 - 10
1976-77	21 - 7	Totals	283 - 74

Coach Crum in action in the 1983 Final Four in New Orleans.

Denny and his assistant coach, Wade Houston, coaching in 1986 at Freedom Hall.

Crum and his mentor, John Wooden, at
Crum's Hall of Fame induction in 1994.

Denny and
Alex Sanders
on the bench
during the
1998-99
season.

ach
m in
8.

Pre-game talk at Freedom Hall (1997-98 season).

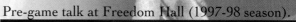

Crum coaching Cameron Murray during the 1998-99 season.

Crum at Freedom Ha (1998-99) wi assistant coac Scott Davenport and Jerry M head trainer.

Crum and Tom Lasorda, v gave a pre-ga talk before UCLA gam Freedom F (1997-9

Alex Sanders taking instruction from Coach Crum (1998-99 season).

Coach Crum and Athletic Director Bill Olsen.

Crum posing with his Hall of Fame plaque in 1994.

Denny accepting the game ball for reaching his 600-win mark at Freedom Hall against Georgia Tech on Jan. 11, 1997.

All Hall did was limit Dawkins to two free throws in the final eight minutes. Try as he would, Dawkins could not shake Hall.

"Jeff was a little fresher—he hadn't had to dodge him or guard him all game," Crum said. "Dawkins is the one they go to down the stretch. He's gotten key baskets for them all year, and we thought it would be a calculated risk worth taking. We decided if somebody was going to beat us, it wouldn't be Dawkins."

With Hall turning into a gem of a defensive player and the other U of L players doing their job in the zone, Louisville limited Duke to 39 percent shooting in the second half. The Blue Devils, American's No. 1 ranked team, got only three baskets in the final 11 minutes. And two of those were follow-up shots.

Duke held the lead until Wagner—working the play Crum put into his offense only the day before—scored from underneath on a pass from Crook with 3:22 to go, giving U of L a 64-63 advantage.

Dawkins dropped in two free throws at the end to give the lead back to Duke. But then Billy Thompson got Mark Alarie off his feet with a perfect head fake and swished a six-footer in the lane. The lead was back in Louisville's favor, 66-65, with 2:47 to go.

Louisville never trailed again. But it needed two big plays from Ellison to hold off the proud Blue Devils.

After running the game clock down 48 seconds and the shot clock to 11, Crum called a timeout.

"We wanted to get the ball to Jeff or Milt, then clear out and let them go one-on-one," Crum said. "If you try to run a set play in those situations, you have to make one or two passes. And with defense as well as they play, it sometimes gets you turnovers."

Hall got a shot about 18 feet out on the wing, but the ball missed everything. However, Ellison was there to grab it and put it in for a 68-65 lead with 41 seconds left in the game.

"I saw the shot was falling short," Ellison said. "I reacted and it seemed I was the only one jumping because I didn't see anyone else around me. I just laid it in."

Fourteen seconds later, Ellison stepped to the foul line. And the man called "Never Nervous" Pervis calmly sank two free throws to put U of L up, 70-65.

"I'm pretty sure I get nervous at times," Ellison said. "But once I made the first one, I relaxed."

Duke center Jay Bilas rebounded a miss by a teammate to pull Duke within three, 70-67 with 19 seconds left. Then, after Thompson missed a bonus attempt from the free throw line for Louisville, Danny Ferry scored on a rebound to cut the Cards lead to just one, 70-69.

Three seconds remained. An inbounds pass went to Wagner, who was fouled. Now there were two seconds left. Louisville 70, Duke 69, and the "Ice Man" on the line.

Hadn't Louisville been there before? Of course, and this time, the results were the same. Wagner buried both free throws to "ice" the win and the NCAA Championship for Louisville, 72-69.

All along, Pervis Ellison knew it would happen that way.

"Kenny," Ellison told his Fairmont Hotel roommate on the morning of the game, "we're going to win the national championship today."

"Pervis, how do you know we're going to win?" Kenny Payne asked.

"Because," said Ellison, "they don't have anybody who can stop 'Ice.'"

"Is that all?" Payne asked.

"Because they don't have anybody who can stop Billy," Ellison said.

"Anything else?" Payne asked.

"Because they don't have anybody who can stop me," Ellison said.

Then—the *Louisville Times* columnist, Rick Bozich, who first reported that conversation, also pointed out Ellison's love for John Wayne westerns. Clearly, Ellison's game-day prediction would make "The Duke" proud.

But it was Ellison's performance in the championship game that had Crum and the U of L players smiling. Ellison had a game-high 25 points, 11 rebounds and always seemed to be in the right place at the right time. In the final four minutes, nearly every big play at both ends involved Ellison. In fact, he stood so much taller than anyone else that he was named the Most Outstanding Player of the Final Four.

With Ellison scoring six of U of L's final 12 points, the "Crunch Bunch" outscored Duke 10-6 in the last four minutes. That raised their dominance over six NCAA tourney opponents to 91-42 in the final four minutes of each game.

"I don't think I took charge," Ellison said. "The ball just came to me."

"We knew we had a height advantage at one spot," Crum said. "We took advantage of our height with Pervis."

"Pervis doesn't say a whole lot in interviews because he's not comfortable with all the praise," said assistant coach Wade Houston. "He understands there are four seniors on this team, and he wants them to get recognition. It's important to him to be known as a team player."

"Ellison was terrific," said Duke coach Mike Krzyzewski. "He played a sensational game. He was a true force inside both offensively and defensively. He does some of the things David Robinson of Navy does, except (Ellison) has the people around him who can take advantage of the things he does."

"After we got through the early part of our schedule," Crum said, "when we got to the tough stretches of games, they've always responded and found a way to win. That's to their credit. They're tough mentally. They work hard and do everything you ask teams to do."

"Ellison made some very athletic moves around the basket," Alarie said. "We knew about his offensive rebounding ability and his blocked shots. But his offensive moves around the basket surprised me."

Crum thought about the final record—32-7—and the 17-game win streak, and he wondered out loud what a lot of others were thinking. "I'm not sure," Crum said, "that we've reached our potential yet. I think if the season went another two or three weeks, we'd really be a great, great team."

Not that the 1985-86 Cards weren't a great team already.

Besides Ellison, Thompson (13 points in the final) and Crook (10) were in double figures. And the Louisville guards—Wagner and Hall—had a large hand in the victory. Duke may have had the upperhand in backcourt scoring, but it was Hall who shut down Dawkins in the closing minutes. And it was Wagner who nailed the clinching free throws in the final seconds.

"We executed when we had to," Wagner said. "I loved that situation at the end. I hadn't done much else. It was a great way to go out—on top of the world."

"I couldn't feel any better," Crum said. "I don't know how I could. That's the way we finished the whole second half of the season. We did what we had to do when we had to do it."

Before the season began, Wagner promised U of L fans, "We will be a dynasty!"

Crum, who does not care for the term, was proud.

"I don't know how exactly you define a dynasty," Crum said. "I guess if anyone since the '70s would warrant that kind of attention, it would be us. But I don't think we're going to be a dynasty like Coach Wooden had at UCLA."

All in all, it was a typical season for Crum and his Cardinals. The coach got hit in the head at Cincinnati when the Bearcat students did their rendition of the "Ice Capades"—throwing ice. The Cards finished strong under Crum's patient hand, a trademark of his teams in the 1980s. And finally, Crum was passed over in Coach of the Year voting. In the National Association of Basketball Coaches' voting, Crum's name appeared on one ballot. That tied him with Minnesota's Jim Dutcher—who resigned halfway through the season!

Crum did not let that bother him, because he was ascending college basketball's mountain and reaching the peak.

No one else stood there in 1985-86 except one coach, Denny Crum.

CHAPTER 8

JOHN WOODEN

Any conversation with Denny Crum either begins or ends with John Wooden. He is a man who had a profound influence on Crum as a player, coach and friend.

"As a player, I learned so much from Coach Wooden," Crum said. "He wasn't fancy, and we didn't do a lot of things that were considered fancy. Coach taught us the fundamentals of the game. He even gave us a lot of leeway in terms of what we did on the floor. And he recognized my strengths."

As a skinny 10th grader at San Fernando High School, Crum volunteered to coach his friends in a Spring-Summer basketball league. Since none of the school coaches were allowed to coach in the league, Crum took the opportunity. The team won the league, and his players nicknamed him "Little John Wooden."

Even listing all of the things he has learned from Wooden is difficult for Crum.

"I don't know if you can put any one finger on it," Crum said. "There were a lot of things: the organization, the planning of practice, the evaluation of your practices, the attention to details, and the profession of teaching and learning. Of all of those things, organization was probably the most beneficial to me. I have a pretty imaginative mind when it comes to offenses and defenses. I think Coach Wooden helped me most on how to organize and plan and teach everything. He's a master teacher. That's where he excels. I learned that more than anything else."

Even though Crum is not concerned about his own basketball legacy, he is certain that Wooden has influenced the college game more than anyone.

"You could probably go back since collegiate basketball first started and never find anyone who has had the impact on the game that he's had," Crum said. "Not only in style, but in terms of how he approached the game. The way he dominated college basketball for so long is mind-boggling. You look around and no one can come close to doing what they did at UCLA. And of course Coach Wooden was the architect of all that. He is probably as versatile a teacher as anyone I have ever seen. He was just a great teacher of the game. He was successful with small players, tall players and all different kinds of teams. I think that versatility and longevity that he enjoyed by being at the top is mind-boggling. When you look at how it is today, nobody can dominate like that. He was the best. You kind of wish he was still coaching."

Wooden's mark lives on through Crum's own style, which still sports several Wooden trademarks.

"I learned basketball as a player and coach under him," Crum said. "We do a lot of similar things. Over the years you change Xs and Os, but the basic underlying philosophy of what you are trying to do—your teaching, philosophy of schedule, mental preparation and all the things that go into having a successful season—are things I learned from him. Whatever successes we've had at Louisville, I give him a lot of the credit because I learned from him."

Some coaches "blow smoke" when they talk about how they regard former mentors, but former U of L assistant coach Bill Olsen said Crum's affection for Wooden could not be more genuine.

"His regard for Coach Wooden is as sincere as anything I know," Olsen said. "I was the freshman coach for Denny when he came here. I come from a Marine background. That kind of regimented approach is what I brought to my coaching. I didn't have the appreciation for the bigger picture that I ended up gaining from Denny. He'd say, 'You need to have more patience. Coach Wooden wouldn't do it this way. This is how we're going to do it.' And he was almost always right."

During Crum's first season at Louisville, he took the Cards to the Final Four, only to lose to Wooden's UCLA team, made up of players Crum recruited.

"I was glad that if we didn't win it, they did," Crum said. "For my close relationship with those kids and Coach Wooden, I was not as unhappy as some people would be."

The night Wooden announced his retirement—at the Final Four after beating Crum's Louisville team in the semifinals—is a night that still sticks with Crum.

"That was an emotional thing," Crum said. "That's what I had taken the Louisville job for—to prove I could be a Division I coach. Then to play Coach Wooden and find out he was going to retire really got to me. But he came back the next night and won another national championship. I was so happy for him. He got to go out as the true champion he always was."

Over the years, Crum gained even more respect for the dynasty Wooden built.

"I was so fortunate to learn under Coach Wooden," Crum said. "When I took the Louisville job and took my first team to the Final Four, I actually thought in my mind that this is how it's supposed to be—I thought we knew more about this than a lot of other guys. I mean, after that first year, I really thought we were supposed to be at the Final Four every year just because that's how it always seemed to be at UCLA. At the time, I just didn't know any better. Looking back, some of my thoughts were very foolish because there is so much that goes into getting your team to that level where they have a chance to win it all. I quickly learned it's a whole lot different as an assistant than as a head coach. As an assistant, you don't get credit when you win, but you don't get blame when you lose. The head coach has those responsibilities. So after my second or third year, I really appreciated even more how Coach Wooden did things. I look back and was so lucky to play for him, coach under him and even coach against him. Of course, I'd rather play against someone else. But just watching Coach Wooden coach was something I'll never forget."

Crum also credits his other two coaches—Vinnie Seekins at San Fernando High School and Collins Jones at Pierce Junior College—with helping shape him as a coach.

"Coach Seekins was just such a down-to-earth person, one of those guys who kept everything simple, never got upset and yelled or screamed," Crum said. "He was a real gentleman as well as a real fundamental coach. He passed away, and I still think of him often."

At Pierce, Jones was similar.

"Coach Jones was a lot like Coach Seekins," Crum said. "He was very religious—a good gentleman. He's just one of the nicest people you'd ever want to be around. Coach Jones always wore a coat and tie, and always wore dress shoes. I can't think of a time he was not meticulously dressed. And he was a first-class person; he never said anything bad about anyone. I just loved to be around him. He was as honest and up front as anyone you've ever found. He impressed me so much. I decided to go to junior college because of him primarily. I had good enough grades to go to UCLA out of high school. But I did not have the money, and UCLA didn't recruit me."

Jones did a solid job on the court as well.

"The program at Pierce had never really been that strong," Crum said. "Coach Jones wanted to make it strong. When he recruited me, he picked up a couple of other pretty good kids. We won two conference championships."

"The thing that helped me as a player—and as an aspiring coach—was that I had real good high school coaches and real good junior college coaches," Crum said.

Jones, in his mid-80s, still follows his former player and assistant coach.

"We've had a lot good experiences together," Jones said. "It's a mutual admiration. We got along very well."

Jones said he is most proud of Crum's level of integrity.

"His character is very high," Jones said. "I'm really very impressed."

While Crum is still very close to Wooden and remained close to Seekins before his death, it was Jones who Crum invited to help his family through the ordeal of Crum's father dying.

"I had the privilege, when his father died, of being the speaker at his funeral," Jones said. "It was such an honor. I appreciated that."

In the summer of 1998, Crum stopped by and saw Jones. And Jones was expecting to see or hear from Crum again in the summer of 1999.

"He very rarely goes through Los Angeles or Salt Lake City without calling me," Jones said. "We have dinner. He usually comes out every summer. He's a great gentleman. I have such a high respect for him. He's been very kind to me. He has a lot of great attributes."

Jones has been watching or coaching basketball for six decades, and he knows where Crum stands in the pecking order of all-time greats.

"There's nobody who knows basketball any better than Denny," Jones said. "He has great insight into the game. He is a wonderful coach. He gets along with his players very well. My impression is that there is no one who knows basketball any better."

Crum even passes the glory to his former coaches with his 1994 induction into the Basketball Hall of Fame.

"I'm very proud of being in there but it is not something I dwell on," Crum said. "I've been so fortunate in my career to play for someone like John Wooden and great high school and junior college coaches. I told my high school coach, 'When I get out of college, I might come back and coach at San Fernando.' And then I told Coach Jones that same thing at Pierce—and of course I did end up coaching at Pierce. I never did become the head coach at UCLA, although I had the opportunity. I probably would have enjoyed coaching at my high school or even just in a YMCA league. I just love coaching, watching kids grow. It is just so rewarding to watch the kids learn and grow and come together as a team. If you are doing it right, you remember the 'teams' more than certain 'individual' players because if they come together as a unit, it is the team accomplishment."

Following is the speech Crum gave during his enshrinement at the 1994 Basketball Hall of Fame Induction Ceremony on May 9, 1994:

"Family, friends, fans and fellow Hall of Famers:

"Two days ago, those of us lucky enough to be in Louisville, Kentucky, watched another great athlete race his way into history. Go For Gin's name will now take its place in gold letters in the paddock of Churchill Downs in a sort of Hall of Fame for race horses.

"I was thinking about what those horses might say if they could talk. It occurred to me that even though they were ferociously competitive on the track, they wouldn't stand around in 'race horse heaven' and argue who could beat the others. Each of them knew what it took to become champions, and their respect for each other would be unequivocal.

"For me, the personal significance of this evening is secondary to the enormous respect I have for the men and women who are honored in the Basketball Hall of Fame. They built the sport of basketball into the popular game it is today. They made it possible for me to be successful, earn a comfortable living and to have the opportunity to influence young lives. To all of them I say thank you from the bottom of my heart.

"I especially want to thank Coach Wooden for everything he has meant to me. For his guidance, his friendship, his love and his willingness to come to Springfield to share this evening with me. To return to my race horse analogy, he is the Man O' War of coaches and the Secretariat of people.

"Basketball reflects the essence of team sports because it's played at such a fast pace. It requires players to know each other and their coaches so well that their skills can be used unselfishly, instantly and instinctively. I've been blessed with coaches and players who have made unselfish commitments to the team's success.

"No one better illustrates that unselfishness than my assistant coach and friend, Jerry Jones, who has shared virtually every minute of my career at Louisville. If I belong here, he belongs here as well. All of my past and present assistants, trainers and doctors also have my gratitude. They have been a critical part of the success of Louisville basketball. And I certainly must pay tribute to coach Peck Hickman, who built the foundation and tradition that I inherited at Louisville.

"Finally, and most importantly, I want to thank my most loyal colleagues, my family, who have made the most substantial sacrifices of all. I love you all.

"In my younger, cockier days I suppose I would have said I expected to be in the Hall of Fame someday. But because I had no idea what it would take to get me there, I also would have thought that it was not important to me. But there are a lot of things youngsters and kids don't know. To me, it is truly very, very important.

"Now that you have placed me here among those who have played and coached the game with great success, I am honored and humbled beyond anything I could have imagined, but I am even more deeply honored by the friends who have come to share this evening with me and my family. For me, your support and love are measures of success that are bigger than basketball and the Hall of Fame.

"The Kentucky Derby has been called the chance of a lifetime in a lifetime of chance. I've been fortunate in my lifetime, in a coaching career, to get the chance to coach and associate with many great players, 14 or 15 of them who are out here tonight. Thanks guys, I love you, too.

"I have seen what a positive force the game and its stars can be for a community. Basketball can certainly arouse, unite and inspire. To borrow a phrase from a great sportswriter, Dave Kindred: 'It is a drama filled with truth, justice and beauty.' I am so lucky to have been able to spend my chance of a lifetime as an actor in that drama. Thank you for your honor and for your contributions to all that is wonderful in sports. God bless all of you."

CHAPTER 9

FUNDAMENTALS

The fundamentals that Crum stresses to his players never go away. While it might have seemed tedious at times in practice, former Cards and NBA star Darrell Griffith looks back at all the fundamental drills and smiles.

"Fundamentals are something you always have to polish," Griffith said. "I have been fortunate to have coaches who do that. You think you know it all, but you don't. Coach Crum taught me some fundamentals that got me to another level. He saw that talent in me. Practices always started off at that level. It didn't surprise me because I knew he was a teacher. You start with fundamentals. He always stresses that. It teaches you that unless you never make a mistake, you can get better. His best players were the most fundamentally sound. And I think you could say that about any great player, that he or she has great fundamental skills."

The number-crunching Crum believes that a focus on the execution of fundamentals is a key ingredient for success.

"Fundamentals are the basic necessity of the game," Crum said. "Coach Wooden would tell you basketball is a game of conditioning, fundamentals and team play. If you watch our team play, we're pretty fundamentally sound, in good condition and we focus on the team play. We averaged 20 assists a game this year (in 1998-99). We stress making that extra pass. You can go back through history and see great teams, and you will see great players—you have to have great players. But they have to be well-coached, fundamentally sound and be willing to give to their teammates. Guys that can and will give of themselves for their teammates."

Wade Houston agrees that Crum's deep roots in fundamentals can be traced back through his basketball "tree" to Wooden.

"I think his philosophy on fundamentals and theory on teaching fundamentals was based on so many things that were done at UCLA and how successful they were there," Houston said. "He modified some of those things and brought them to Louisville. They were very good fundamentals."

Crum's continued focus on fundamentals is something that also led to the impressive run he's had for almost three decades as a head coach at Louisville.

"He's a fundamentalist, that's why he wins games in the long run, and that's why his teams constantly improve," former assistant coach Bobby Dotson said. "Team play—the points will be equally distributed—is also a key. The better players get more shots, but there's something there for everyone. His attitude toward having his players find and accept their roles can't be overlooked."

Assistant coach Jerry Eaves has embraced Crum's concepts.

"We always make the extra pass when we can," Eaves said. "And we look for the bounce pass to create a lay-up or find the right spot on the floor for our shot."

Dotson said the passing drills were always stressed.

"One of the things I remember is the two-handed pass—that way if you are about to throw it and see it's going to be intercepted, you can pull it back," Dotson said. "The overhead pass, making the back cut—I think that's what Denny mastered, one of the kinds of marks he has made on the game."

After all the time Crum spent in his own backyard shooting all those years, it is not surprising that Crum has always put an emphasis on shooting.

"We spent a lot of time on shooting," Dotson said. "We ran drills to shoot the shot the offense created for you. We practiced using the glass from the proper angle."

Dribbling drills also dot Crum's daily practice ledger.

"Everyone on the team—centers, guards, forwards—worked on dribbling," Dotson said. "We would work up and down the court every day. We'd work on the crossover, keep the ball in front of you, reversing it—that's the way we'd start. Denny wanted the players to dribble and be quick, but to be under control and not to hurry. He also had them work on coming to a two-footed stop and to always keep your body balanced. That's another thing that can't be overemphasized enough—body balance—because you have to have that in any sport."

Crum's teams are also known for being in top condition. But that is a part of the process itself more than it is a focus.

"We didn't run a lot of sprints at the end of practice, but we did a lot of full-court stuff," Dotson said. "It was part of the process, rather than a project. We would do full-court drills. That kept them in condition."

The set-up of the practices was also very regimented.

"His practices are very organized," Dotson said. "Denny's even more of a supervisor now than he was then. The assistants are more on the front line now. Denny's role is doing what he does best: preparing and teaching. He just loves to coach and teach."

Gary Tuell mimicked Crum's teaching skills—and still does as the coach at Augusta State College in Georgia.

"If you don't do the fundamentals well, you don't have a chance," Tuell said. "You have to execute, or you are not going to win. The way he teaches in a game was invaluable for me."

A cerebral coach, Crum is known to analyze numbers at an incredible pace.

"He is extremely honest," Tuell said. "He's more intelligent than 99 percent of the coaches in the business. One time I asked him, 'Why do you win so often?' He looked at me and tapped his forehead with his finger. He said, 'I have the ability to see all 10 players on the floor; most guys can't.' Denny is just tremendous with numbers."

Crum spends time on fundamentals throughout the season because he knows his players probably don't do much fundamental work in the summer.

"Denny believed that from October 15 to March 15, that was team time—the time to work on things that would help execute his system and improve each player's ability with the basic tenets of that system," Tuell said. "Now, from March 15 to October 15, the guys could do the other stuff—the dunking and the behind-the-back passes—the individual skills. But when fall practice started, it was all about the team and perfecting the system."

CHAPTER 10

EMERGING FROM THE SHADOW CAST BY UK

As the 1972-73 season wound down, Crum lit into the *Louisville Courier-Journal*. He felt slighted because U of L's Allen Murphy had been selected the conference "Sophomore of the Year," and it gained only a small story inside the sports section. At the same time, the University of Kentucky's Kevin Grevey won a similar honor in the Southeastern Conference. Grevey's award received greater play and a big headline.

"I didn't like the fact that the newspaper buried Allen's achievement and played up Grevey's," Crum said. "I don't want to take anything away from Grevey—he's a fine player—but it's just not fair to slight Allen. He's just as good as Grevey."

Junior Bridgeman said the issue was ongoing.

"What a lot of people have forgotten," Bridgeman said, "is that we were a Louisville team trying to prove to people that we were just as good·as Kentucky, UCLA and the others. Our confidence level wasn't as high in those days because a lot of people in the area thought Kentucky was THE team and we were second rate. That hurt our confidence as a team, and it hurt us. No matter how much Denny said on our behalf, the city of Louisville had a lot of UK supporters at that time. It affected what we thought about ourselves as a team. We'd beat somebody and go back to the dorm and there'd be UK and its 'Fabulous Freshmen' or 'Super Sophomores' on TV. It had an effect."

Few know the depth of the UK-U of L rivalry better than former Kentucky coach Eddie Sutton.

"I knew Denny long before I went to Kentucky," Sutton said. "In Kentucky, that was a fierce rivalry. I'll tell you the way I saw it: When I was at Kentucky, and where I am now, I see it as a difference once you cross the border out of Kentucky. Nationally, the program at the University of Louisville is held in the same regard as the University of Kentucky's program. But if you live within the borders of the Commonwealth of Kentucky, there are more supporters for the Wildcats than the Cardinals. That doesn't mean Louisville doesn't have supporters in western Kentucky or eastern Kentucky because they do. But since UK basketball got bigger earlier under Coach Rupp, it gave them a lot of support as representing the state. Certainly, that has changed over the years in terms of Louisville getting more and more support. And Denny should get some of the credit for that."

Derwin Webb came to Louisville from neighboring Indiana to play for the Cards in the late 1980s and early 1990s.

"The funny thing is, I'm from Indianapolis where the big rivalry was Indiana-Purdue," Webb said. "I got here (to Louisville) and it was like, 'Man, that was nothing compared to Louisville and UK.' When I played, we'd walk through shopping malls, and folks would say, 'I don't care if you only win one game this year—just beat Kentucky.'"

Crum inadvertently fanned the flames of the rivalry when he took the job in 1971 by telling reporters he was "not overly impressed" with the University of Kentucky's 1971-72 recruiting class, telling the *Courier-Journal's* Dave Kindred that his own prized recruit Allen Murphy "would eat any of UK's guys alive." If that wasn't enough, when Crum was asked to compare UK's recruiting class with the ones he helped bring to UCLA, Crum smiled and said, "UK's wouldn't compare."

"I wasn't being a pop-off," Crum remembers. "I was being honest. I knew about Kentucky and their great basketball tradition. But when I thought of college basketball, I thought of UCLA, not Kentucky. In my opinion Coach Wooden was—and always will be—the greatest coach in the history of the game. I had a hard time understanding why everybody was so upset about the things I said—how could anybody ignore the success of Coach Wooden and the UCLA program?"

Purdue coach Gene Keady—who is part of that IU-Purdue rivalry—admires the way Crum handles his own in Kentucky.

"What can you say about the rivalry with Kentucky?" Keady asked. "Denny overcame the attitude that Kentucky was a state with one Division I basketball power. He won two national titles in a state where basketball is king. He could have been the UCLA coach— make no mistake about it, that was his job if he wanted it—and he could have picked up the foundation Coach Wooden built and won national titles at UCLA. But he chose to build his own dynasty at Louisville. That's what got him to the Hall of Fame."

Although everyone else connected to the game played up the rivalry, one who didn't was Crum.

"When the game with UK finally came up, Coach Crum kept stressing to us, 'Remember, this is just another game,'" Webb said. "He said, 'Play as hard as you can. If we win, it will be great. But if we lose, it will still be good because we can learn from it. Just play the best you can.' That's why playing for Denny was such a great joy, because it taught me a lot about life. The 'bad' things that happened used to get me down. Through Denny, I learned to always keep in mind that the earth keeps spinning, and you have to move on, because people see how you handle defeat, whether it is on the court or off the court."

Former Crum assistant Wade Houston said the schools, while within the borders of the same state, could not have been more different.

"I think it's a lot like Auburn against Alabama, or UCLA against USC," Houston said. "These kinds of rivalries are competitive and there is not going to be much love lost. If Louisville were a team that was beaten every year by the University of Kentucky, then the match-up wouldn't have the passion of the rivalry. The people around the state thought of UK as the state university. They had a lot of advantages and a higher profile—when they lobbied for state dollars, they even had the advantage. They see another school in the state that is not the so-called 'state university.' Then they see that school beat them, and it was hard to take. We were thought of, for a long time, as kind of an inner-city team that wasn't supposed to challenge the 'state university,' which was UK."

Houston, who went on to coach at Tennessee, said the Kentucky-Louisville "Dream Game" in 1983 was about more than pride for both schools.

"That was a huge event," Houston said. "The atmosphere was so thick you could cut it with a knife. The teams hadn't played in 20 years or something. We got to go play in front of friends and family. The way the game happened, the way the game was played—overtime and having to come back from a 16-point deficit—was just something for the ages. What a game! It was euphoria when we won. The sun was shining brighter the next day, and we were going to the Final Four."

Current Augusta State College and former Crum volunteer assistant coach Gary Tuell said the rivalry intensified when Rick Pitino brought his successful formula to UK.

"Denny took so much heat from his own fans because of Kentucky," Tuell said. "I really saw an irony when Rick Pitino was coaching at UK. When Denny came to Louisville, he was considered brash and arrogant. Well here comes Pitino to UK, and he's cocky, brash, the whole bit—the mirror image of Denny when he first came to Louisville. But because of the era Pitino came in, being that way was more acceptable. Plus, Pitino puts out a really good image on TV and shaking hands with boosters. But I'll take Denny because I love that competitive fire of his."

Crum was not as image-conscious as Pitino.

"He's not a self-promoter, he'll tell you exactly what he thinks," Tuell said. "He won't hide from questions or run. He's not interested in the PR or BS. That's what I admire about him."

Crum's former assistant, former U of L athletic director Bill Olsen, said the rivalry with UK is one of the things that makes being the coach of Louisville a challenge.

"Louisville is not an easy job," Olsen said. "There aren't a lot of jobs where the state university—Kentucky—is synonymous with college basketball success and its roots. Louisville is basically an urban university surrounded by other great basketball programs."

While the 600 wins of Crum's teams are impressive, carving a niche in UK crazy Kentucky is, former LSU coach Dale Brown says, one of Crum's biggest accomplishments.

"He's in a state with one of the greatest college basketball programs of all time in the University of Kentucky," Brown said. "To survive that—and to create his own powerful legacy at the same time—is an incredible compliment in itself."

Included in the UK rivalry is the "Dream Game" in March of 1983 when Louisville beat UK with a berth in the Final Four on the line. In this Mideast Regional Championship in Knoxville, Tenn. Louisville won in overtime, 80-68.

"I've never been hung up on the rivalry—to me, every game is a learning experience for our guys," Crum said. "But that was a very good game. Afterward, cheerleaders and fans from the two teams stood, arms intertwined, as 'My Old Kentucky Home' was played. Governor John Y. Brown gave a speech to the legislature about how we should play every year. That whole thing was really good for everyone involved, and in my opinion, college basketball."

CHAPTER 11

PLAYING UNDER CRUM

Junior Bridgeman went on to the NBA's Milwaukee Bucks and the Hall of Fame after being the first player Crum recruited to Louisville.

"Obviously, there are a whole lot of things that I learned from him," said Bridgeman, who now owns 78 Wendy's fast-food restaurants and lives in Louisville. "But there is one thing that sticks out in my mind, and it is the most important of all—it has stuck with me to this day.

"When you go to college, you are at a time in your life when you are between the feelings of being a boy or girl and becoming a man or woman," Bridgeman said. "You hear 'growing up' or 'becoming an adult' and you think to yourself, 'What does that mean?' You are away from home for the first time. A coach has a tremendous amount of influence on you, from how to view yourself to what it takes to be successful. Coming from high school, I remembered the 'rah-rah' atmosphere to get fired up emotionally for games—a fever pitch. But in college, Denny was not that way."

Bridgeman recalls Crum talking to the players.

"We have been over what you have to do to be successful as a player, and this is what you have to do as a team," Crum told Bridgeman and his teammates. "It's up to you to find the motivation that it will take for you to succeed. You have to develop that yourself. I can coach you, but I can't make you grow up and make decisions for you. Where you go from here, on the court or in life, is going to result from the choices you make, how hard you work and how well you can work with a group, in basketball or life."

Bridgeman said, "For the first time after that talk, I thought about it: I can motivate myself. I can work hard. And that's the type of attitude that carries on into life. You can't depend on—you should not need—someone else to motivate you."

That talk sticks with Bridgeman.

"He made you grow up," Bridgeman said. "That's the most important, meaningful thing I received from my education at Louisville under Coach Crum. That's such a big step for a lot of young people. Not everyone is going to be fortunate to continue and go on and play like I did. But no matter what you do, when you leave home or college, your parents are not going to be there to hold your hand and push you along. If you are going to be successful, it will come from within. That message is so important—think about it—yet it gets missed a lot of time. Sure, you can—and should—have people who tell you, 'You must do this, and do that, to be successful.' But even if that advice is good, you have to go after it yourself. When you come out of high school, or you go to college, those four years are critical in finding out what life is all about. Coach Crum tells you from the get-go that the most important game is the game of life, not basketball. To that end, what he teaches you—and I know he's smart enough to do this on purpose—are things that you apply to life, not just basketball. That ranges from being responsible to knowing when you need to be home at night—we had no curfew, but he could tell—to your dedication to yourself and the team."

The father-figure image is something most former players bring up first when asked about Crum.

"Personally, he means a lot to me," said former player Derwin Webb. "Whenever a situation away from home comes up that I need a father figure to talk to, it's Denny. He's been like a second father to me."

The equal-treatment-for-everyone policy that Crum stuck to meant a lot to the players.

"He treats everyone the same," Webb said. "Whether you are the star or the 12th man, if you do something wrong, you are punished, and if you do something right, you get rewarded whether it is with playing time or whatever. The bottom line is this: If you put out 100 percent for Denny, he'll put out 100 percent for you.

That's the promise he makes to all of his players, and he's always stood by that."

Webb's most memorable interaction with Crum came during Webb's senior season in 1992.

"My senior year, we lost a game to Houston," Webb said. "I was devastated. I was the first one in the locker room, grabbed a chair and threw it against the blackboard—it broke either the chair or the blackboard, I don't remember which—maybe both. Coach Crum came in, and we were there alone. He asked me, 'Derwin, why'd you do that?' I said, 'Coach, we should not have lost.' Coach said, 'Son, this game is over; you learn from it and move on.' That taught me something that would help me not just in basketball, but more importantly, in life. You run into different obstacles, but you learn and you work through it, and everything is going to be fine. He tried to teach us to be young men more than basketball players."

Another thing Bridgeman won't forget is how Crum always geared the team for the big prize—the NCAA Tournament.

"I felt his strength in preparing our teams for the season was important to our success," Bridgeman said. "He didn't run a six-week boot camp to prepare you to win the first five games, then go .500 the rest of the year."

Former Cardinal Robbie Valentine, now executive director of the Sports and Education Program for the Gheens Foundation, Jefferson County Public School systems, and the Boy Scouts, shares a family-type relationship with Crum to this day.

"Denny and I have a special bond," Valentine said. "I was 18 when I went to U of L, and I had never had a father. I learned so much from him, and he was willing to offer that extra care and insight because he knew I had only one parent. Denny taught me about being honest, about not having to yell to be successful. He taught me that the best way to take care of yourself in a team setting is to treat others the way you want to be treated, and to keep a good attitude and treat people with respect. It sounds silly, but not a lot of 18-year-olds know all that. But then, you get out of college, and you are 22 or 23, and you see where what he taught you is about so much more than basketball, it's about life. I've learned a lot from that man. I have total respect for him."

Valentine will also remember Crum for something else, other than the victories.

"The wins and longevity are what people will remember the most because that's just how society is," Valentine said. "What I will remember is seeing figures showing how his graduation rate has gone higher and higher. Denny Crum knows the importance of forcing—not just pushing—kids to get their degrees. And he makes YOU get it—not Denny, not anyone else at U of L can get it for you; only you can do it. Denny does not have curfews or anything like that because he knows that if someone wants something, it is up to them to get it done. You can stay out until 2 a.m., but he will know it—believe me, he will know. You can skip class, but he'll know that too, and you will pay for it—because that was your choice. It's the same thing with someone who does go to class and does study—they get to enjoy the reward of that, not Denny, because that is also their choice. His deal is he puts his trust in you, and that makes you grow up on your own. And come on, let's face it, when you are 18, it is time to grow up. I never heard Denny yell, scream or cuss. All he does is make you accountable for your choices, good or bad."

That Crum's true colors are never painted just right by the media bothers former players.

"I guess what has bothered me the most is seeing people take shots at his reputation," Valentine said. "I just love the man. He's provided so much leadership and direction to those of us who, at such a young age, really needed it. There are stories that Denny would never tell you about former players he went to the wall—and beyond—to help out. It does not matter whether you have made all the right choices or all the wrong choices, Denny is there to help you out. His view of it is this: 'If I bring them here, it's my responsibility to take care of them for the good and the bad.' He's not going to kick a guy out unless that guy keeps refusing to try. Denny will give second and sometimes third chances if he sees potential and commitment. Denny just can't turn his back on someone in need.

And I don't see where people have the right to deem that a fault. If anything, it's an endearing attribute."

Bridgeman, in the NBA Hall of Fame after a stellar career with the Milwaukee Bucks—who retired his number—said Crum would have won NBA titles had he moved into the pro ranks to coach.

"There is absolutely no question he could have been a huge success in the NBA, especially with the way he maintains his composure," Bridgeman said. "In the NBA, the college coaches who rely on rah-rah won't make it. With Denny, it was all about the team, the execution, the system, the preparation, the self-motivation—that kind of formula works at any level, and it's the only way to do it in the NBA."

Valentine never was a Darrell Griffith or Junior Bridgeman, but the quality of his experience at U of L rivals anyone's.

"My role was kind of ironic at Louisville," Valentine said. "The year after my class, there was a lot of talent. So I was not going to be one of the stars by any means. But Denny saw what I brought to the team, and he always used me as a leader. Sometimes that meant helping my teammates off the court, sometimes it meant helping from the bench. I had a role that was very meaningful to our team, even though I was not one of the best players. You can't treat every kid the same because they are all different. That's one of Denny's strengths—seeing where players are strong or where they need development. He creates an environment where everyone can reach their potential. And when that happens, the team is that much better. That's why it's funny to hear people talk about how they were surprised a certain year's Louisville team made it deep into the NCAA Tournament even though it wasn't expected to—that kind of success happens when players reach their potential and execute their role on the team. It's a great part of Denny and his system that's never really been noticed outside of the program."

Webb, who went to law school before joining the Cardinals athletic department administration, said Crum's longevity is what's most impressive.

"As much as coaches move around, to be that committed to one school—and have the community and school be that committed to him—is something you won't see, a coach staying 30 years," Webb said.

The incredible numbers Crum has posted on the court, Bridgeman said, cast too long of a shadow over what Crum has done for his former players off of it.

"He's a competitor, and he really enjoys competition," Bridgeman said. "He is also very, very good with the numbers. Yes, he is in the Hall of Fame, and he's got a couple of national championships, and the 600 wins at Louisville—you can go on and on and still not touch all the records. But the thing that is lost when folks write or talk about Denny is that if you ever asked him to do anything, he'd go out of his way to do it. He does not do it because Louisville wants him to or requires him to. He does it because he loves it. In 30 years at Louisville, he feels a need or necessity to try to help people. That's one thing about Denny that has not been written about. Yet it really is the best story about him because it shows what is inside his heart. I have seen and heard a lot of people go to Denny for help over the years. I have never—not a single time—heard that Denny said no."

Former Card Brian Kiser still sees that side of Crum.

"I've seen that happen," Kiser said. "The way it works is if you have worked hard and you have good character, he knows that, and he'll do what needs to be done to help you out. He's a very fair individual."

If the media doesn't respect Crum enough, his former players more than make up for it.

"He's done so much for us as players," Valentine said. "We all probably lean on him a little too much at times for speaking appearances, but he'd never tell a former player no—if he can help out, he will somehow, someway find a way to do it. He's just so very loyal."

"What he went through with (former assistant coach and player) Scooter McCray is the perfect example of Denny's loyalty," Valentine said. "A lot of coaches would have fired Scooter just to make themselves look good and get the heat off their back. He knew what Scooter did was resolvable, and now you won't see Scooter in that circumstance again. It was so heart-warming the day of the press conference (in February 1999, announcing the NCAA ban of U of L's post-season tournament plans had been lifted and Scooter McCray, facing a banning under the sanctions before they were lifted, was also freed to resume his coaching career). The first words out of Denny's mouth weren't for himself or anything like that. No, he said he was happy that Scooter's coaching career could get back on track, and he was happy for the players on the team, that they'd have the chance to accept a post-season bid, if they were selected. But that's who he is, the father, the teacher, looking out for his 'own.'"

Kiser was going to play basketball at the U.S. Military Academy at West Point before Crum came calling. After seeing Kiser play in an all-star game, Crum talked to Kiser.

"I couldn't believe how tall Coach Crum was—I guess standing next to all those 6-9 guys on TV made him look shorter than he actually was," Kiser said. "I hadn't been recruited by any big schools, so when Coach Crum came by, I expected him to ask me to walk-on. He offered me a scholarship. He had confidence and good character—and Louisville was the biggest school that had recruited me—so I accepted."

Kiser was a sharp-shooting forward for the Cards. Now with the Kentucky office of the Fellowship of Christian Athletes, Kiser considers Crum a role model.

"I remember him saying, 'Life is a game of percentages—you have to think through things," Kiser said. "Coach Crum is a lot like my Dad is in terms of being understated. In the Bible it says 'Everyone should be slow to speak, slow to become angry and quick to listen.' That sums up Coach Crum's attitude a lot. Very rarely will you see him become angry—he does a great job of keeping his cool, and that's why his nickname is 'Cool Hand Luke.'"

Kiser added with a smile, "That face might get a little red, but with the red blazer he wears, that balances it out."

Crum's patience and sense of fairness are something Kiser treasures.

"He really helped me with the way he didn't yank me out of the game when I'd miss a couple of shots," Kiser said. "He knew I could do it, so he'd stay with me, and then I'd start knocking them down. This is why: His whole philosophy, 'If you can't get it done in practice, you can't get it done in the game, and if you can get it done in practice, you will get it done in the game.' From a player's perspective, when it comes to playing time, he's so fair with that. He plays people based on how they play in practice. I really admire that. He stuck by his guns. It was a tremendous privilege to play for him—he was so patient with me."

Unable to tell Crum face to face what the U of L coach did for him, Kiser sat with a pen and paper after graduation to sum up his feelings.

"I wrote Coach Crum a note after I graduated," Kiser said. "It was just something to thank him for all he did for me. I signed it, 'From the worst defensive player you ever coached, Brian Kiser.' But I kept hustling on defense to make up for my shortcomings. And I got the job done the best I could."

When Crum retires, the face of Louisville will change.

"It is almost a given that he'll always be here, so when he does retire, it is really going to change the face of Louisville," Kiser said. "Along with Muhammed Ali, Coach Crum is the most famous person to ever be from Louisville."

His players appreciate Crum's sense of humility.

"I never did hear him blow his own horn, and with everything he's accomplished, there's little question he has the resume´ to back it up if he was that way," Kiser said. "But the truth is that is just not Coach Crum. At the same time, there was no doubt who was in charge, though. He's the type of guy whose actions spoke for him."

Kiser also saw where Crum gave his assistant coaches room to grow.

"By the time I went through there," Kiser said, "the assistant coaches pretty much ran the practices and got us all on the same page. That way Coach Crum was able to do what he loves the most, and that was to teach."

And that's what Crum does first and foremost—teach.

"He won't just blast you for making a mistake," Kiser said. "You just know that if you work hard and do what needs to be done, things will take care of themselves. He doesn't even require that you score a certain amount. He just asks that you play defense, rebound and run—those three things—and you will play for Coach Crum, whether you were a high school All-American or a walk-on. The good scoring opportunities come from those three things and playing smart. If you didn't do those things, you'd sit."

While Crum's acclaim for what he does off the court falls short of what is deserved, his worth as a coach will one day, Valentine said, be the measuring stick—that and the fact that Crum's passion for the game itself might never be rivaled.

"There are some people who simply have a love for the game of basketball, and Denny has it," Valentine said.

Kiser's biggest memory is Crum's first pre-game "non-speech."

"We went out for our first big game, and I'll never forget it," Kiser said. "I was ready for this big speech to get us going. He looked at us, sensed that, and said, 'I'm not going to give a win-one-for-the-Gipper thing here. The motivation needs to come from you.' Looking back, what a great thing that was. Think about it: Emotion only goes so far. You see teams come out all fired up and five minutes into the game they've sunk back down because it's worn off. Or they come out so fired up they can't concentrate, and they make mistakes. Coach Crum, by the way he dealt with us—treating us like adults—never let that happen."

Darrell Griffith, back in Louisville after a national title with the Cards and a stellar NBA career with the Utah Jazz, appreciates what he learned from Crum.

"Any time in a coaching environment, coaches will direct you when you are trying to make a career out of basketball," Griffith said.

"They teach you about the game. I learned a lot from him. You have to be a student of the game to learn, and that's what Coach Crum appreciated, I think, about me."

Griffith was tall enough to play small forward. Instead, he stayed at guard under Crum, something Griffith believed help take him to the next level in the NBA.

"It was a situation where he realized my potential was at guard," Griffith said.

Griffith also appreciated the way Crum handled himself.

"Coach Crum is always laid back," Griffith said. "He's not a coach who likes to have the spotlight. He likes coaching, enjoys winning. That's what makes him happy. It's not the notoriety. To have the success he's had and survive at one high-profile place like Louisville for that long, you'd have to be the way he is. He's the leader of the pack. He knows the kids look up to him, and the importance to give second chances, but to keep people on track. He also understands his role as a leader in the community. If he was the kind who panicked or lost his cool, people would see that, and those who look up to him would imitate that. So that level-headedness is to be admired."

CHAPTER 12

COACHING UNDER CRUM

Former assistant coach Bobby Dotson said Crum's composure is a key to his success.

"He avoids the peaks and the valleys, which is something Coach Wooden stressed a lot to keep things on an even keel," Dotson said.

"He is very patient—I have said that over and over," said current assistant Scott Davenport. "His ability to stay at an even keel and apply that patience are his greatest attributes. You could have the greatest practice or greatest game, everyone's buzzing around, kids are fired up, but Denny stays the same. The practice is bad, or we lose, yet he retains that ability to remain patient. It's easy when things are going perfect. But who is the captain when the waves get a little rough, a little rocky? Denny's always there, 'Mr. Consistet.'"

Jerry Jones was an assistant coach at Pepperdine when Crum was a UCLA assistant.

"I got to know him when our freshman team played UCLA," Jones said. "The thing that stuck me the most was how confident he was in what he was doing. You could tell he really trusts his ability.

"His mood rarely changes," Jones said. "His demeanor never changes before, during or after a basketball game. He's always level-headed. He takes the victories with the defeats. He is one of the best I've ever seen at handling a defeat the right way. I've never heard him jump all over a basketball team after a defeat. But I've also never heard him go overboard in praise because there is going to be a next week, a next time, and you have to play every game the same way. If you play up-and-down, you aren't always going to win the games you are supposed to win. That consistency is something that can't be overrated."

"Denny is the same, win or lose—he's a gentleman," former assistant coach Bill Olsen said. "His attitude was that we'd win with class, and we'd lose with class. On or off the court he's not someone who complains. He's always very positive. He looks into the future and doesn't focus on what happened in the past. It has served him well. I don't know whether it comes from Coach Wooden or if this comes from his background. He's more like Coach Wooden than anyone who coaches today. Many wanted to imitate Coach Wooden, but few had the ability to do that. Coaches grow a lot, and Denny has since he left UCLA. It is just that he saw a great person and coach in John Wooden, and he modeled himself in that manner."

Olsen said Crum is in a class of his own in terms of consistency.

"I don't know anybody in a high pressure sport like college basketball who maintains the composure and cool during a basketball game like he does," Olsen said. "It has always carried over onto the floor with our players."

Part of that consistency comes from Crum's ability to focus.

"He is able to focus better than anyone I'm aware of on the important things and not be distracted by things that aren't important," Olsen said. "He was a student of the game from the time he picked up the ball. He found he wanted to coach before he was even out of high school. So he has a great understanding of the game. I've never seen anyone who can make adjustments during a game like he is able to. He was able to convey a confidence that I think carries over to the players. The players who came to Louisville grew on the floor and off the floor because of him. He treated the youngsters the way their parents wanted, with respect. He made them grow in a gentle and nice way."

Jones said Crum's sincere outlook for his players—and others— is something that is not touted, but very much a key to the long run he's had.

"I think one of the biggest things that is overlooked about Denny Crum is that he truly cares about people—he has a genuine concern for people," Jones said. "That he likes to help people is a tremendous asset."

An ability to change with the times in terms of how he interacts with his players has also helped the long-time Louisville coach, and that too is linked to Crum's consistency as a person and coach.

"The game has changed a lot in recent years, but Denny built a game plan on a series of steps and progressions," Olsen said. "The learning experience was well thought out, and he'd add to it as we went along. For new players who weren't accustomed to the Louisville system and how complicated it really is, it takes time to adjust to it. That's why our teams always come on strong at the end of the year and play well in the post-season—because Denny looks at the big picture."

Former NBA and Louisville standout Jerry Eaves, another Crum assistant coach, also points to the even keel.

"The consistency—there are no highs and lows for Denny," Eaves said. "You always want to keep yourself on an even keel. For life in general, to be successful, you have to avoid the severe mood swings."

The consistent behavior is something ingrained in Crum.

"That goes back to his coaching beliefs, balance," assistant coach Scott Davenport said, "You must practice what you preach, and he would share that. He demands that of coaches and players. If you are the teacher, one of the greatest ways to lead is by example."

Crum's care for those in his charge—assistants, players, trainers, support staff, former players—often goes unnoticed outside the program.

"He has a great ability to keep a team together—players, coaches, trainers, everyone," Davenport said.

Like his late father, Crum, a math major himself, has always been interested in numbers, from analyzing to application.

"As I study him, he has the ability to be very analytical, to make decisions based on percentages, not emotions, although he has great intuition," Davenport said.

The assistant coaches are also grateful that Crum has allowed them to grow, something a lot of coaches don't provide if they run a dictatorial program, directing every move.

"It allows you to grow, especially in this profession," Davenport said. "He allows you to do your job. He values your input. If it's practice prep, game prep, recruiting, he allows you to do your job."

Being an assistant coach under Crum puts the emphasis on "coach" rather than simply "assisting."

"It has been very good for me," Eaves said. "I have talked to assistant coaches at other colleges and a lot of them are there just to recruit, not to teach. In addition to recruiting, Denny gives us the opportunity to teach."

"As I look back on my career," Jerry Jones said, "I could never have been at a place where I had as much to say or contribute as I did at Louisville. What he does is that after the coaches learn the system, and he has confidence in them as far as teachers go, he allows them to coach. That's why you don't see much of a turnover on his staff. You enjoy working for Coach Crum because he puts trust in you. If you need help, he will do it. But it is your job. Part of that means you will make mistakes—but that's part of the job too, as is learning from those mistakes."

Crum is always aware of the process in the big-time, big-exposure game of college basketball.

"We keep the big picture in focus. It is not just the next game, the next season—it is an approach that all the time we have to get better, and it is ongoing, 24 hours a day, 365 days a year whether it is recruiting or film, whatever," Davenport said.

The only "drawback" to Crum is what is perhaps his most endearing quality—loyalty. He'll go to the wall and back for former players and assistant coaches. He will give them every chance to succeed, and he will support them when they fail, making sure they are responsible and accountable for their mistakes.

"If it's possible, he is loyal to a fault," Davenport said. "But in our society, as competitive and cutthroat as it is, maybe we need more of that."

Former assistant coach and U of L athletic director Bill Olsen admires that loyalty.

"His loyalty to his family, friends and players is something that in some circles is perceived as a weakness," Olsen said. "But it is one of his strengths—tell me, what better characteristic is there than loyalty? Not many. Yes, there are cases where that hurt Denny because people let him down. But he still pushes them to make it right and be successful with their lives—whether it is as a parent, player, coach, husband or brother—and I do not see how that is anything but admirable."

Eaves has also seen Crum apply that loyalty to former players and assistants.

"He is with you through the good and the bad," Eaves said. "You don't find that very often in this business, a very cutthroat business. You can ask any of his assistants and they will tell you the same thing."

That relationship—between Crum and his players—usually only blossoms after their playing days are done in terms of Crum getting close to them personally. Crum knows his role as a coach is to lead.

"As a player, you have to be able to coach them," Eaves said. "Sometimes it takes a little distance to do that. But you can definitely still talk to him. On the floor there's no question who is in charge of a Denny Crum team—Denny."

Crum's confidence might not be spoken, but its presence is always perceived.

"There's no question that Denny is, absolutely, a very confident person," Eaves said. "You have to be in his position to enjoy all the success he's had."

Crum's legacy, like his unspoken sense of confidence, remains secure.

"Those of us who have been around him speak all the time about what he's accomplished," Eaves said. "I know the one who comes after Denny, and then the one after him, will be compared to what Denny did, and no one will be able to meet that expectation of what he's done here as long as he's been here. No way anyone can ever touch that."

Former assistant and current Augusta (Georgia) State coach Gary Tuell said Crum remains a private guy.

"Sadly, I'm not sure he'll get the acclaim he deserves," Tuell said. "He's not a self-promoter. Denny doesn't seek the spotlight like some guys do. He's a private guy who is not interested in people thinking he's great. He's satisfied with who he is. He doesn't need attention to feel good about himself. He's often overlooked. What he's done is incredible. But I don't think—for whatever reasons—he'll get the respect he deserves."

That respect grows when the year-in and year-out difficulty of Louisville's schedule is taken into consideration. The Cards' schedule annually ranks as one of the top 10 or so most difficult in the nation.

"The continuity, the leadership having a Denny Crum who was out here for this successful run, is incredible," Olsen said. "The schedule is always difficult. As an assistant coach, we always worked for the most difficult schedule we could get. That makes the win-loss record even more impressive."

It also keeps the team focused.

"Players don't burn out when you approach things the way Denny does," Olsen said. "A lot of teams are ready to go on spring break when March rolls around—it's almost like losing is not that big of a deal. But Denny's teams are hitting their peak at that time and aren't ready to hang it up."

Crum's ability to teach has led to his success.

"Most great coaches are great teachers," Jerry Jones said. "You are not going to succeed in coaching unless you are a great teacher. Denny learned that from Coach Wooden. With Denny's ability to communicate with student-athletes, he looks upon coaching as his classroom.

"The reason you never hear him talk about the 600 wins or national championships," Jones said, "is because that's not what Denny is trying to accomplish with his coaching career—not that he doesn't want to win because he does. But the wins are not the paramount thing. It is the teaching, the competing, the consistency and helping young people grow. The only time he talked about any of his accomplishments with me was when he was elected to the

Basketball Hall of Fame. I said, 'What do you think about that, Denny?' He said, 'Well, I guess it's exciting.' I think to Denny that represents the fact that he's done something well over a long period of time."

Crum's mind doesn't stop working just because the game has started, something his assistants learned to emulate over the years.

"He's the best game coach I've ever been around—he's a remarkable game coach," Tuell said. "There were so many times when I was there and he'd draw up stuff to take advantage of the team, things I had never seen done by other coaches. There are coaches who can do that—know what they want done—but to do it and explain it in one minute's time is a difficult task. He's such a clear communicator."

CHAPTER 13

TOP COLLEGE COACHES ON CRUM

Not a member of the college basketball coaching fraternity like most others in his position, Denny Crum spends his time worrying more about those in his own program than slapping backs with those outside his program.

"I think the numbers will speak for themselves," University of Arizona Coach Lute Olson said. "Over the years he has had such great basketball teams. A lot of coaches are very social in their nature—and I don't count myself among those, either. But all of us in the coaching fraternity see, appreciate and respect what Denny's done."

The endurance factor is something most coaches relate when talking about Crum.

"He's been one of those guys who has been able to do it over a lot of years," Olson said.

Olson's association with Crum goes back—way back—to the 1960s.

"I first knew Denny back when he was the head coach at Pierce Junior College because I was coaching high school in that area," Olson said. "When he moved to UCLA, I went to Long Beach City College. So I had already known a lot about him for a long time."

Purdue coach Gene Keady said Crum has built on that UCLA pedigree.

"He has a good system," Keady said, "and it's no secret he got it from John Wooden. But Denny has added his own touch to it and created a system of his own."

One thing that goes unnoticed to a degree in the long-tenured coaches is that the times have required coaches to change the way they deal with players and the school administration.

"There are some coaches who can adjust to different times and different kids," Olson said. "Denny has been one of those guys who has been flexible enough to deal with the changes in young men and yet has maintained his fundamental ideas of the game. They're still running the same offense basically that he did at Pierce, and he refined it under Coach Wooden. He's put in his own things, and that's one of the reasons he's been such an outstanding coach."

Keady said that the ability to adapt has served Crum well.

"He's a firm disciplinarian, but he's adjusted to the 1980s and 1990s with the proper fine-tuning to how he handles things," Keady said. "Denny does handle anything that comes up; it's just that he's not going to drag the player out into the newspaper for it to hold him and say, 'Look what I did.' No, he's going to do it behind closed doors and make sure that player learns a lesson. He knows in his heart he's handled it right, and he doesn't need the public pat on the back because he truly is in it to help his players in the game of life."

While moving on is an option, Olson, like Crum, chooses to stay put.

"Back when I took Iowa to the Final Four—and we lost to Denny's Louisville team—Al McGuire came up to me after the game," Olson said. "Al said, 'Well what are you going to do next year?' I said, 'What? We just went to the Final Four.' Al said, 'So, you gonna stay?' I said, 'I hadn't thought about leaving, why?' Al said, 'My feeling is that no coach should stay for more than four or five years. Once you have done that and built up a program, you move. There is no way in the long run that you can win with the media and some of the boosters and some of the other things for a long period of time.' I understand what Al was saying. There have been a lot of times when I've thought about that as good advice from Al— and Al always had a feel. He's off the wall sometimes, but his understanding of people is pretty good. That's what's amazing about Denny. To be in a hot bed like Louisville and survive—and excel— for that long is amazing in this day and age. You have to have outstanding discipline to deal with those pressures over a period of time. Based on what I've seen and heard, he loves his lifestyle and quality of life there. When I had chance to move on, I thought about how all but one of our children live here in Tucson, and nine of our 12 grandkids are here. To some people, the quality of life and your family situation are more important than moving to maybe more money or maybe a better situation."

Missouri Coach Norm Stewart agrees that himself, Crum, Mount St. Mary's Jim Phelan, Indiana's Bobby Knight, UTEP's Don Haskins and the few others who have stayed two-plus decades are a dying breed.

"I think all of us are saying that," Stewart said. "To move—that seems to be the trend. Coaches don't seem to, for whatever reason, stay or last more than four to six years at a school, sometimes even three. In that regard I think Denny and a few others have set a standard that might not be equaled that often in the future."

And Olson would also like to face a Crum team early in the season rather than come tournament time.

"When you look at his record, you know he's done a good job," Olson said. "The most telling thing is what he's done with teams from the beginning of the year to the NCAA Tournament. You don't make the kind of improvement his teams have made through the year unless you aren't just an outstanding bench coach, but a practice coach as well, to get those teams to reach—and sometimes exceed—their potential."

One of his biggest rivals, former University of Kentucky coach Eddie Sutton, holds Crum in the highest regard.

"I have a great respect for Denny as a basketball coach," Sutton said. "I consider him one of the greatest college coaches that we have ever seen. First of all, his basketball philosophy is sound," Sutton said. "He emphasizes good sound defense, and Denny also is sound in his offensive approach—they will run with the ball when they have the opportunity, yet they are disciplined to play in the half-court offense if they have to. His players play hard to a high level."

Off the court, Sutton said, is where Crum has also made his mark.

"I think he's a quality human being as well," Sutton said. "He's been a real asset to the college coaching profession. We came up about the same time. We both came from great backgrounds, being fortunate to coach with the giants—Denny having worked under UCLA Coach John Wooden and myself under another legend, Henry Iba. In that respect, both of us were very fortunate."

Sutton, now at Oklahoma State in the Big 12 Conference, still beams when he talks about the length of Crum's successful run at Louisville.

"Here's a guy who has won a couple of national championships and has a remarkable record staying at the same school for nearly three decades," Sutton said. "I can't see anyone who knows anything about basketball not holding him in high esteem. He's one of the best. Any coach in our profession that I know of feels that way about Denny. And he knows as well as anyone else that you can't always worry about what everyone else thinks."

Former Missouri coach Norm Stewart, himself comfortable being tethered to the Tigers for a long run, says Crum built upon a solid basketball upbringing.

"He's got a little bit of everything," Stewart said. "You look at his background; he came out of the UCLA system and obviously that's a great foundation to have. He's been able to go add his own things and his own twists to it. He's been successful over a long period of time. He's fundamentally sound and does a good job of teaching. I think for anyone to win consistently and keep coming back to the tournament almost every year, you have to be sound fundamentally; you have to be a good manager. But the key is to be consistent, and that's where Denny really shines."

The Missouri coach also appreciates the way Crum has provided opportunities for his former players and assistant coaches.

"I see Denny as a person who has added to the coaching profession by giving a lot of people opportunities," Stewart said. "When he retires, he will have left something for the game. Not only has he done a great job at Louisville, he has brought something to that community for a long period of time. As a person I think he's given some things outside of the game. His involvement in so many charitable efforts—the Coaches vs. Cancer comes to mind—I think that shows that he has a good heart."

Purdue coach Keady agrees.

"When coaches are talking about Denny, one of the first things you'll hear is them praising his loyalty to his former players," Keady said.

Crum is hard to get to know, Keady admits, but those who wait to judge him and get to know him are rewarded.

"Denny has a strong personality, yet at the same time he is often a man of few words, so sometimes people take him wrong until they get to know him," Keady said. "When you first play against Denny, you might not judge him right. But I know him as a great competitor and a good friend. If you talk to his former players, they'd tell you they'd go to war for him, and he's the one they'd want in their foxhole with them."

Former Crum assistant and former Tennessee head coach Wade Houston said Crum has gradually opened up to the members of the so-called "coaching fraternity" in recent years.

"Once he started to serve on some of the committees (at the coaches' meeting held annually after the Final Four)," Houston said, "I think he became more involved with the other coaches. It used to be, Denny would come to the Final Four, and then when it was over, he'd go golfing, hunting or fishing. His feeling was that there was just so much to do from the time the season started to the end that when you had time to go and clear your head, you should take that opportunity. I don't know a lot of coaches who have the same feel for the outdoors—or realize that there just has to be a time to get away from it all, at least for a while."

Keady takes it one step further.

"He's a guy that if we retire, I would like to live next door to him," Keady said. "I'd like it to be in Palm Springs so we could golf everyday. But you know what? He might not leave Louisville. That's his home, and he loves the life he has in Kentucky."

Another misconception about Crum is in regard to recruiting.

"It's funny," Keady said, "whenever I hear someone say that Denny isn't a recruiter, I laugh—because anyone saying that hasn't had to face those kids in a game against Denny's teams. He's a GREAT recruiter. If you had to play his teams, you'd KNOW he's a great recruiter."

LSU's former coach Dale Brown says Crum's legacy won't overtake the misconception until Crum retires—and by that time, Brown says, Crum's legacy will be secure.

"It's amazing what he's done, but the perception of him has not caught up to his accomplishments," said Brown. "First of all, Denny is a very understated guy. He's not like many of the new breed of college coaches you see now. He's not flamboyant, and he doesn't seem to be swallowed up with vanity. He's unique in that regard. Think about how many coaches who won national championships are even still coaching in college basketball—there are not that many. Look at how many coaches have been to the Final Four more than twice, look at career wins and win percentages—you'll see Denny high on all those lists. I don't think he's ever been credited for the job he's done. Another reason is he's not a big on-camera buff."

Brown says that Crum's lack of intentional endearment—or kissing up—to the media will not tarnish his record when he retires.

"I read an article that said, 'Who could have known that Crum would show up to coach or the Cardinals to play? You never know at Louisville. It results in their bland, unemotional performances in the clutch,'" Brown said. "That is so unfair! It is so preposterous that some are knighted as great coaches and some are not. There are some who get so much credit, but you know them personally and you just shake your head wondering why the media has held them up. Maybe it's because he didn't cater to the right people. It will be interesting to see someone try to equal his record—especially staying at the same school. Someone coming up now taking the same school to six Final Fours—it'll never happen. He'll be appreciated more after his retirement. Whoever replaces him eventually at Louisville will struggle to get them where he has them.

Maybe he just didn't brown-nose the 'right' people. Denny is extremely honest. When he says something, he means it. He does not try to manipulate his words in any way—he's just not out to impress everybody. I find Denny to be rather quiet and shy. But Denny has the record to do his speaking for him. Denny came up under the tutelage of John Wooden, the greatest coach of all time and one of the greatest human beings. Just by osmosis look how much more he had than us when he became the coach at Louisville."

Back when sportswriter Mark Purdy was at the *Cincinnati Enquirer*, he penned this of Crum and U of L: "His teams have an image problem. People think of Louisville as the log flume ride of college basketball: splashy, wild, out of control and dangerous. Well, the Cards do often run, and they do often seem to be in 18 places at once. But if you watch them closely, they are not out of control. They may throw a stupid pass now and then, but they don't make it a habit. They are shrewdly reckless and creatively audacious. During timeout huddles, Crum has been known to diagram brand-new plays and install defenses they've never even practiced. The allegedly wild and crazy players seldom seem confused . . . the UCLA dash and the Louisville flash are close cousins."

CHAPTER 14

ALWAYS A COMPETITOR

Former U of L assistant coach Bobby Dotson has seen Denny Crum's competitive nature as well as anyone.

"I don't think people realize what a competitor he is. He doesn't cry and moan when he loses, but it kills him to lose," Dotson said.

One story in particular from Dotson's tenure under Crum comes to mind.

"Every spring we (the assistants and Denny) would go to Florida," Dotson said. "Wade Houston and I played Denny and Jerry Jones in golf. They just killed us year after year. After we played—every single time—we would refigure our handicaps because that was the most fair thing to do, so we did it that way. So one day, we beat them. But the day before that, Denny had been in the hospital with a kidney stone—so we hadn't refigured our handicaps from the day before that."

Crum realized this fact while walking toward the clubhouse after the 18th hole.

"Hey wait, since I wasn't here, we didn't adjust my handicap," Crum said.

Dotson looked over his shoulder and said, "Coach, all the rest of us three had adjusted our handicap based on those scores."

"Yeah, but we didn't figure my score from last time, and you guys KNOW that," Crum answered. "Let's throw this out and figure it the right way."

"Coach," Dotson said, "No way. It's over, and you lost."

The foursome went to lunch, and Crum was quiet. They played for just $10 that day, but according to Dotson, "By Denny's sour face, you'd have thought we played for a million."

Dotson wanted Crum to get over the defeat. Crum, however, knew better: With his math-sharp mind, he had done the tally in his head and knew—although he did not tell the others—that actually he and Houston, with the updated score, would have won by two strokes instead of losing by one stroke.

Crum put his $10 on the table to pay the debt for himself and Jones.

"Now," Crum said to Dotson, sliding the money toward him, "I will see what kind of man you are—if you take this money, that will tell me."

Dotson took the money.

"Coach," Dotson said, "I don't get it with you. We go to Syracuse, get blown out on national television, and you don't say a word. We go to Kentucky and get beat in a game where the arena is shaking, and you don't change your mood. Now, I don't understand this, all this rinky-dinky golf match for a lousy 10 bucks and you are getting all bent out of shape."

Crum shook his head. "The difference from the Syracuse and Kentucky games is this, and this only," Crum said, leaning forward in his chair. "You might have thought we didn't get a couple of calls in those games, but the officiating is part of the game, and those guys do the best they can—and calls go both ways. But today, on this golf course—since you guys know we didn't figure my scores from last time in—you are cheating!"

"Denny was looking for sympathy because he was about to pass a kidney stone," Houston said. "He wasn't going to get it from us— we were competing, and kidney stone or not, we beat them."

Dotson still gets a laugh out of the memory.

"And let me tell you something else, don't ever play him in cards," Dotson said. "With the way that mind of his crunches numbers, he's tough."

"There's no question about it," Houston said. "He's a fierce competitor."

Golf pro Gene Sullivan is one of Crum's closest friends. "I've never been around someone who can't stand to lose as much as

Denny," Sullivan said. "We have played ping-pong, pool, golf—you name it, and he will do anything within his power to win—whatever type of sport, he will do whatever it takes to win. Even if he was a businessman in an insurance agency, he'd be the best in the market.

"He really is a 14 handicap from the back tees," Sullivan said. "But if the match is on the line and he needs a birdie or par to win, he becomes a scratch golfer just because of his will to win. I played with him once, and he was at 90 already on the 17th tee—just struggling that day. We figured out what we needed to win, and he'd have to go birdie-par, or par-birdie. Of course, he did, and we won. He's an excellent putter because his concentration is so great."

That sense of competition drives Crum to learn more about things that are outside of basketball.

"He's very knowledgeable about a lot of things," Sullivan said. "If he doesn't feel like he knows enough about something, he'll go find out about it through a book or listening to someone who is an expert. He loves going to movies, and he loves reading Louis L'Amour—that guy can't write enough books for Denny."

Radio commentator Jock Sutherland said Crum still keeps to himself more often than not, but his competitive side is hard to conceal.

"It's funny because after all these years, you'd think I have lots of stories, but I really don't," Sutherland said. "Unless he's in a crowd he's comfortable with, he's shy. In a group he's comfortable with, he has his own style of humor. I played golf with him a couple times, and he's competitive on the course—there is nothing he is not competitive at."

The sense of competitiveness drives Crum, but it is backed by the confidence necessary for someone in Crum's position.

"Denny is the most confident person I know," Sutherland said. "He would have been good at whatever he did—if he were a plumber, he'd be a great plumber. If he were a rocket scientist, he'd be leading the pack. He's smart with anything. He has an aptitude with numbers and percentages."

Former assistant coach Wade Houston was able to apply that

competitiveness to the business world after he moved on from Louisville to take the head coaching job at Tennessee. He started his own business, which he still runs in Louisville, while his son, Allan Houston, plays for the New York Knicks in the NBA.

"I've learned a lot from Denny and have taken that into the business world, but competing is the first thing that comes to mind," Houston said. "There's so much competition in going after accounts, competition for trying to attract top-quality employees, and you can take the lessons from college basketball and apply it to the business world—whether it is being properly prepared, making adjustments as needed or what have you."

Sutherland makes a point to state that he speaks freely about Crum, without fear of repercussion.

"Denny has no leverage on me," Sutherland said. "I say these things about him because they are true. As a person, in 18 years I have never heard him cuss—not even once. I respect him a lot as a man. He always seems to be fair. He's always fair with his players. He's so loyal to his coaches and players. As a former coach myself, I really appreciate the loyalty Denny shows to his coaches and players, even after they've graduated."

Watching hundreds of coaches and teams over the years, Sutherland has drawn some conclusions about Crum's system.

"Denny has mastered his system, just totally mastered it," Sutherland said. "He is the best coach in the last three minutes in America. He's also a master at reading defenses. He sees where there is a soft area. He'll call a timeout and take advantage of it. He's the best I ever saw at that.

"The thing about Denny is he always stays very strong within himself," Sutherland said. "He comes over to the table for his post-game show the same way after a loss as he does after winning a national championship. He's not too much on the highs or the lows. I remember seeing him coming over to me after the championship game—when they beat Duke for the title. And I recall a game we should not have lost at Towson State. He looked the exact same. I wish I could have known him before I finished my coaching career because I would have liked to have taken his disposition toward the game and the way he kept his priorities in line. I ruined a lot of weekends for myself and my family when I coached. So being around Denny, I learned you really don't have to do that to be a coach."

Sutherland admits that Crum, without even really knowing it, helped Sutherland through the toughest time of his life.

"The time I joined the broadcast team for Louisville was in 1982," Sutherland said. "My wife had died. I was going through an awfully bad time. My bonus in life has been my time at Louisville. I've always been grateful for the way Denny accepted me. I'm back now to where I need to be. I had been, as a coach, riding a 10 and had fallen all the way to a one, losing my wife and coaching. When this job came along, it gave me something to grab ahold of."

Crum's sense of competitiveness is balanced by the secure inner-confidence. To that end, Sutherland is one person who will really miss Crum.

"One of the things I admire about him a lot is that he has never told me what I could or could not say on the radio," Sutherland said. "I speak my mind—what I see to be the truth—always to the listeners. So many coaches out there are so paranoid. They wouldn't want anyone saying anything that disagrees with the program. In the good times or bad times, Denny is always the same way. I admire him a whole lot for that. He has so much confidence in his own judgment that he's not concerned with what the radio broadcasters or writers think. That's something, when I'm done with Louisville, I will always remember. I will always admire him for that."

CHAPTER 15

LIFE—AND LONGEVITY— IN LOUISVILLE

Denny Crum's basketball legacy will—and does—stand on its own merit. But he will always be linked to UCLA Coach John Wooden. And when Crum was only three years into his Louisville tenure, Wooden's UCLA team beat the Cards in the semifinals at the Final Four.

"We had a great team. I knew that we would be strong for the next two seasons, and I was still several years away from the mandatory retirement age. The thought of retirement wasn't really on my mind that afternoon," Wooden said. But after the game, Wooden could think of nothing else but retirement. "When it ended, I walked over to congratulate Denny and to tell him that this was one of the greatest games I had ever been associated with. Then I saw all the interviews and bright lights associated with championship night, and it dawned on me that I didn't want to do this anymore."

The rumors started flying that Crum's departure to UCLA from Louisville was imminent. Like a lot of media-fed rumors, this one had little basis in fact, just innuendo. Crum distanced himself from the talk, saying he wanted to win a national title at Louisville. Word got to UCLA that Crum was not interested, and he was not even a candidate.

"I think his plan was to show everybody he could coach and then go back to UCLA," said former assistant Jerry Jones. "I don't think he had any idea what this basketball program was or what it could become when he came here. He got caught up in the atmosphere, and he was amazed by it."

A couple of years later, Crum did receive an offer to coach the Bruins. It was late in the 1976-77 season when UCLA and Wooden's successor, Gene Bartow, were getting ready to meet Louisville at the NCAA Tournament's West Regional in Pocatello, Idaho. Bartow was in the bleachers at the Minidome on March 11 when Louisville showed up for its practice.

"Where's Denny?" Bartow asked a U of L athletic department official. "Bring him up, would you please—I want to talk to him."

Crum showed up a few minutes later. Following in Wooden's footsteps had exacted a huge toll on Bartow in a very short time, just two seasons.

"Denny," Bartow said, "you want this job? You can have it. I can't take it anymore. I'm getting out."

Bartow said the Los Angeles media was relentless in its criticism.

"Everyday," Bartow told Crum, "there's a letter to the sports editor saying UCLA should bring back Denny Crum. Who needs it?"

Crum was as sympathetic as he was interested.

"Have you already given your resignation to them?" Crum asked.

"Several weeks ago," Bartow said.

The offer from UCLA athletic director J.D. Morgan—who hadn't even bothered to contact Crum when Wooden stepped down—came shortly after Crum's talk with Bartow.

"I seriously considered the UCLA offer," Crum said. "When I left there (UCLA, for the interview), I really felt I was going to accept the job."

So Crum promptly went home and announced he would not leave Louisville.

"When I came to the University of Louisville, my goal was to win a national championship," Crum said. "I haven't accomplished that yet."

The decision was as personal as it was professional.

"The more I thought about the community and the friends I have made here," Crum said, "and the more I thought about the university and the program we had built, I just decided it would be dumb to leave. And the more I thought about it, the dumber I thought it would be."

So he stayed at Louisville, a decision he never fathomed would go that way when he first left UCLA for the Cardinals.

"When I first took the job here, I could never have thought about being here more than 20 years down the road," Crum said. "I guess the longevity and consistency of the program is something that you take great pride in. It's certainly not something many people could predict. Most coaches don't stay at the same schools very long. So to be able to do that gives you a feeling of accomplishment and a feeling of pride."

The job offers he received could not approach the quality of life he found in Louisville.

"I have always loved living here so much, and the interest in basketball is tremendous," Crum said. "I don't ever look back, or at least I try not to. I have had the opportunity to move on so many times, but it was never something where I wanted to leave Louisville."

The NBA came calling, but Crum never called back.

"I've had the chance to coach in the NBA," Crum said. "But at that time, I would not have made much more money in the NBA than I was making here—they weren't paying coaches like they are now. I would have had to be on the road that much more. Plus I was a little skeptical of having to deal with the prima donnas—not that all are that way, but it's no secret that some are. I have really enjoyed college coaching. It's a wonderful experience, teaching these kids and watching them grow."

While success at UCLA would have been all but guaranteed, Crum's not so sure that he believes in the "grass is always greener" theory.

"You never know when moving from one place to another about how things will work out," Crum said. "It didn't take me long to figure out I liked living here. I learned quickly that this would be a great place to live, raise kids and where people have an interest in what I do. Given the overall quality and cost of living, you would have a hard time finding a better place to be than Louisville, Kentucky."

Living in Louisville, Crum was soon turned on to horse racing. In the past decade, Crum's involvement has continued to grow in the sport.

"I have always had an interest in horses, and I've always loved races themselves," Crum said. "I've been involved in it myself for 10 years or better. I really enjoy it. I currently breed and race my own horses. One of these days I want to take one from birth, train it and race it myself to see if I can do it and do it successfully. They're like athletes. They're just really good athletes. And the good ones are just incredible. I'm trying to figure them out, how to do it all—how to get them to be their best at the right time. All the things you have to do are like what you do in any other sport. The only thing is the horses can't talk back to you—but that actually makes it harder. If an athlete has a muscle pull and feels it, you'll know about it because he can tell. But with a horse, they won't stop, they'll just push. This is a thousand-pound animal on spindly legs, and if you don't have patience, you never will get one right. I really enjoy the industry and the competition. It's a tremendously challenging field. It's a lot of fun for me as well as a very challenging and competitive business."

Former assistant Bill Olsen said the horse-racing hobby will probably become a career for Crum when he retires.

"It was somewhat ironic that he fell in love with Louisville," Olsen said. "And look at him now: He loves horse racing, and he works in the same town as Churchill Downs. It's like Louisville and Denny Crum were made for each other."

The analytical process in horse racing is something Crum thrives on.

"The strategy of placing a horse where you need to place him and moving him to the finish line where he's ahead of anyone else is what drives Denny's interest in horse racing," Olsen said. "The coaching aspect, playing the percentages, the attention to detail, the preparation, the even keel, the consistency—it's all there in horse racing, and those are what Denny excels at, so it is a logical match."

"The real reason Coach Crum stayed here is because of the fact he really enjoys the lifestyle of Kentucky and in the community," Jerry Jones said. "And when these jobs come open, they come open for a reason, and that has to be taken into consideration. Being from California, Denny already knew what the West coast offered, but by then he knew that Kentucky had everything he enjoys."

And, like most other hobbies, the competition drives him.

"Absolutely," Crum said. "when I quit playing slow-pitch softball and basketball recreationally, I had to have something to fill that void. Here, horse racing is a major pastime."

"I like what this area has to offer—I also like to hunt and golf," Crum said. "I had kids in school here who did not want to leave."

Crum's other main hobby is fly-fishing, something he took up—and soon mastered—after he moved to Louisville.

"The thing that allows me to unwind and get back to a normal existence is my free time in the summer," Crum said. "There's nothing more relaxing than fishing. Fish don't live in ugly places. We floated six days in Alaska (in 1998) on a river and saw only one other raft in those six days. You can get back into the wilderness and experience the challenge of catching different kinds of fish, finding different ways to get them to take your bait, or lure. I don't eat fish. I just catch them and release them. It's a sporting thing. I also like it a lot for the camaraderie you build with your fellow fishermen, especially when you're with them for six or seven days in a row in the back country. You get to share with Mother Nature herself and all her offspring. It would be watching a pair of eagles fishing, or a mother bear with her cub standing in waist-high water trying to catch salmon and trout as they swim by. It's really a special treat to be out in a natural setting."

Former assistant coach Jerry Jones said Crum takes an unspoken pride in his charitable causes.

"The charity is part of who Denny is as a person," Jones said. "He would rather not let the word get out about all he does—how many people do you know like that? Usually, they're sending press releases to the paper and TV stations to hype the charity work they do. It's unbelievable to Denny that people think his charity work is something special—to him it is something that is just the right thing to do. He's just not an egomaniac. If he did call the press and get attention for the charitable causes he works for, he'd probably get a boost in his public image and people would appreciate him more. But then, the charitable act would not be genuine, and Denny could not live with himself if that was the case."

Crum's charity work is something he enjoys doing without any fanfare or publicity.

"He can't say no to anybody," Dotson said. "Anyone he can help—one kid, a group or organization—he's always there for them. Denny does not promote Denny. He just goes about his business. He doesn't have a lot of coaching friends, whereas someone like Dean Smith has his fraternity. Some people might think that he does the charity work because it is expected from a state university like Louisville. But that's what kills me, Denny does the work because he enjoys it. You could write a book about everything he has done on his own time because he won't tell the newspapers and media about it. He is content with the action itself and how it makes him, and those he is doing it for, feel. He does not need—and won't accept—a public pat on the back because that belies the meaning of the word 'charity' in itself to Denny."

Crum is also generous to his friends—and even to strangers he meets on the golf course.

"Denny is an extremely generous person," said Jock Sutherland, who does color commentating on the U of L basketball network. "We were playing golf, and I noticed he had a nice new driver. Denny said, 'Do you like it? I can get you one.' And he did. Another time we were playing, and a guy said he liked Denny's clubs. After we were done, he told the guy, 'Here, take these clubs and play them—see if you like them. If you do I can get you some.' Same thing with some shoes he was wearing one day at practice. I remarked that they were nice, and I hadn't seen them before. Of course, Denny said, 'Hey, I can get you a pair.' He always wants to give his friends something."

"I am with him three or four days a week, and he will never tell anyone about what he does for charity," Sullivan said. "He is chairman of this thing for cystic fibrosis, which has raised something like $100,000. But he's in it to help people suffering from that, not to help his public image. To Denny, promoting himself would belie the charitable effort itself. To me, the way Denny handles it is the essence and true meaning of charity—done for the right reasons, for the right people. He actually sleeps very little. He has a drive to help people. That's only intensified—not backed off at all—since his mother and father passed away."

Like Sutherland, golf pro and Crum confidante Gene Sullivan has seen Crum giving stuff away on the golf course.

"I got Denny a nice driver, and some guy named, I think, Joe from Seattle was one of Denny's golfing partners," Sullivan said. "I guess Joe commented on the driver. So I get a call from Denny, 'Hey, I need another one for me.' I said, 'What? I just got that for you yesterday.' He said, 'I know, but I met this guy who really liked it, and I gave him mine.' That's just Denny."

But the best memory of Crum for Sullivan took place at a General Electric assembly plant.

"One thing that does stand out in my mind is a time I was talking to a guy from the General Electric plant in this area that has thousands of employees," Sullivan said. "This guy says, 'We had our employee of the year presentation, and the guy who won was asked if this was the greatest moment of his life.' Well, the guy was a big Louisville fan, and he said, 'Well, it's great, but I'd rather shake Denny Crum's hand.' Denny and I were headed out one morning a couple of days later, and I told him the story because I thought it was neat.' Denny said, 'Gene, exit here.' I said, 'Denny, we've still got about five miles left to get where we're going.' Denny said, 'No, how about we go see this guy at the plant and shake his hand.' We showed up at the plant. Denny came up to the guy and extended his hand, 'Hi, I'm Denny Crum. Congratulations on Employee of the Year. You must've worked hard.' The guy almost passed out! I heard they had to send the guy home later that day because he was just so shocked. But did Denny want any ink for that? No way, because that was not the reason he went out there."

CHAPTER 16

THE STATE OF THE GAME

I n 30-plus years of coaching college basketball, Denny Crum has seen a lot of changes, especially societal ones, that have forced college coaches to adjust to new roles and attitudes.

"For players coming up today, it's really difficult," Crum said. "So many people are pulling at them from different directions. There is so much recognition, and everyone is recruiting them. They get a lot of attention. And to a 16- or 17-year-old high school junior or senior, that makes a lot of things get out of focus—namely some of the things that are really important and matter the most, from academics to a situation that is the best for them, not just best for a coach or sponsor. The summer league coaches are pulling on them, their family members are pulling maybe another way, and some kids have various hangers-on who just want to associate with them to get their own piece of the spotlight. In the high school situation, the really good players get so much recognition that it is hard for them to keep everything in the proper perspective. They get advice from people who don't have their best interests at heart. And if that's the case when decision time comes, they might pick a school for the wrong reason."

The changes in the game have come, gone, and some have come back.

"If you were to talk to old timers, they would say taking away the jump ball after the basket was the most dramatic change," Crum said. "And it probably was up to that time. The dunk was eliminated, then it was put back in—I'm glad it was reinstalled. But I don't think there has ever been a change in the game that rivals the three-point shot. It not only has changed the game, but the way it is scored. It's had a change on offense and defense. It's enabled the little guy to get back into the game, making them a more important contributor. It's probably had more impact than anything I've ever seen."

Being a coach means being a teacher, a role he takes seriously and holds close to his heart.

"I really think the world of all my former players," Crum said. "I'm proud of the successes they've had. It's really a lot of fun to get together with a group of them. I like to talk to them about what they learned, things they figured out down the road after they had left college. It just means so much to have a player come back a few years later and say, 'Thanks, you taught me a lot about discipline,' or 'Now I see the reason why we ran so many drills, and now I do the same thing with my own children.' When you look back on it, it makes what you've done seem so much more special. So many of them didn't appreciate things until they got out in the real world."

That does not always mean celebrations—indeed, each player and every team goes through a period of struggle.

"You have to be there for your players during the good times, and the bad times too," Crum said. "The good times are easy because everyone is happy, and really, they get a sense of almost 'too high' because the focus can get lost, so you try to keep emotions from getting too high. When things are bad, the kids need you just as much as before, even more. But the truth of the matter is that you only prosper through adversity—that's something I heard from Coach Wooden, too. The good times are easy and fun. But the bad times are where you learn to negotiate the obstacles or work through a tough run of luck. That's where the character comes in. And if you think about it, that's where the seeds for significant accomplishments are planted. You do hard work, you do what you are supposed to, and there is a reward—the 'good' times. Now, if that is a meaningful reward, you were probably able to work through the 'bad' times."

Through those challenges comes character.

"The fun part of the job to me," Crum said, "is looking back at the adversity you had and how you worked through it. For a lot of kids, the challenge of college—academically, socially and athletically—is like nothing else they have been faced with before."

Noted for his fairness, Crum knows each team, each player has unique qualities.

"There are characteristics of individuals that make them all different," Crum said. "Therefore, you can't treat them all the same way. That does not mean you should be unfair. But since everyone is different, you have to understand that and work through that. Some kids you can't raise your voice to; others you do just to get their attention. Some kids pick up a drill on the first time. Some take several times, several weeks even, to get it down. So you have to take every young person's unique characteristics into consideration or you are not giving them your best effort to help them succeed."

In a society of changing values and motivation, Crum's job has forced him to adapt.

"With the way recruiting has developed, there are some kids who expect to be handed something—even if that's just a promise of playing time, or being a starter—and that's not the way to do it," Crum said. "The competition when kids get to college is so tough that it just doesn't work that way—you can't make those kinds of promises. That can turn a parent off. But as a parent of boys myself, I'd rather have them get a healthy dose of the truth so they go into the experience with their eyes wide open, rather than pick a place based on a promise or guarantee that will likely not be followed through on."

Sports give anyone, with varying abilities, the chance to succeed.

"In athletics, you really only get what you earn—they're just aren't any shortcuts," Crum said. "Even though some players get more recognition, it does not mean others can't be successful. They are all important and have to be treated that way—so they feel, believe and know they are important."

The media has also changed: At one time the television sported three networks plus public broadcasting. Now, there are literally hundreds of channels. Throw that in with the magazines and newspapers—plus the burgeoning Internet media—and the information superhighway, once a "county road" is now a dozen lanes wide.

"Everything today is so visible," Crum said. "With the rise in cable sports channels and satellite dishes, there is so much going on out there that everything is readily accessible. A really good thing, or bad thing, happens and it is known nationwide immediately. You don't always get a chance for explanation or context—it's just all out there."

That has brought coaches and teams into the spotlight and under the microscope like never before.

"One of the things that has happened in the coaching profession today is that more is expected of coaches," Crum said. "And that's demanded because of the visibility of the sport. I know that, personally, I try to do my best with every team. Sure, there will be years when things go better than others. But if there's a slip-up or a lower win total, it's not because I've tried less. In the good years, when we go to a Final Four or deep into the NCAA Tournament, it is not because I've tried harder. My effort is always the best I can do, and that's all I—or any coach—can offer, our very best effort."

Coaches coming up nowadays can find their way to the top in a hurry through a variety of means, whether it's quick success or sending players to the NBA. But Crum knows meaningful success doesn't always come from instant success.

"I think the main thing is that they've got to pay their dues," Crum said. "They've got to be able to make sure they have everything in place to make it in the long run. Most colleges want to hire guys on the basis of their ability to recruit, not the basis of what they know about the game of basketball. So up-and-coming coaches have to remember two things: One is be prepared and able to take advantage of the opportunity. Most guys want to start out at a high level—Division I—and it doesn't work out that way. I started in junior high. Most guys want the college level to start out at, yet they're not ready for it. You have to learn all about coaching, and, of course, recruiting is important—but there are so many other things in running a program. You have got to be prepared to understand the game, what it's all about and be able to teach the game. That way, wherever you get hired, you will be able to have success. And that will help on the recruiting end of it. A lot of coaches are hired based only on what they've done on the recruiting end."

"Most coaches feel like they know enough about recruiting and basketball that they could, if they had to, do it alone, even without an assistant coach," Crum said. "Part of your success—and a big part, at that—comes from the people you surround yourself with. Your assistant coaches will help determine your success, or your degree of success. You have to be loyal to these people, teach them and encourage them to go. A lot has been made out of the fact that my assistants have a lot of input and responsibility. But you know, I would not want to hire a coach who did not want to keep improving and taking on more responsibility, or going a different direction. I have the final word, but I still learn from my assistant coaches—and players. I learn from talking to my administrative assistant, Judy Cowgill, and I learn from talking to our trainers. You take in a lot of information from a lot of sources, you process it and that's how you make decisions. There's no such thing as too much knowledge. Now, when you get a lot, it comes down to how you digest it and apply it. You can't apply everything you learn, and you can't try everything everyone suggests. But you have to have an open mind while at the same time, not forgetting what got you to where you are in the first place."

High school coaching has also grown in stature.

"There are some great high school coaches—some of the best coaching goes on in high school—and most don't recruit because the players come from their geographic area for the most part," Crum said. "But the best coached teams I've ever seen are high school teams. And when I go to high school games, I feel like more often than not the teams with the most talent just don't seem to be as fundamentally sound. That's why you might see a team with two or three highly recruited players lose in the state tournament to a team with maybe one NAIA and one Division III players on it— because the second team works on fundamentals, is not concerned about the recognition, and the players aren't as distracted. Those wins in high school are never forgotten. A lot of major college players recall their high school basketball memories as readily as they do their college ones."

Part of a small circle of coaches who stay at one university their whole career, Crum points to it as just a sign of the times.

"I think that mentality is reflected in other businesses because people just seem to move around more," Crum said. "If there are universities that will pay you more and do more for you, there might be a better situation out there for particular coaches. For a long time, the only way to get a good raise was to move to another school. But then the school whose coach left had to pay more to get another coach, so perhaps had the money been there, the coach would not have left in the first place."

The perfect example, Crum says, of one coach to stay at one place and enjoy success is not himself, but rather Wooden.

"When I was at UCLA as his assistant, they had been winning and continued to win when I left," Crum said. "The only common factor was Coach Wooden. He's the one who set the thing up. He had a lot of success, and people will never forget that. Looking back, the times were different—everything was different then. You didn't go to the NCAA Tournament unless you won your conference. I remember a couple of years when UCLA had some great teams and didn't go to tournaments. One of those years was when Cal won a national championship—that happened when I was still there. I look back on it, try to evaluate what they did then, things going on now, not a whole lot of change other than the three-point shot. (Cal Coach) Pete Newell had his team playing fundamentally sound, and as a unit—the team knew its individual roles, and executed everything so selflessly. Guys like Pete Newell, I always admired."

In recent years, Crum has become more involved with the "coaching fraternity." To that end, he took an active role in the National Association of Basketball Coaches (NABC).

"My NABC involvement helped me get to know the other coaches better," Crum said. "The best thing is what we've been able to accomplish. In the eight or nine years I have been involved, we've been able to get more involved with a lot of things going on—and that in itself is a good thing. We've had a lot of success impacting things in the game that impact the kids and the coaches. The whole experience with NABC has been really good for me. We have an office right by the NCAA office, and it's just worked out tremendously as we try to get our view communicated to the NCAA about issues we want to focus on."

Crum succeeded Duke Coach Mike Krzyzewski as president of the NABC starting with the 1999-2000 season.

"That's really helped spur my interest in a lot of things to help the game," Crum admitted.

Crum's Cards have also had several brushes with the NCAA. The most recent, a ban on post-season handed down before the 1998-99 season, was overturned. But Crum said there were still important lessons to be learned and mistakes not to be repeated.

"We've had a couple of mistakes by assistant coaches, and I take responsibility for anything they do because they work for me, and I work for the University of Louisville," Crum said. "There has to be an accountability, and that will always be my responsibility. Our mistakes were not intentional; in fact, they were inadvertent and isolated in some cases. But a mistake is a mistake, and just like you make your players learn from their mistakes, the head coach and his coaching staff have to as well. So I sure hope we've made our last mistake with the NCAA rules. We have a new compliance staff and meetings every month. So we'll work as hard as we can and keep the communication open so we don't bring any other problems our way again."

The highlights on dozens of cable channels a night is crowd pleasing, but it does not please the skill level of fundamental-based players.

"I think a lot of that has changed," Crum said. "There are so many great individual players that kids see on television, and the kids try to emulate them. They spend more time working on the fancy stuff and dunks than they do on the fundamentals. The fundamentals of the game are not nearly as apparent as they were. That does not mean there aren't great college players because there are. There are still a lot of talented players coming into college, but on the whole they just aren't as fundamentally sound as in the past."

Fundamentals do need to be practiced in college and at the high school level, but the roots of solid fundamental play should begin when a boy or girl first picks up a basketball.

"The fundamentals are a result of what they're taught at the lower levels," Crum said. "Kids who have extraordinary talent stand out, and most coaches won't say no. They give those players a lot more freedom. Most are not the superstar type, so they don't get taught the basic fundamentals. It is hard to be successful if your team is not fundamentally sound, no matter what system you run. That's why we spend an hour to two hours a day on fundamentals."

Crum points to his mentor, Wooden, as an example of the importance of fundamentals.

"If you were to ask Coach Wooden what makes a great college team, he would tell you conditioning, fundamentals and team play," Crum said. "Conditioning is not hard to do. The team play comes as a result of what you do in practice and what you require of the players. The fundamentals have to be learned and practiced constantly. If you are not fundamentally sound as a team, you are not going to beat a team that is completely fundamentally sound, even if you have the higher talented players in a lot of cases. There are a lot of kids with good talent who can't make the proper pass, can't make a proper pivot jump stop—there are a lot of things that aren't visible to the television viewer that can make a huge difference in a game. You have to set the pick without moving, take a charge, make a pass in a way that is most efficient, use the proper form on shooting, know what hand to dribble with, and when to switch."

Focusing on fundamentals makes a decent team good, or a good team great.

"Like in 1980—our team wasn't picked to win a national title either," Crum said. "I don't do things a whole lot differently in practice in terms of how much time we spend on fundamentals— which is a lot of time, and effort. Even when we have most of our kids coming back, we still teach it over and over and over again.

They can pick up bad basketball habits over the summer. You want them to be able to do certain things. There is a right way to do them and a wrong way to do them. It is easy to get out of sync. Some of the summer coaches may or may not focus on basic fundamentals, yet that's where players need the most work."

While players can exceed their coach's, and their own, expectations, some players simply have limits because of their athletic ability.

"It depends on the talent level," Crum said. "A lot of times you can be very encouraging and a player won't play Division I. But if a kid is completely fundamentally sound and has some quickness and/or talent, he can in all likelihood play somewhere, at some level. Players need to learn to execute the right way—they even need to learn to lift weights the right way. You take that, add that to some ability, find someone who is properly taught, and they will have a chance. They have to have some physical tools—some that can't be taught. But a lot of things they have to learn—and things you have to learn are what carry you to the next level, not just the talent. You could go to the YMCA and see some incredible players putting on a show. But then you ask, 'Where did you play Division I ball?' And the answer often is, 'I didn't play in college.' To play college basketball, a lot of other things have to be put into place as a player, academically and socially. You have to learn a lot of things to play college basketball."

The national titles Crum has won draw the most attention, but the two are as different as night and day—or just as different as Crum is today compared to when he took over in 1971 at U of L.

"The first championship was totally different than the second one," Crum said. "The first one had a lot to do with proving that I could do it. Since we were there in the Final Four my first year, and UCLA beat us and then in our second trip, UCLA again beat us, the big question was, 'Can you win the big one?' In 1980 when we won the thing, for me it was more a feeling of relief. I was thrilled, but I was more relieved than I was totally happy about it. There was a lot of pressure there. In 1986 when we won it, it was a different feeling for me. Not that I'm downplaying the 1980 team, it was just a different feeling. There wasn't that pressure. I was happy and elated for our team and fans and everyone. That 1986 team was a group of overachievers. They had seven losses that year, but they did what we asked them to do."

Still, that 1986 team did not have the talent of several other former Crum-coached Cards.

"There were three or four Final Four teams that were better," Crum said. "The 1983 team was better, but Milt Wagner had a hand problem, and we lost him. In 1977, we beat Marquette at Marquette, and they ended up the national champions. We had the best team in the country that year, but we didn't even get to the Final Four (losing to UCLA in the NCAA West Regional, 87-79). We just were not the same team after Larry Williams broke his foot. We had really good teams that at times—for whatever reason—did not win. And then we had several teams that were not picked to win and maybe did not have the high-profile talent, but did go to the Final Four, or—in the case of the 1986 team—won it all. But that is part of the appeal of team sports. You find a way to compete, you define roles for players and help them grow into that role—and a lot of that is them committing their effort and attitude—and then you give it your best shot."

For all the changes around the sport, the game itself has not changed as much.

"A lot of the game has to do with experience and mental approach," Crum said. "In that regard it's a complete dichotomy because the situation surrounding college sports has really changed, but the game itself really has not. There have been rule changes that changed some things, but it's still really the same game of scoring on offense and preventing scoring defensively, and not making mistakes or breakdowns."

That means the core of Crum's coaching philosophy is the same.

"But from the standpoint of dealing with kids and people treating them fairly, the philosophy is still pretty much the same,"

Crum said. "You teach them to get along with everyone as a group rather than seeing themselves as just individuals."

Therein lies the most meaningful success.

"I appreciate the players on the teams who gave of themselves for the betterment of the team," Crum said. "That means so much, and they take that into life. There might be a time when they are working for IBM, and they think they have a better way to do it than the guy giving the presentation. But the boss picked that guy for a reason, so you have to bite the bullet. You don't cause a scene, you don't pout and put down the other guy, you don't yell at the boss and you don't stomp out of the meeting—presentation is a big part of any message. You could have the greatest message in the world, but if your manner is such that no one wants to listen to you, no one will ever hear that message. So you go along and make the best of things, even encouraging others. Then, if the other guy's plan doesn't succeed, you offer to step up. And you not only succeed, but you are regarded as an important part of that team at IBM because you are both successful and a team player, and that's something that companies look for."

Not a believer in "free rides" for student-athletes who won't put in the academic time, Crum simply likes to see players succeed in the classroom.

"I don't object to the various standards and various propositions the NCAA requires," Crum said. "But I know it has cost a lot of players a chance. That being said, I think high academic standards are good, and we must demand our student-athletes to work hard at their studies in college. Certain individuals have valid reasons for not being as far along academically as others, including learning disabilities and the environment they come from. I don't think you can disregard kids because they had it 'rough' growing up. Given the proper opportunity and support in college, a lot of those kids would surprise you with how well they do."

Still in contact with hundreds of former players, Crum likes nothing more than to visit with those players and listen to what they are up to, the challenges they face and the successes they experience.

"I think I'm like most college coaches in that I am just as appreciative, happy for, and proud of the success of our kids when they graduate and move on," Crum said. "I feel good for players who keep playing. But some of the ones who mean the most are the ones who are teachers, coaches, doctors and engineers—I am just as proud of the ones whose playing careers ended at Louisville and were able to move right into the 'real world' and find a niche. We get as much joy watching their successes—or more—than we do of our own accomplishments. People who teach—and that's what college coaches are, teachers—love what they're doing. We get very close to our students, who in this case are also our players. It seems like more and more the players come back and thank me for what I did for them on and off the floor, and I can't tell you how much that means to me. You get pretty close to your players as people, students and athletes. To me, the irony is how close you get when you're out of school. A lot of them come back and thank me for everything on and off the floor. The feeling that you had a positive impact on their lives—that is what it is all about. You try and do the right thing and teach them meaningful lessons, and they never forget that."

DENNY'S DOZEN: CRUM'S 12 KEYS TO SUCCESS

1. **Remember–We are all teachers:** "Coaches are teachers, parents are teachers, older siblings are teachers, you are a teacher to your friends—and of course teachers are teachers," Crum said. "If you are a parent, you have to remember that you are teaching every time you interact in front of your children. If you come home from work and start bad-mouthing co-workers and complaining, you are teaching your children how to act. Always be aware of what you are saying in front of your children. If you raise your voice or your hand to your children, the chances are they will repeat that later in life. If you work hard and try to set a positive example, your children will imitate that as well. What you teach your children—what they learn early in life—will stay with them forever in a lot of cases, and they will translate that to their children, and your grandchildren, as well. Being a teacher is an enormous responsibility. It is not always easy to do the right thing, but life sure is easier when you've done the right thing."

2. **Loyalty—but responsibility through accountability:** "Without loyalty, what else is there? I believe in people who are close to me. I am also not foolish enough to believe they are all perfect. I know human beings are not perfect. With mistakes comes growth. Do not abandon someone close to you because they have failed. Help them learn, and both you and that person close to you can be better off for the mistake in the long run. With that being said, demand accountability if someone in your charge has made a mistake. Help them learn where they fell short and how they can avoid such pitfalls in the future. Rules and laws exist for a reason. Sometimes, the simple truth is that we all fall short. Move forward, but never forget where you stepped out of bounds because it will keep you in-bounds in the future."

3. **Always be prepared to seize the moment:** "Proper preparation is a key in any venture, from sports to business to personal interaction and beyond. Perhaps you are not chosen for a plum assignment at work. Be prepared to step in if called upon, either to assist or—if the need arises—to take over. If you are prepared, it will show through in both your work results and your attitude. You will carry more confidence into meetings and other interactions with internal and external customers. In basketball, failing to prepare almost always leads to substandard performance. That poor performance has a ripple effect, giving that person a poor attitude and bringing those around that person down as well. Learn what you need to do to be properly prepared, not just for one occasion, but because it will prevent you from having to go back and re-learn things or make excuses for why you could not, when called upon, get the job done."

4. **Never lose sight of the big picture:** "You lost a game last night. You lost an account at work yesterday. You won a game yesterday, or you picked up a new account. Deal with everything with the big picture in mind. Keep pursuing the immediate obligations, but never forget how they fit into the bigger picture. It is like a puzzle: You have to have the smaller pieces, or you will have no puzzle. At the same time, if you don't have a grasp of the big picture, you will not get a clear picture of the final puzzle until all the little pieces are assembled in proper order. Keep the big picture in mind, and it will give a constant context and perspective to the 'little pieces.' Certainly, the smaller pieces are critical—essential—to make the big puzzle complete. But with the big picture in mind, you will understand what each step of the journey means and where it fits in as you consider the destination."

5. **Remember that lessons in sports can be translated to lessons in life:** "In more than 30 years as a college basketball coach, my biggest goal has been to positively impact the lives of the young men I coach. I know that what they do in college—what they learn—will affect them well into their lives after they leave college. If you miss a game-winning shot, it can be like failing to close a business deal. But perhaps you can work on better circumstances and execution if you have a chance to take that shot—or close that deal—the next time. Maybe you make a bad pass during a game because you thought the play was different and your pass went to a place where no teammate was standing because he broke left when you thought he'd turn right. That could be like not getting a memo to a co-worker in time or in the right format, or perhaps that person needed the project yesterday and is out of town, but you didn't take time to read the memo. You can prevent both from happening the next time by communicating better, or knowing what the other person expects, or where that person is going to be, whether it is on the court or in the office. There is no shame in failure. There is a problem, though, if you can't learn from it. I have always believed that if you can glean one morsel of positive from a negative moment, you can regard that perceived failure as a success."

6. **Make time for those in need:** "Whatever you have, you can probably use to influence someone in need in a positive way. We are all blessed with certain gifts and talents. To share those gifts to help someone in need helps not just that person, but yourself. Indeed, you gain a greater understanding of others' situations—and ideally a greater appreciation for your own life—when you encounter those in need. Sometimes just five minutes of your time can help someone for days and weeks, maybe even longer. I am always flattered when folks come to me to speak or for counsel. I consider it a privilege to help wherever I can. Through every opportunity there is room for growth. Approach each chance to influence someone as an opportunity, not as an obligation."

7. **Don't be fooled; the grass is not always greener:** "How many times have I had the chance to leave Louisville? Too many to count. But Louisville has what I want. I had children in school here. I have interests in horse racing and the outdoors, and this is an area of the country that is second to none in both of those areas. There were opportunities for more money, but when you factor in what we would have had to sacrifice, whether it be in our friends, hobbies, or lifestyle, it would have been too costly on our personal lives to move on. Just about anyone can tell you several things they don't like about their job, but is the new job you are looking at without any hassle? Certainly there are times and circumstances where moving on is the right decision. But don't be fooled that when you leave your hometown that you are trading it for Utopia. On top of that, every situation is only what you make it to be. If you have a bad attitude and choose to see only the negative, you simply will not be happy—no matter where you are. If you choose to find the positive, you will be happier. Just remember, when you move on, to properly look into just what it is you are taking on because you might leave something that means a lot to you. And in a lot of positions, there are times when you leave and you can't go back—either for an extended period of time, or perhaps forever."

8. **When you judge others, you are ultimately selling only yourself short:** "With the new era of media and the proliferation of Internet media, you can get a whole lot of information in a short period of time. Some of it is very good information, but some of it might not be in the right context or be presented with the genuine perspective. To that end, don't judge others on what you hear third- or fourth-hand. You might meet someone and have all kinds of prejudices about who they are, where they are from or what they have done. You will one day meet someone that you have prejudged and find some very special qualities about that person that you never heard of—a kid who has had a rough go who has a heart of gold, or an interest that parallels an interest of yours. But if you keep that prejudice and let it prevent you from even striking up a conversation, you are putting up a wall that won't let some very special people into your world. And you are the one who is going to suffer out of it—from not meeting some very unique people who could lend you a perspective or some other information you might never attain if you keep those walls up."

9. **Fundamentals–Stay sharp on the basics:** "In basketball, there is no question that to have success, your players all have to be very good at dribbling, passing and shooting. If you are in the computer field, you have to stay sharp on all the new technologies while always remaining cognizant of the basic functions and commands. Sometimes, we get into routines and we find shortcuts—some of those shortcuts are good, but some lead to the development of bad habits. Especially if you are a teacher, you want to avoid shortcuts that teach bad habits. Every so often, take time to practice—or perhaps even re-learn—the basics that you need to constantly be familiar with to be successful. A lot of us chose—or fell in love with—a particular career field because of the so-called 'basics.' Practicing these not only makes you sharper, but can rekindle the passion you felt when you first chose that career."

10. **Don't be afraid to give a kid a chance:** "One of the players to have the greatest influence on me was Derek Smith, a young man who excelled at U of L before playing in the NBA. Derek came back and graduated before he tragically died of a heart ailment. Derek came from the most meager background of any kid I have ever been around. I found him hard to understand when we spoke at first because his English skills were poor. When Derek graduated with his degree, I was so proud of him. With the help of tutors and all his hard work, he really pushed himself to a level that I am not sure either of us thought he could achieve. Kids who come from certain backgrounds have more problems than others with the standardized tests, yet that does not mean they are not qualified to do college work. Certainly, there are times when a kid comes here with low test scores, and they end up not making it. But the ones who do make it show that the possibility exists—that with the right circumstances, they will achieve heights in the classroom no one could have envisioned. If you go strictly by the standardized tests, you are going to exclude a lot of kids from the opportunity to get an education and improve themselves. Derek was the perfect example of someone making the most of his chance. Before he died, he was really active and involved with helping kids. Had he not been given a chance, he would not have been able to enjoy the accomplishments he ended up achieving by going to college."

11. **Be aware of peripheral opportunities associated with your career field:** "One factor that has really gotten me more involved with my peers over the years is the National Association of Basketball Coaches (NABC). I found out that a lot of coaches share the same concerns I have. In some cases, I've learned things about issues I was either not familiar with, or needed more information on. If your work offers to send you to a seminar—or if you hear about something on your own—investigate it. It might be well worth your while. You could come back with information that would not only help you personally, but might help your company. That kind of initiative is appreciated. And you are going to be better for the experience in a lot of ways. You have to remember that other people in your field are often at these seminars. You will likely make job contacts for the future as you network with others in your field. You might find a better job, or you might find out that your job is better than you previously believed before you got out and learned what else was out there, how other companies do business, or how your responsibilities and compensation compare to others in similar positions with other companies."

12. **Have other interests, expand horizons and continue to learn:** "Enjoying the beauty of the outdoors through fishing and hunting has really brought me a nice, comfortable sense of perspective. I also enjoy golfing. And of course my interest in horse racing only continues to grow. Some of these hobbies just help me get away and clear my head while doing something I really enjoy. Others help me hone the way I approach competition or the way I interact with people. You might not want to float down a river in Alaska for a week, but if you have an interest in, say, home improvement or learning more computer skills, why not take a class at the local university or community college? You could take your spouse or a friend with you as you forge a bond through a common interest. The inner accomplishment you get from learning a new skill or just honing an existing one will make you feel better about yourself and will continue to stimulate your mind."

YEAR-BY-YEAR RESULTS

1971-72
(WON 26, LOST 5)
COACH: Denny Crum
CO-CAPTAINS: Jim Price and
Al Vilcheck

Date	Site	UL	OPP
Dec. 1	**Florida (A)**	**69**	**70**
Dec. 4	Bellarmine (H)	116	58
Dec. 8	Dayton (H)	88	60
Dec. 11	Kansas (A)	74	65
Dec. 21	Alabama (H)	89	70
Dec. 22	SMU (H)	96	62

Holiday Festival Tournament
(New York, N.Y.)

Dec. 27	Syracuse (N)	103	81
Dec. 28	St. Peter's (N)	126	80
Dec. 30	Fordham (N)	96	82
Jan. 8	Cincinnati (A)	84	76
Jan. 12	Dayton (A)	71	64
Jan. 15	Bradley* (A)	75	71
Jan. 22	Drake* (2 OT) (A)	79	77
Jan. 24	No. Texas St.* (H)	95	72
Jan. 26	St. Louis* (H)	77	59
Jan. 29	Bradley* (H)	52	46
Feb. 2	**Memphis State* (H)**	**69**	**77**
Feb. 5	Drake* (H)	92	75
Feb. 9	Wichita St.* (H)	65	64
Feb. 12	Tulsa* (A)	84	66
Feb. 19	Wichita St.* (A)	69	60
Feb. 23	Cincinnati (H)	93	73
Feb. 27	St. Louis* (A)	84	78
Feb. 29	No. Texas St.* (A)	90	85
Mar. 2	**Memphis State* (A)**	**65**	**80**
Mar. 6	Tulsa* (H)	102	83

MVC Playoff
(Nashville, Tenn.)

Mar. 11	Memphis St. (N)	83	72

NCAA Midwest Regional
(Ames, Iowa)

Mar. 16	Southwestern La. (N)	88	84
Mar. 18	Kansas St. (N)	72	65

NCAA Finals
(Los Angeles, Calif.)

Mar. 23	UCLA (N)	77	96
Mar. 25	No. Carolina (N)	91	105
		2607	2237

*MVC game

1972-73
(WON 23, LOST 7)
COACH: Denny Crum
CAPTAIN: Game Captains

Date	Site	UL	OPP
Nov. 30	Vanderbilt+ (H)	57	66
Dec. 2	Georgetown Col. (H)	66	57
Dec. 6	Dayton (H)	75	58
Dec. 9	Butler (H)	90	67
Dec. 18	Navy (H)	68	52
Dec. 20	Florida (H)	69	57
Dec. 23	Utah (A)	84	67

Rainbow Classic
(Honolulu, Hi.)

Dec. 27	Fordham (N)	100	73
Dec. 29	Hawaii (A)	95	82
Dec. 30	**No. Carolina (N)**	**86**	**89**
Jan. 4	No. Texas St.* (H)	76	69
Jan. 6	Detroit (H)	76	58
Jan. 13	Wichita St.* (2 OT) (A)	78	75
Jan. 17	Dayton (A)	74	73
Jan. 20	**St. Louis* (A)**	**51**	**61**
Jan. 25	**Memphis St.* (A)**	**76**	**81**
Jan. 27	**No. Texas St.* (A)**	**64**	**78**
Jan. 29	New Mexico St.* (H)	91	64
Feb. 1	Bradley* (H)	91	74
Feb. 3	St. Louis* (H)	88	49
Feb. 5	**Cincinnati (A)**	**79**	**81**
Feb. 8	Memphis St.* (H)	83	69
Feb. 15	Drake* (A)	80	77
Feb. 17	Bradley* (A)	84	78
Feb. 22	West Texas St.* (A)	85	70
Feb. 24	Cincinnati (H)	91	81
Mar. 1	Tulsa* (H)	69	62
Mar. 3	Drake* (H)	66	60

NIT
(New York, N.Y.)

Mar. 17	American (N)	97	84
Mar. 20	**Notre Dame (N)**	**71**	**79**
		2361	2091

*MVC game
+Game played in Convention Center.

1973-74
(WON 21, LOST 7)
COACH: Denny Crum
CAPTAIN: Game Captains

Date	Site	UL	OPP
Dec. 1	**Cincinnati (H)**	**58**	**65**
Dec. 3	Houston (H)	87	81
Dec. 5	Dayton (H)	75	68
Dec. 8	Butler (A)	91	81
Dec. 15	Florida St. (H)	90	78
Dec. 18	Clemson (A)	74	70
Dec. 22	Bradley* (H)	74	65

Citizen's Fidelity Bank
Holiday Classic

Dec. 27	Eastern Ky. (H)	91	75
Dec. 28	**Alabama (H)**	**55**	**65**
Jan. 5	Tulsa* (A)	78	75
Jan. 9	**Cincinnati (A)**	**70**	**77**
Jan. 12	Drake* (A)	87	82
Jan. 19	Memphis St. (H)	94	81
Jan. 23	Dayton (A)	90	72
Jan. 28	Drake* (H)	75	73
Jan. 31	No. Texas St.* (H)	97	81
Feb. 2	West Texas St.* (H)	99	73
Feb. 7	**New Mexico St.* (A)**	**73**	**76**
Feb. 9	West Texas St.* (A)	81	62
Feb. 14	**Memphis St. (A)**	**71**	**78**
Feb. 19	Wichita St.* (H)	106	90
Feb. 23	St. Louis* (A)	93	85
Feb. 28	St. Louis* (H)	95	85
Mar. 2	Bradley* (OT) (A)	87	84
Mar. 4	Illinois St. (H)	117	107
Mar. 7	Detroit (H)	89	74

NCAA Midwest Regional
(Tulsa, Okla.)

Mar. 14	Oral Roberts (A)	93	96
Mar. 16	Creighton (N)	71	80
		2361	2179

*MVC game

1974-75
(WON 28, LOST 3)
COACH: Denny Crum
CAPTAIN: Game Captains

Date	Site	UL	OPP
Dec. 2	Houston (A)	91	87
Dec. 5	Dayton (A)	76	65
Dec. 14	Florida St. (A)	84	75
Dec. 18	Clemson (H)	90	75
Dec. 21	Marquette (A)	80	69

Citizen's Fidelity Bank
Holiday Classic

Dec. 26	Western Ky. (H)	107	81
Dec. 27	Florida St. (H)	79	61
Jan. 4	Bradley* (OT) (H)	82	80
Jan. 7	Cincinnati (H)	82	74
Jan. 9	West Texas St.* (A)	53	51
Jan. 11	New Mexico St.* (A)	82	69
Jan. 18	Drake* (OT) (H)	55	53
Jan. 23	St. Louis* (A)	78	70
Jan. 25	**Bradley* (A)**	**59**	**65**
Jan. 30	New Mexico St.* (H)	51	42
Feb. 1	No. Texas St.* (H)	112	67
Feb. 6	Wichita St.* (A)	62	57
Feb. 8	**Tulsa* (A)**	**77**	**82**
Feb. 13	Drake* (A)	86	66
Feb. 16	St. Louis* (H)	75	68
Feb. 20	Wichita St.* (A)	85	76
Feb. 22	Tulsa* (H)	104	79
Feb. 25	West Texas St.* (H)	75	69
Mar. 1	No. Texas St.* (A)	92	73
Mar. 4	Memphis St. (H)	84	79
Mar. 6	Dayton (H)	83	67

NCAA Midwest Regional
(Tulsa, Okla.)

Mar. 15	Rutgers (N)	91	78

NCAA Midwest Regional
(Las Cruces, N.M.)

Mar. 20	Cincinnati (N)	78	63
Mar. 22	Maryland (N)	96	82

NCAA Finals
(San Diego, Calif.)

Mar. 29	**UCLA (OT) (N)**	**74**	**75**
Mar. 31	Syracuse (OT) (N)	96	88
		2519	2186

*MVC game

1975-76
(WON 20, LOST 8)
COACH: Denny Crum
CAPTAIN: Game Captains

Date	Site	UL	OPP
Nov. 29	Memphis St. (A)	79	75
Dec. 6	Murray St. (H)	78	59
Dec. 9	Cal Poly (H)	84	70
Dec. 13	**DePaul (H)**	**76**	**78**
Dec. 16	St. Louis (H)	87	71
Dec. 20	Manhattan (H)	78	71

Louisville Holiday Classic

Dec. 26	Kentucky St. (H)	106	93
Dec. 27	Texas A&M (H)	102	88
Jan. 3	**West Texas St.**		
	(OT) (H)	**78**	**84**
Jan. 6	**Cincinnati (A)**	**73**	**77**
Jan. 10	**Providence (A)**	**60**	**63**
Jan. 13	Idaho St. (2OT) (A)	52	51
Jan. 15	Tulsa (A)	78	68
Jan. 17	Drake (H)	95	79
Jan. 19	Wichita St. (H)	56	52
Jan. 22	West Texas St. (A)	69	57
Jan. 28	Dayton (H)	83	74
Feb. 1	So. Illinois (H)	98	93
Feb. 4	Morehead St. (H)	90	68
Feb. 7	Bradley (A)	74	71

Feb. 14 Drake (A) 85 73
Feb. 17 Tulsa (OT) (H) 98 90
Feb. 21 Marquette (H) 62 72
Feb. 26 So. Illinois (A) 73 72
Feb. 28 Wichita St. (OT) (A) ... 74 78
Mar. 1 Bradley (H) 107 89
Metro 6 Tournament
(Louisville, Ky.)
Mar. 5 Memphis St. (H) 76 87
NIT
(New York, N.Y.)
Mar. 16 Providence (N) 67 73
2238 2076

1976-77
(WON 21, LOST 7)
COACH: Denny Crum
CAPTAIN: Game Captains
Date   Site   UL OPP
Dec. 1 Vanderbilt (OT) (A) ... 81 76
Dec. 4 Syracuse (H) 75 76
Dec. 6 Va. Commonwealth (H) 89 60
Dec. 8 Idaho St. (H) 89 68
Dec. 11 Purdue (A) 70 72
Dec. 18 Marquette (OT) (A) ... 78 75
Dec. 22 Tenn.-Chattanooga (H) 81 71
Louisville Holiday Classic
Dec. 28 Rutgers (H) 76 68
Dec. 29 Creighton (2OT) (H) ... 69 66
Jan. 3 Florida St.* (OT) (H) ... 78 75
Jan. 8 Tulane* (A) 90 81
Jan. 15 Marshall (H) 104 85
Jan. 19 Cincinnati* (H) 83 77
Jan. 22 St. Louis* (A) 74 55
Jan. 24 Long Island (H) 107 68
Jan. 27 Dayton (H) 76 71
Jan. 29 Rhode Island (H) 105 87
Feb. 5 Memphis St.* (H) 111 92
Feb. 6 Providence (H) 68 64
Feb. 9 SW Louisiana (H) 103 82
Feb. 12 Las Vegas (A) 96 99
Feb. 15 Tulsa (A) 91 67
Feb. 19 Memphis St.* (A) 77 87
Feb. 22 Northeast Louisiana (H) 95 65
Feb. 25 Georgia Tech* (H) 91 80
Feb. 27 No. Carolina (A) 89 96
Metro Conference Tournament
(Memphis, Tenn.)
Mar. 4 Georgia Tech (N) 55 56
NCAA West Regional
(Pocatello, Id.)
Mar. 12 UCLA (N) 79 87
*Metro Conference Game. 2380 2106

1977-78
(WON 23, LOST 7)
COACH: Denny Crum
CAPTAIN: Game Captains
Date   Site   UL OPP
Nov. 30 Providence (A) 51 57
Dec. 3 Vanderbilt (H) 96 66
Dec. 7 Michigan (A) 88 85
Dec. 10 Robert Morris (H) 104 68
Dec. 13 Purdue (H) 68 66
Dec. 19 Dayton (H) 69 63
Dec. 22 Marquette (H) 61 60
Louisville Holiday Classic
Dec. 28 LaSalle (H) 113 85
Dec. 29 Georgia (H) 70 73
Jan. 3 Memphis St.* (H) 78 75
Jan. 7 Cincinnati* (A) 78 75
Jan. 14 Georgia Tech* (H) 90 84
Jan. 18 SW Louisiana (A) 78 75
Jan. 22 Florida St.* (H) 66 70
Jan. 26 Tulane* (A) 105 82
Feb. 1 Marshall (A) 85 69
Feb. 4 Cincinnati* (H) 83 76
Feb. 7 Tulane* (H) 115 86
Feb. 11 St. Louis* (A) 63 61
Feb. 14 Georgia Tech* (A) 59 69
Feb. 17 Florida St.* (A) 70 81
Feb. 19 Minnesota (A) 71 72

Feb. 23 Ball St. (H) 104 84
Feb. 25 Memphis St.* (H) 115 97
Feb. 27 St. Louis* (A) 94 59
Metro Conference Tournament
(Cincinnati, Ohio)
Mar. 2 Tulane (N) 93 64
Mar. 3 Memphis St. (N) 67 62
Mar. 4 Florida St. (N) 94 93
NCAA Midwest Regional
(Tulsa, Okla.)
Mar. 12 St. John's (N) 76 68
NCAA Midwest Regional
(Lawrence, Kan.)
Mar. 17 DePaul (2OT) (N) 89 90
*Metro Conference Game. 2493 2215

1978-79
(WON 24, LOST 8)
COACH: Denny Crum
CAPTAIN: Game Captains
Date   Site   UL OPP
Seawolf Classic
(Anchorage, Ak.)
Nov. 24 Penn St. (N) 89 58
Nov. 25 Lamar (N) 90 68
Nov. 26 NC State (N) 66 72
Dec. 2 Tennessee (H) 82 61
Dec. 6 Michigan (H) 86 84
Dec. 9 Idaho (H) 101 54
Dec. 12 Ohio State (A) 69 85
Dec. 16 West Virginia (H) 106 60
Dec. 23 Providence (H) 88 70
Louisville Holiday Classic
Dec. 28 Wisconsin (H) 70 53
Dec. 29 Mississippi St. (H) 73 80
Jan. 4 Tenn.-Chattanooga (H) 94 70
Jan. 6 SW Louisiana (H) 73 60
Jan. 8 Marshall (H) 112 64
Jan. 13 Maryland (A) 99 84
Jan. 16 Dayton (A) 77 76
Jan. 18 Cincinnati* (A) 82 77
Jan. 20 Florida St.* (A) 67 65
Jan. 24 St. Louis* (H) 80 65
Jan. 28 Virginia Tech* (H) 82 72
Jan. 31 Florida St.* (H) 84 71
Feb. 3 Cincinnati* (H) 88 85
Feb. 5 Memphis St.* (H) 103 82
Feb. 8 Tulane* (A) 77 66
Feb. 10 Marquette (A) 55 71
Feb. 15 St. Louis* (A) 78 62
Feb. 17 Memphis St.* (A) 53 60
Feb. 18 Duke (A) 72 88
Feb. 24 Tulane* (H) 95 71
Metro Conference Tournament
(Memphis, Tenn.)
Mar. 2 Virginia Tech (N) 68 72
NCAA Midwest Regional
(Dallas, Tex.)
Mar. 10 South Alabama (N) 69 66
NCAA Midwest Regional
(Cincinnati, Ohio)
Mar. 15 Arkansas (N) 62 73
*Metro Conference Game. 2590 2245

1979-80
(WON 33, LOST 3)
COACH: Denny Crum
CO-CAPTAINS: Darrell Griffith and
Tony Branch
Date   Site   UL OPP
Dec. 1 South Alabama (H) 75 73
Dec. 5 Tenn.-Chattanooga (H) 87 63
Dec. 8 Tennessee (A) 77 73
Dec. 13 UNC-Charlotte (H) 93 76
Dec. 14 Western Ky. (H) 96 74
Dec. 19 Ohio St. (H) 75 65
Dec. 22 Utah (A) 69 71
Hawaii Rainbow Classic
(Honolulu, Ha.)
Dec. 28 Princeton (N) 64 53
Dec. 29 Illinois (N) 64 77
Dec. 30 Nebraska (N) 65 58

Jan. 3 Tulsa (H) 78 58
Jan. 5 Kansas St. (H) 85 73
Jan. 8 St. Louis* (H) 94 65
Jan. 12 Memphis St.* (A) 69 48
Jan. 19 Tulane* (A) 76 59
Jan. 22 Marquette (H) 76 63
Jan. 25 St. Louis* (A) 99 74
Jan. 27 Florida St.* (H) 79 73
Jan. 31 Tulane* (H) 64 60
Feb. 3 St. John's (A) 76 71
Feb. 4 Memphis St.* (H) 88 60
Feb. 6 Cincinnati* (A) 88 73
Feb. 9 Providence (A) 79 73
Feb. 11 Virginia Tech* (OT) (A) 56 54
Feb. 14 West Virginia (A) 90 78
Feb. 16 Cincinnati* (A) 61 57
Feb. 18 Virginia Tech* (H) 77 72
Feb. 21 Iona (N) 60 77**
Feb. 24 Florida St.* (A) 83 75
Metro Conference Tournament
(Louisville, Ky.)
Feb. 29 Memphis St. (N) 84 65
Mar. 1 Florida St. (H) 81 72
NCAA Midwest Regional
(Lincoln, Neb.)
Mar. 8 Kansas St. (OT) (N) .. 71 69
NCAA Midwest Regional
(Houston, Texas)
Mar. 14 Texas A & M (N) .. 66 65
Mar. 16 Louisiana St. (N) 86 66
NCAA Finals
(Indianapolis, Ind.)
Mar. 22 Iowa (N) 80 72
Mar. 24 UCLA (N) 59 54
2770 2411
*Metro Conference Game
**Game played at Madison Sq. Garden

1980-81
(WON 21, LOST 9)
COACH: Denny Crum
CAPTAIN: Game Captains
Date   Site   UL OPP
Hall of Fame Game
(Springfield, Mass.)
Nov. 22 DePaul (N) 80 86
Dec. 4 Tulsa (A) 60 68
Dec. 6 Oklahoma St. (A) 71 72
Dec. 13 Maryland (H) 78 67
Dec. 20 Utah (H) 59 78
Dec. 22 Minnesota (H) 56 62
Winston Tire Classic
(Los Angeles, Calif.)
Dec. 29 No. Carolina (N) 64 86
Dec. 30 So. California (N) 79 50
Jan. 3 Kansas St. (A) 47 64
Jan. 5 Tulane* (A) 73 53
Jan. 10 Cincinnati* (A) 83 68
Jan. 17 Florida St.* (H) 98 78
Jan. 18 Missouri (A) 71 49
Jan. 22 Memphis St. (OT) (A) 55 60
Jan. 27 Providence (H) 71 55
Jan. 29 St. Louis* (H) 61 57
Jan. 31 Virginia Tech* (H) 92 70
Feb. 2 US International (H) 86 68
Feb. 4 Tulane* (H) 85 58
Feb. 7 Florida St.* (OT) (A) .. 82 73
Feb. 9 Virginia Tech* (A) 71 66
Feb. 13 Marquette (A) 79 60
Feb. 16 Memphis St.* (H) 95 65
Feb. 18 Iona (H) 91 57
Feb. 23 Cincinnati* (A) 81 67
Feb. 25 St. Louis* (A) 97 85
Feb. 28 Western Ky. (H) 90 75
Metro Conference Tournament
(Louisville, Ky.)
Mar. 6 Virginia Tech (N) 81 68
Mar. 7 Cincinnati (H) 42 31
NCAA Midwest Regional
(Austin, Tex.)
Mar. 14 Arkansas (N) 73 74
*Metro Conference Game. 2251 1970

1981-82
(WON 23, LOST 10)
COACH: Denny Crum
CAPATIN: Game Captains

Date	Site	UL	OPI
	Wendy's Classic		
	(Bowling Green, Ky.)		
Dec. 4	Tulane* (N)	55	54
Dec. 5	Western Ky. (A)	71	66
Dec. 9	Purdue (A)	73	71
Dec. 12	Tennessee St. (H)	83	58
	Suntory Ball		
	(Tokyo, Japan)		
Dec. 17	Pennsylvania (N)	76	68
Dec. 20	**Oregon St. (N)**	**56**	**62**
Dec. 23	Morehead St. (H)	103	70
Dec. 26	**DePaul (A)**	**68**	**75**
Jan. 2	Duke (H)	99	61
Jan. 4	Florida St.* (H)	79	57
Jan. 7	St. Louis* (H)	89	53
Jan. 9	**Virginia Tech* (OT)(A)**	**74**	**75**
Jan. 13	South Alabama (A)	76	68
Jan. 16	Cincinnati* (A)	74	58
Jan. 17	**Missouri (A)**	**55**	**69**
Jan. 23	**Virginia Tech* (H)**	**76**	**78**
Jan. 24	**Virginia (H)**	**56**	**74**
Jan. 30	**Florida St.* (A)**	**65**	**71**
Feb. 3	Tulane* (H)	61	56
Feb. 6	**Memphis St.* (OT) (A)**	**65**	**74**
Feb. 7	St. John's (H)	70	60
Feb. 13	Cincinnati* (A)	67	53
Feb. 18	St. Louis* (A)	99	69
Feb. 22	Memphis St.* (H)	65	61
Feb. 25	Cleveland St. (H)	95	74
Feb. 28	Marquette (H)	80	68
	Metro Conference Tournament		
	(Memphis, Tenn.)		
Mar. 5	St. Louis (N)	76	44
Mar. 6	Florida St. (N)	97	73
Mar. 7	**Memphis St. (A)**	**62**	**73**
	NCAA Mideast Regional		
	(Nashville, Tenn.)		
Mar. 13	Middle Tennessee (N)	81	56
	NCAA Mideast Regional		
	(Birmingham, Ala.)		
Mar. 18	Minnesota (N)	67	61
Mar. 20	Ala.-Birmingham (A)	75	58
	NCAA Finals		
	(New Orleans, La.)		
Mar. 27	**Georgetown (N)**	**46**	**50**

*Metro Conference Game. 2434 2128

1982-83
(WON 32, LOST 4)
COACH: Denny Crum
CO-CAPTAINS: Scooter McCray and
Rodney McCray

Date	Site	UL	OPP
	Great Alaska Shootout		
	(Anchorage, Ak.)		
Nov. 26	Florida (A)	80	63
Nov. 27	Washington (N)	58	47
Nov. 28	Vanderbilt (N)	80	70
Dec. 1	Santa Clara (A)	84	56
Dec. 4	**Purdue (H)**	**63**	**69**
Dec. 8	Eastern Ky. (H)	82	53
Dec. 15	South Alabama (H)	94	77
Dec. 18	Oklahoma St. (H)	67	66
Dec. 21	NC State (H)	57	52
Dec. 28	**UCLA (A)**	**72**	**76**
Jan. 3	Cincinnati* (A)	65	58
Jan. 5	Ky. Wesleyan (H)	79	58
Jan. 8	Florida St.* (A)	96	69
Jan. 12	Duke (A)	91	76
Jan. 15	DePaul (H)	63	58
Jan. 17	Tulane* (A)	63	55
Jan. 22	So. Mississippi* (H)	63	48
Jan. 26	Rutgers (N)	54	49
Jan. 29	**Virginia (H)**	**81**	**98**
Feb. 2	Cincinnati* (A)	79	73
Feb. 5	Lamar (H)	85	60
Feb. 7	Florida St.* (H)	89	63

Date	Site	UL	OPP
Feb. 9	Tulane* (H)	73	56
Feb. 12	Marquette (A)	81	73
Feb. 19	Memphis St.* (A)	75	66
Feb. 22	Wright St. (H)	71	55
Feb. 26	Western Ky.* (A)	73	62
Feb. 28	Murray St. (H)	66	58
Mar. 2	Virginia Tech* (A)	73	64
Mar. 6	Memphis St.* (OT) (H)	64	62
	Metro Conference Tournament		
	(Cincinnati, Ohio)		
Mar. 12	Memphis St. (N)	71	68
Mar. 13	Tulane (N)	66	51
	NCAA Mideast Regional		
	(Evansville, Ind.)		
Mar. 20	Tennessee (N)	70	57
	NCAA Mideast Regional		
	(Knoxville, Tenn.)		
Mar. 24	Arkansas (N)	65	63
Mar. 26	Kentucky (OT) (N)	80	68
	NCAA Finals		
	(Albuquerque, N.M.)		
Apr. 2	Houston (N)	81	94

*Metro Conference Game. 2682 2309

1983-84
(WON 24, LOST 11)
COACH: Denny Crum
CAPTAIN: Game Captains

Date	Site	UL	OPP
Nov. 26	**Kentucky (A)**	**44**	**65**
Nov. 30	**Purdue (A)**	**83**	**90**
Dec. 3	So. Methodist (H)	89	65
Dec. 7	Iowa (H)	79	58
Dec. 12	Indiana St. (H)	105	69
Dec. 17	NC State (A)	83	79
	Western Airlines-Chaminade Classic		
	(Honolulu, Ha.)		
Dec. 25	**Houston (N)**	**73**	**76**
Dec. 26	**Chaminade (A)**	**72**	**83**
Dec. 28	Hawaii Pacific (A)	89	71
Jan. 2	Morehead St. (H)	85	50
Jan. 5	Iona (N)	93	81
Jan. 7	Cincinnati* (A)	51	37
Jan. 14	Virginia Tech* (OT) (H)	83	79
Jan. 18	Cincinnati (H)	78	64
Jan. 22	UCLA* (H)	86	78
Jan. 25	Florida St.* (H)	95	71
Jan. 28	**Marquette (H)**	**60**	**65**
Jan. 30	So. Mississippi* (A)	63	56
Feb. 1	Tulane* (H)	62	56
Feb. 4	LaSalle (A)	93	88
Feb. 6	**Florida St.* (A)**	**60**	**75**
Feb. 8	So. Mississippi* (H)	63	56
Feb. 11	**Virginia (H)**	**45**	**50**
Feb. 13	**Virginia Tech* (A)**	**74**	**76**
Feb. 18	Memphis St.* (A)	85	78
Feb. 20	Wright St. (H)	90	69
Feb. 22	Western Ky. (H)	69	60
Feb. 26	**DePaul* (A)**	**63**	**73**
Feb. 29	Tulane* (A)	61	60
Mar. 3	Memphis St.* (H)	68	58
	Metro Conference Tournament		
	(Memphis, Tenn.)		
Mar. 8	Cincinnati (N)	62	55
Mar. 9	**Virginia Tech (N)**	**61**	**69**
	NCAA Mideast Regional		
	(Milwaukee, Wis.)		
Mar. 16	Morehead St. (N)	72	59
Mar. 18	Tulsa (N)	69	67
	NCAA Mideast Regional		
	(Lexington, Ky.)		
Mar. 22	**Kentucky (A)**	**67**	**72**

*Metro Conference Game. 2575 2358

1984-85
(WON 19, LOST 18)
COACH: Denny Crum
CAPTAIN: Game Captains

Date	Site	UL	OPP
Nov. 24	Indiana (A)	75	64
Dec. 1	Va. Commonwealth (H)	67	55
	Wendy's Classic		
	(Bowling Green, Ky.)		
Dec. 7	**Louisiana Tech (N)**	**64**	**73**
Dec. 8	St. Francis (N)	76	63
Dec. 15	Kentucky (H)	71	64
Dec. 17	Tampa (H)	87	55
Dec. 20	Hawaii-Hilo (A)	80	75
	Western Airlines-Chaminade Classic		
	(Honolulu, Ha.)		
Dec. 22	**Chaminade (A)**	**65**	**67**
Dec. 25	**Oklahoma (N)**	**72**	**90**
Dec. 29	**Loyola-Chicago (H)**	**81**	**93**
Jan. 3	Santa Clara (A)	72	67
Jan. 9	Tulane* (H)	52	51
Jan. 12	Florida St.* (A)	63	62
Jan. 16	**So. Mississippi* (A)**	**63**	**72**
Jan. 19	**Memphis St.* (H)**	**66**	**69**
Jan. 21	**South Carolina* (A)**	**59**	**64**
Jan. 24	**Cincinnati* (A)**	**54**	**56**
Jan. 26	NC State (H)	84	78
Jan. 30	**Virginia Tech* (H)**	**61**	**81**
Feb. 2	DePaul (H)	77	73
Feb. 6	**Cincinnati* (H)**	**63**	**69**
Feb. 9	**Virginia* (A)**	**65**	**74**
Feb. 11	Virginia Tech* (A)	70	65
Feb. 16	So. Methodist (A)	64	72
Feb. 18	So. Mississippi* (H)	88	71
Feb. 20	Florida St.* (H)	83	72
Feb. 24	**UCLA (A)**	**65**	**75**
Feb. 26	**Tulane* (A)**	**56**	**68**
Feb. 28	South Carolina* (H)	70	54
Mar. 2	**Memphis St.* (A)**	**59**	**66**
	Metro Conference Tournament		
	(Louisville, Ky.)		
Mar. 7	South Carolina (H)	74	61
Mar. 8	**Memphis State (H)**	**74**	**81**
	NIT (Broadbent Arena)		
	(Louisville, Ky.)		
Mar. 14	Alcorn State (H)	77	75
	NIT		
	(Louisville, Ky.)		
Mar. 20	South Florida (H)	68	61
Mar. 24	Tenn.-Chattanooga (H)	71	66
	NIT Finals		
	(New York, N.Y.)		
Mar. 27	**UCLA (N)**	**66**	**75**
Mar. 29	**Tennessee (N)**	**84**	**100**

*Metro Conference Game. 2588 2583

1985-86
(WON 32, LOST 7)
COACH: Denny Crum
CAPTAIN: Game Captains

Date	Site	UL	OPP
	Big Apple NIT		
	(Cincinnati, Ohio)		
Nov. 22	Miami (Ohio) (N)	81	65
Nov. 24	Tulsa (N)	80	74
	Big Apple NIT		
	(New York, N.Y.)		
Nov. 29	**Kansas (N)**	**78**	**83**
Dec. 1	**St. John's (N)**	**79**	**86**
Dec. 7	Purdue (H)	77	58
Dec. 10	Iona (H)	88	75
Dec. 14	Western Ky. (H)	73	70
Dec. 18	Indiana (H)	65	63
Dec. 28	Kentucky (A)	64	69
Jan. 4	Wyoming (H)	94	62
Jan. 6	Eastern Ky. (H)	86	55
Jan. 9	**Memphis St.* (A)**	**71**	**73**
Jan. 13	So. Mississippi* (A)	59	54
Jan. 15	Florida St.* (A)	85	64
Jan. 18	Syracuse (H)	83	73
Jan. 20	**Cincinnati* (H)**	**82**	**84**
Jan. 25	**Kansas (A)**	**69**	**71**
Jan. 28	LaSalle (H)	72	60
Feb. 1	UCLA (H)	91	72
Feb. 3	South Carolina* (H)	74	72
Feb. 6	Virginia Tech* (H)	103	68
Feb. 8	**NC State (A)**	**64**	**76**
Feb. 10	Virginia Tech* (A)	93	83
Feb. 13	Cincinnati* (A)	74	58

Feb. 15 DePaul (A) 72 53
Feb. 17 So. Mississippi* (H) 83 74
Feb. 19 Florida St.* (H) 89 67
Feb. 22 Houston (A) 76 59
Feb. 24 South Alabama (H) 66 55
Feb. 26 South Carolina* (A) 65 63
Mar. 2 Memphis St.* (H) 70 69
Metro Conference Tournament
(Louisville, Ky.)
Mar. 8 Cincinnati (H) 86 65
Mar. 9 Memphis St. (H) 88 79
NCAA West Regional
(Ogden, Utah)
Mar. 13 Drexel (N) 93 73
Mar. 15 Bradley (N) 82 68
NCAA West Regional
(Houston, Texas)
Mar. 20 No. Carolina (N) 94 79
Mar. 22 Auburn (N) 84 76
NCAA Finals
(Dallas, Texas)
Mar. 29 LSU (N) 88 77
Mar. 31 Duke (N) 72 69
*Metro Conference Game. 3096 2694

1986-87
(WON 18, LOST 14)
COACH: Denny Crum
CAPTAIN: Game Captain
Date   Site   UL OPP
Great Alaska Shootout
(Anchorage, Alaska)
Nov. 28 Northeastern (N) (OT) 84 88
Nov. 29 Washington (N) 54 69
Nov. 30 Texas (N) 70 74
Dec. 6 Eastern Kentucky (H) . 98 86
Dec. 8 Fairleigh Dickinson (H) 82 74
Dec. 10 Western Kentucky (A) . 60 58
Dec. 13 DePaul (H) 68 75
Dec. 17 Tampa (H) 68 60
Dec. 23 Indiana (A) 58 67
Dec. 27 Kentucky (H) 51 85
Jan. 3 Rutgers (H) 79 49
Jan. 5 Nevada-Reno (H) 92 77
Jan. 7 Florida State* (A) 73 64
Jan. 10 Wyoming (A) 67 64
Jan. 14 Southern Miss* (A) ... 69 76
Jan. 18 Purdue (A) 73 88
Jan. 20 Virginia Tech* (H) 84 62
Jan. 22 Cincinnati* (H) 81 69
Jan. 28 Memphis State* (H) ... 48 64
Jan. 31 Kansas (H) 58 62
Feb. 2 South Carolina* (H) ... 90 62
Feb. 5 Virginia Tech* (A) 90 71
Feb. 7 North Carolina St. (H) . 87 75
Feb. 11 South Carolina* (A) ... 59 55
Feb. 14 Syracuse (A) 71 99
Feb. 16 Southern Miss* (H) (OT) 85 84
Feb. 18 Florida State* (H) 87 71
Feb. 22 Memphis State* (A) ... 57 58
Feb. 25 Cincinnati* (A) 81 69
Feb. 28 UCLA (A) 86 99
Metro Conference Tournament
(Louisville, Ky.)
Mar. 7 Southern Miss (H) 78 71
Mar. 8 Memphis State (H) ... 52 75
*Metro Conference Game. 2339 2302

1987-88
(WON 24, LOST 11)
COACH: Denny Crum
CAPTAIN: Game Captains
Date   Site   UL OPP
Bank One/Big Four Classic
(Indianapolis, Ind.)
Dec. 5 Notre Dame (N) 54 69
Dec. 12 Kentucky (A) 75 76
Dec. 16 Cleveland State (H) ... 93 79
Dec. 19 Indiana (H) 81 69
Dec. 22 Eastern Ky. (H) 87 69
Rainbow Classic
(Honolulu, Hawaii)

Dec. 28 So. Methodist (N) 87 79
Dec. 29 NC State (N) 75 80
Dec. 30 Mississippi St. (N) 86 62
Jan. 4 South Alabama (H) 80 69
Jan. 6 Georgia Tech (H) 61 62
Jan. 9 Florida State* (A) 76 83
Jan. 16 UCLA (H) 92 79
Jan. 18 Western Kentucky (H) . 84 71
Jan. 20 Cincinnati* (OT) (A) ... 91 89
Jan. 23 Purdue (H) 85 91
Jan. 26 Dayton (A) 90 59
Jan. 28 Southern Miss* (A) 92 95
Jan. 30 Memphis State* (A) ... 68 72
Feb. 1 Virginia Tech* (H) 107 99
Feb. 3 South Carolina* (H) ... 68 53
Feb. 6 Houston (H) 73 69
Feb. 13 NC State (A) 89 101
Feb. 15 Cincinnati* (H) 90 78
Feb. 17 Florida State* (H) 82 62
Feb. 20 So. Carolina*(2OT)(A) . 98 88
Feb. 24 Southern Miss* (H) ... 94 84
Feb. 27 Virginia Tech* (A) 87 82
Feb. 29 Memphis State* (H) ... 71 69
Mar. 2 Austin Peay (H) 84 78
Mar. 5 DePaul (A) 58 77
Metro Conference Tournament
(Memphis, Tenn.)
Mar. 12 South Carolina (N) 89 57
Mar. 13 Memphis State (N) 81 73
NCAA Southeast Regional
(Atlanta, Ga.)
Mar. 17 Oregon State (N) 70 61
Mar. 19 Brigham Young (N) ... 97 76
NCAA Southeast Regional
(Birmingham, Ala.)
Mar. 24 Oklahoma (N) 98 108
* Metro Conference Game. 2893 2668

1988-89
(WON 24, LOST 9)
COACH: Denny Crum
CAPTAIN: Pervis Ellison and
Kenny Payne
Date   Site   UL OPP
Big Apple NIT
(Cincinnati, Ohio)
Nov. 18 Xavier (A) 83 85
Nov. 30 Vanderbilt (A) 62 65
Bank One/Big Four Classic
(Indianapolis, Ind.)
Dec. 3 Indiana (A) 101 79
Dec. 6 Murray State (H) 83 51
Dec. 8 Western Kentucky (A) . 81 69
Dec. 10 Dayton (A) 95 68
Dec. 17 Oklahoma State (H) ... 92 90
Dec. 21 Eastern Kentucky (H) . 76 40
Dec. 31 Kentucky (H) 97 75
Jan. 4 Virginia (H) 74 71
Jan. 7 DePaul (H) 81 67
Jan. 9 Virginia Tech* (H) 82 73
Jan. 11 South Carolina* (H) 75 52
Jan. 15 Georgia Tech (A) 67 65
Jan. 22 Nevada-Las Vegas (H) 92 74
Jan. 26 Southern Miss* (A) ... 95 76
Jan. 29 Ohio State (H) 79 85
Feb. 1 Virginia Tech* (H) 108 95
Feb. 4 Memphis State* (A) ... 101 85
Feb. 6 Florida State* (H) 78 81
Feb. 8 Cincinnati* (A) 69 66
Feb. 12 UCLA (A) 75 77
Feb. 16 Florida State* (A) 78 77
Feb. 20 Memphis State* (H) ... 67 72
Feb. 22 Southern Miss.* (H) ... 96 83
Feb. 25 South Carolina* (A) ... 73 77
Mar. 1 Cincinnati* (H) 71 77
Mar. 4 Notre Dame (A) 87 77
Metro Conference Tournament
(Columbia, S.C.)
Mar. 11 Memphis State (N) 71 70
Mar. 12 Florida State (N) 87 80
(continued on page 136)
NCAA Midwest Regional

(Indianapolis, Ind.)
Mar. 16 Ark.-Little Rock (N) 76 71
Mar. 18 Arkansas (N) 93 84
NCAA Midwest Regional
(Minneapolis, Minn.)
Mar. 24 Illinois (N) 69 83
*Metro Conference Game. 2714 2441

1989-90
(WON 27, LOST 8)
COACH: DENNY CRUM
CAPTAIN: Game Captains
Date   Site   UL OPP
Maui Classic
(Lahaina, Maui, Hawaii)
Nov. 24 Chaminade (N) 89 70
Nov. 25 Missouri (N) 79 82
Nov. 26 Villanova (N) 83 69
Bank One/Big Four Classic
(Indianapolis, Ind.)
Dec. 2 Notre Dame (N) 84 73
Dec. 4 Cleveland State (H) 104 77
Dec. 6 Vanderbilt (H) 101 75
Dec. 9 Western Kentucky (H) . 75 61
Dec. 16 New Mexico (H) 78 49
Dec. 18 Austin Peay (H) 93 59
Dec. 30 Kentucky (A) 86 79
Jan. 4 Cincinnati* (H) 66 71
Jan. 7 UCLA (H) 97 80
Jan. 11 South Carolina* (A) ... 79 66
Jan. 14 Florida State* (A) 73 66
Jan. 18 Tulane* (A) 109 96
Jan. 20 Memphis State* (H) 86 69
Jan. 27 DePaul (A) 62 66
Jan. 29 Southern Miss.* (H) 105 88
Feb. 1 Virginia Tech* (H) 96 69
Feb. 4 Ohio State (A) 88 91
Feb. 6 Florida State* (H) 69 50
Feb. 8 South Carolina* (H) ... 95 77
Feb. 10 Georgia Tech (H) 84 94
Feb. 15 Virginia Tech* (A) 97 78
Feb. 17 Virginia (A) 72 56
Feb. 20 Memphis State* (A) ... 68 82
Feb. 24 Nev.-Las Vegas (A) ... 81 91
Feb. 27 Tulane* (H) 99 85
Mar. 1 Cincinnati* (A) 86 71
Mar. 3 Southern Miss.* (A) ... 73 71
Metro Conference Tournament
(Biloxi, Miss.)
Mar. 8 Tulane (N) 79 66
Mar. 9 Memphis State (N) 76 73
Mar. 10 Southern Miss. (N) 83 80
NCAA West Regional
(Salt Lake City, Utah)
Mar. 15 Idaho (N) 78 59
Mar. 17 Ball State (N) 60 62
*Metro Conference Game. 2933 2553

1990-91
(WON 14, LOST 16)
COACH: Denny Crum
CAPTAIN: Game Captains
Date   Site   UL OPP
Bank One/Big Four Classic
(Indianapolis, Ind.)
Dec. 1 Indiana (N) 52 72
Dec. 12 DePaul (H) 94 75
Dec. 15 Prairie View A & M (H) . 100 76
Dec. 17 Western Kentucky (A) . 86 79
Dec. 19 Cleveland State (H) 95 80
Dec. 22 George Mason (A) 85 80
Dec. 29 Kentucky (H) 85 93
Jan. 3 Cincinnati* (A) 64 72
Jan. 5 UCLA (A) 81 88
Jan. 7 South Carolina* (H) ... 64 67
Jan. 10 Memphis State* (H) ... 56 65
Jan. 12 Florida State* (A) 66 77
Jan. 14 Tulane* (A) 79 73
Jan. 19 South Alabama (H) ... 85 83
Jan. 24 Southern Miss* (H) ... 81 84
Jan. 26 Nev.-Las Vegas (H) ... 85 97
Jan. 30 Virginia Tech* (H) 79 86

Feb. 2	Southern Miss* (A)	66	77
Feb. 6	South Carolina* (A)	67	70
Feb. 9	Florida State* (H)	88	72
Feb. 13	Virginia Tech* (A)	56	72
Feb. 16	Memphis State* (A)	73	91
Feb. 20	Southwestern La. (H)	104	77
Feb. 24	Georgia Tech (A)	69	82
Feb. 26	Tulane* (A)	95	72
Feb. 28	Cincinnati* (H)	68	61
Mar. 1	Notre Dame (H)	65	59

Metro Conference Tournament
(Roanoke, Va.)

Mar. 7	Southern Miss (N)	83	76
Mar. 8	Memphis State (N)	72	70
Mar. 9	Florida State (N)	69	76

*Metro Conference Game. 2312 2302

1991-92
(WON 19, LOST 11)
COACH: Denny Crum
CAPTAIN: Game Captains

Date	Site	U	LOPP
Nov. 23	Howard (H)	102	73
Dec. 5	Notre Dame (A)	84	81
Dec. 10	Maryland (H)	96	79
Dec. 14	George Mason (H)	85	66
Dec. 19	Morehead State (H)	90	76
Dec. 21	Louisiana State (A)	93	92
Dec. 28	Kentucky (A)	89	103
Jan. 2	Houston (H)	60	56
Jan. 4	Tulane* (H)	83	87
Jan. 9	Va. Commonwealth* (A)	57	66
Jan. 11	Kansas (A)	85	78
Jan. 16	South Florida* (H)	60	47
Jan. 18	Wyoming (H)	68	60
Jan. 23	Southern Miss* (H)	88	74
Jan. 25	Georgia Tech (H)	65	73
Jan. 28	Virginia Tech* (A)	78	68
Jan. 30	UNC Charlotte* (A)	68	77
Feb. 2	UCLA (H)	64	78
Feb. 6	UCC Charlotte* (H)	73	63
Feb. 8	Xavier (N)#	86	73
Feb. 13	South Florida* (A)	66	69
Feb. 16	DePaul (A)	81	84
Feb. 18	Va. Commonwealth* (H)	89	71
Feb. 22	Arizona State (A)	63	62
Feb. 27	Tulane* (A)	87	72
Feb. 29	Southern Miss* (A)	70	82
Mar. 7	Virginia Tech* (H)	79	59

Metro Conference Tournament
(Louisville, Ky.)

Mar. 13	Va. Commonwealth (H)	65	74

NCAA West Regional
(Tempe, AZ)

Mar. 20	Wake Forest (N)	81	58
Mar. 22	UCLA (N)	69	85

*Metro Conference Game. 2324 2186

1992-93
(WON 22, LOST 9)
COACH: Denny Crum
CAPTAIN: Game Captains

Date	Site	U	LOPP
Dec. 5	Michigan State (N)	73	69
Dec. 9	Vanderbilt (A)	88	90
Dec. 12	Kentucky (H)	68	88
Dec. 16	DePaul (H)	93	88

Kuppenheimer Classic
(Atlanta, Ga.)

Dec. 19	Georgia Tech (N)	85	87
Dec. 28	Maryland (A)	67	72
Jan. 2	Oral Roberts (H)	122	76
Jan. 7	South Florida* (A)	98	75
Jan. 9	UNC Charlotte* (A)	69	57
Jan. 11	Xavier (H)	76	73
Jan. 14	Va. Commonwealth* (H)	77	68
Jan. 16	Kansas (H)	77	98
Jan. 21	Southern Miss* (A)	85	81
Jan. 24	Arizona State (A)	85	59
Jan. 28	Virginia Tech* (A)	76	65
Jan. 30	Va. C'wealth* (OT) (A)	90	88
Feb. 4	South Florida* (H)	78	61
Feb. 6	Southern Miss* (H)	86	71

Feb. 11	Tulane *(A)	60	62
Feb. 14	Nevada-Las Vegas (A)	90	86
Feb. 16	Western Kentucky (H)	77	78
Feb. 21	Houston (H)	81	89
Feb. 25	UNC Charlotte* (H)	69	64
Feb. 27	Tulane (H)*	94	67
Mar. 4	Virginia Tech* (H)	82	61
Mar. 7	Notre Dame (H)	83	68

Metro Conference Tournament
(Louisville, Ky.)

Mar. 13	UNC Charlotte (H)	71	59
Mar. 14	Va. Commonwealth (H)	90	78

NCAA Midwest Regional
(Indianapolis, Ind.)

Mar. 19	Delaware (N)	76	70
Mar. 21	Oklahoma State (N)	78	63

NCAA Midwest Regional
(St. Louis, Mo.)

Mar. 25	Indiana (N)	69	82

*Metro Conference Game. 2513 2293

1993-94
(WON 28, LOST 6)
COACH: Denny Crum
CAPTAINS: Greg Minor,
Dwayne Morton

Date	Site	U	LOPP
Nov. 27	Kentucky (A)	70	78
Dec. 4	Michigan State (H)	77	68
Dec. 8	Morehead State (H)	107	71
Dec. 11	Eastern Kentucky (H)	90	66
Dec. 18	Wyoming (A)	72	55
Dec. 22	Western Ky. (OT)(H)	78	73

Rainbow Classic (Honolulu, Ha.)

Dec. 28	UC Santa Barbara (N)	76	53
Dec. 29	Florida (N)	83	68
Dec. 30	Hawaii (N)	85	79
Jan. 4	George Mason (H)	132	87
Jan. 6	South Florida* (H)	80	56
Jan. 8	Va. C'wealth (OT)(H)	89	93
Jan. 13	Virginia Tech* (H)	95	76
Jan. 15	Georgia Tech (H)	88	68
Jan. 20	Tulane* (A)	83	76
Jan. 22	Southern Miss* (H)	70	69
Jan. 27	Virginia Tech* (A)	74	63
Jan. 29	Va. Commonwealth* (A)	94	74
Feb. 3	UNC Charlotte* (H)	76	55
Feb. 6	Vanderbilt (H)	78	62
Feb. 10	South Florida* (A)	65	50
Feb. 12	Tulane (H)	77	73
Feb. 17	UNC Charlotte* (A)	62	64

7-Up Shootout (Orlando, Fla.)

Feb. 20	Temple (N)	63	68
Feb. 23	Louisiana State (H)	82	64
Feb. 26	Notre Dame (OT) (A)	85	82
Feb. 28	Howard (H)	108	65
Mar. 2	Southern Miss* (A)	82	75
Mar. 6	UCLA (A)	72	75

Metro Tournament(Biloxi, Miss.)

Mar. 12	Virginia Tech (N)	76	67
Mar. 13	Southern Miss (N)	69	61

NCAA West Regional
(Sacramento, Calif.)

Mar. 18	Boise State (N)	67	58
Mar. 20	Minnesota (N)	60	55

NCAA West Regional
(Los Angeles, Calif.)

Mar. 24	Arizona (N)	70	82

*Metro Conference Game 2737 2339

1994-95
(WON 19, LOST 14)
COACH: Denny Crum
CAPTAINS: Tick Rogers, Brian Kiser

Date	Site	U	LOPP
Nov. 23	Jackson State (N)	90	64
Nov. 25	Brigham Young (N)	60	75
Nov. 26	Villanova (N)	81	82
Dec. 3	Michigan State (A)	71	85
Dec. 5	Western Carolina (H)	108	76
Dec. 10	Eastern Kentucky (H)	89	75

Kuppenheimer Classic, Georgia Dome
(Atlanta, Ga.)

Dec. 17	Georgia Tech (A)	77	72
Dec. 22	UNLV (A)	89	72
Dec. 29	Dayton (A)	92	78
Jan. 1	Kentucky (H)	88	86
Jan. 5	Va. C'wealth* (A)	63	67
Jan. 7	Notre Dame (H)	80	72
Jan. 12	Virginia Tech* (A)	62	61
Jan. 14	Southern Miss* (H)	72	74
Jan. 19	UNC Charlotte* (A)	82	86
Jan. 21	Tulane* (A)	73	76
Jan. 23	San Francisco (H)	82	61
Jan. 26	Virginia Tech* (H)	78	74
Jan. 28	UNC Charlotte* (H)	79	57
Jan. 30	Towson State (A)	69	81
Feb. 2	South Florida* (H)	66	65
Feb. 4	Tulane* (H)	71	56
Feb. 9	South Florida* (A)	79	64
Feb. 12	Temple (H)	48	53
Feb. 16	Southern Miss* (A)	63	74

Worchester Centrum
(Worcester, Mass.)

Feb. 19	Massachusetts (N)	76	91
Feb. 25	DePaul (A)	81	82
Mar. 2	Va. Commonwealth* (H)	80	64
Mar. 5	UCLA (H)	73	91

Metro Tournament (Louisville, Ky.)

Mar. 10	Va. Commonwealth (N)	80	64
Mar. 11	Tulane (N)	81	80
Mar. 12	Southern Miss (N)	78	64

NCAA Midwest Regional
(Austin, Texas)

Mar. 17	Memphis (N)	56	77

*Metro Conference Game

1995-96
(WON 22, LOST 12)
COACH: Denny Crum
CAPTAINS: Tick Rogers, Brian Kiser

Date	Site	U	LOPP

San Juan (Puerto Rico) Shootout

Nov. 24	American (P. Rico) (N)	90	86
Nov. 25	Va. Commonwealth (N)	83	74
Nov. 26	Auburn (N)	78	82
Nov. 30	Boston College (A)	67	81
Dec. 2	Michigan State (H)	79	59
Dec. 6	Morehead State (H)	119	61
Dec. 9	Texas (H)	101	78
Dec. 13	Eastern Ky. (H)	87	70

Jeep Eagle Classic (Atlanta, Ga.)

Dec. 16	Georgia Tech (N)	77	88
Dec. 20	Murray State (H)	81	72
Dec. 23	Kentucky (A)	66	89
Dec. 30	Towson State (H)	96	72
Jan. 3	Saint Louis* (A)	67	63
Jan. 7	DePaul* (A)	81	71
Jan. 10	UNC Charlotte* (H)	66	78
Jan. 13	St. John's (A)	64	86
Jan. 17	UAB* (A)	78	70
Jan. 21	Southern Miss* (H)	87	61
Jan. 24	Saint Louis* (H)	61	57
Jan. 27	UCLA (A)	78	76
Jan. 31	South Florida* (A)	57	54
Feb. 3	Memphis* (H)	74	56
Feb. 8	Tulane* (H)	65	68
Feb. 10	UAB* (H)	81	66
Feb. 15	UNC Charlotte* (A)	67	64
Feb. 22	Cincinnati* (A)	72	66
Feb. 25	Memphis* (A)	54	57
Feb. 28	Marquette (2 OT)(H)	79	80
Mar. 2	Massachusetts* (H)	59	62

Conference USA Tournament
(Memphis, Tenn.)

Mar. 7	Tulane (N)	82	80
Mar. 8	Cincinnati (N)	81	92

NCAA Midwest Regional
(Milwaukee, Wisc.)

Mar. 15	Tulsa (OT) (N)	82	80
Mar. 17	Villanova (N)	68	64

NCAA Midwest Regional
(Minneapolis, Minn.)

Mar. 21	Wake Forest (N)	59	60

*Conference USA Game

1996-97
(WON 26, LOST 9)

COACH: Denny Crum
CAPTAINS: Alvin Sims, DeJuan Wheat

Date	Site	UL	OPP
Big Island Invitational (Hilo, Hawaii)			
Nov. 29	Montana State (N)	92	78
Nov. 30	Illinois (N)	70	60
Dec. 1	Colorado (N)	92	82
John Wooden Classic (Anaheim, Ca.)			
Dec. 7	LSU (N) (OT)	93	87
Dec. 11	Dayton (H)	80	67
Market Square Arena (Indianapolis, Ind.)			
Dec. 14	Purdue (N)	88	72
Dec. 16	Wright State (H)	65	57
Dec. 21	Arkansas (A)(OT)	91	88
Dec. 23	Tennessee State (H)	102	54
Dec. 29	Boston Col. (H) (2OT)	89	85
Dec. 31	**Kentucky (H)**	**54**	**74**
Jan. 3	UAB* (A)	93	79
Jan. 6	UNC Charlotte* (A)	92	81
Jan. 11	Georgia Tech (H)	60	56
Jan. 15	Houston* (H)	92	78
Jan. 19	Texas (A)(OT)	85	78
Jan. 23	**Memphis* (H)**	**58**	**64**
Jan. 25	UCLA (H)	74	71
Jan. 28	DePaul* (H)	71	54
Jan. 30	Cincinnati* (H)	81	70
Feb. 2	**Temple (A)**	**44**	**67**
Feb. 6	**Saint Louis* (H)**	**62**	**64**
Feb. 9	**Memphis* (A)**	**59**	**79**
Feb. 15	Houston* (A)	70	66
Feb. 17	South Florida* (H)	75	64
Feb. 20	**Marquette* (A)(OT)**	**71**	**79**
Feb. 22	Southern Miss.* (A)(OT)	75	72
Feb. 26	UNC Charlotte* (H)	72	71
Mar. 1	**Tulane* (A)**	**71**	**83**
C-USA Tournament (St. Louis, Mo.)			
Mar. 5	South Florida (N)	69	58
Mar. 6	**UNC Charlotte (N)**	**60**	**64**
NCAA East Region (Pittsburgh, Pa.)			
Mar. 14	Massachusetts (N)	65	57
Mar. 16	New Mexico (N)	64	63
NCAA East Regional (Syracuse, N.Y.)			
Mar. 21	Texas (N)	78	63
Mar. 23	**North Carolina (N)**	**74**	**97**
*Conference USA Game		2631	2482

1997-98
(WON 12, LOST 20)

COACH: Denny Crum
CAPTAINS: Game Captains

Date	Site	UL	OPP
Puerto Rico Shootout			
Nov. 27	Hofstra (N)	76	66
Nov. 28	Illinois (N)	58	57
Nov. 29	**Georgia Tech (N)**	**69**	**73**
Great Eight Classic (Chicago, Ill.)			
Dec. 3	**North Carolina (N)**	**72**	**81**
Dec. 6	**Purdue (H)**	**69**	**87**
Dec. 9	**Arkansas (H)**	**83**	**100**
Dec. 17	Morehead State (H)	84	54
Delta Airlines Classic (Atlanta, Ga.)			
Dec. 20	**Georgia Tech (N)**	**86**	**94**
Dec. 22	**Mississippi (H)**	**70**	**74**
Dec. 27	Kentucky (A)	79	76
Dec. 29	Southeast Missouri (H)	91	69
Jan. 3	**Marquette* (H)**	**70**	**71**
Jan. 6	St. John's (H)	73	67
Jan. 8	DePaul* (H)	73	57
Jan. 10	**Syracuse (A)**	**65**	**69**
Jan. 15	**UAB* (A)**	**53**	**55**
Jan. 18	**Cincinnati* (H)**	**57**	**71**
Jan. 20	Saint Louis* (H)	87	81
Jan. 22	**UNC Charlotte* (A)**	**75**	**84**
Jan. 25	**UCLA (A)**	**82**	**88**
Jan. 29	**Cincinnati* (A)**	**61**	**67**
Jan. 31	**Saint Louis* (A)**	**55**	**64**
Feb. 5	**South Florida* (H)**	**60**	**62**
Feb. 7	Tulane* (H)	81	62
Feb. 12	Houston* (A)	72	69
Feb. 15	**UNC Charlotte* (H)**	**68**	**73**
Feb. 19	**Marquette* (A)**	**52**	**57**
Feb. 21	**Memphis* (A)**	**75**	**93**
Feb. 25	**Southern Miss* (H)**	**62**	**72**
Feb. 28	**DePaul* (A)(OT)**	**85**	**82**
C-USA Tournament (Cincinnati, Ohio)			
Mar. 4	South Florida (N)	75	64
Mar. 5	**Cincinnati (A)**	**50**	**64**
*Conference USA Game		2267	2303

1998-99
(WON 19, LOST 11)

COACH: Denny Crum

Date	Opponent	UL	OPP
11/22	Western Kentucky (H)	99	78
12/05	Mississippi (A)	69	88
12/07	Towson State (H)	106	73
12/17	North Carolina (A)	72	77
12/19	*DePaul (H)	90	63
12/21	Dayton (A)	68	65
12/26	Kentucky (H)	83	74
12/30	Morgan State (H)	95	47
01/02	Michigan State (A)	57	69
01/06	*Saint Louis (H)	93	70
01/10	*South Florida (A)	95	74
01/13	*Marquette (A)	78	63
01/17	*DePaul (A)	71	68
01/21	*Cincinnati (H)	55	81
01/23	UCLA (H)	70	82
01/28	*Saint Louis (A)	52	62
01/30	*UNC Charlotte (H)	47	58
02/04	*Memphis (H)	89	76
02/06	*Marquette (H)	81	77
02/11	*UNC Charlotte (A)	79	68
02/14	Georgia Tech (H)	78	58
02/16	*Houston (H)	106	78
02/18	*Tulane (A)	80	75
02/21	*Cincinnati (A)	78	91
02/25	*UAB (H)	91	60
02/27	*Southern Miss (A)	58	59
03/04	Saint Louis (N)	70	61
03/05	UAB (N)	77	68
03/06	UNC Charlotte (N)	59	68
03/11	Creighton (N)	58	62
		2304	2093

*Conference USA Game

KEY DATES IN CRUM'S CAREER

■ April 17, 1971: Denny Crum, a young assistant coach to legendary UCLA Coach John Wooden, is introduced as Louisville's new basketball coach. Crum replaces John Dromo, who resigned because of health problems.

"I believe in running, shooting and pressing," Crum said at the press conference announcing that he was taking over the Louisville program. "In other words, putting pressure on your opponent at both ends of the floor. I know Louisville is a good basketball school in a top conference. Anybody who has had the success they've had over the years is bound to have something going for them. I don't think there's any limitation on the potential of U of L basketball. It's a good basketball area. And there's no reason you can't win here."

■ December 1, 1971: Louisville falls 70-69 to the University of Florida in Crum's debut as the Cardinals' coach.

"We hadn't practiced very hard going into the game," Crum said. "After the game, I told our team I had a better way to do it."

Crum was right, and "his way" led to a 15-game winning streak following that first loss.

■ December 4, 1971: Crum gained his first victory at Louisville as the Cards beat Bellarmine 116-58. It was, at the time, just two points short of the Louisville scoring record for one game. That game also marked Crum's first game in Freedom Hall, where he has won better than 80 percent of his games.

■ March 11, 1972: With a 72-65 win over Kansas State, fourth-ranked Louisville earns a berth in the NCAA Final Four in Crum's debut season. (At the time, Crum became the first coach ever to guide a team to the Final Four in his first full season.)

"Coming from UCLA, I thought that was the way it's supposed to be every year," Crum said of the trip to the Final Four. "Obviously, it doesn't always work out that way. But at the time, I didn't know any different."

The Cardinals were eventually eliminated in the NCAA Tourney semifinals by UCLA, which went on to win its 44th consecutive game on the way to a sixth straight NCAA crown under John Wooden.

■ March 29, 1975: Seniors Junior Bridgeman and Allen Murphy lead Louisville to the NCAA Final Four—Crum's second appearance in the Final Four in four years at U of L. But again it is UCLA that knocks the Cards out. The game was, at the time, widely referred to as the best college basketball game ever. The Bruins won 75-74 in overtime.

"I'm disappointed," Crum said at the time, "but I can't feel disappointed at all with the way we played. We tried against a great team with a great tradition, and we almost won. And I could not be prouder of a bunch of guys than I am of these. This was one of the best basketball games I've ever been involved in as a player or coach."

■ December 6, 1975: Crum gains his 100th win in just the second game of his fifth season as Louisville beats Murray State 78-59 in Freedom Hall. After trailing by three in the first half, U of L outscores the Racers 50-28 in the second half on the way to the victory.

■ August 27, 1977: Crum makes his mark on the international scene, coaching the U.S. team to the gold medal at the World University Games in Sofia, Bulgaria, with an 87-64 win over Russia in the championship game. Two of his Louisville players, Darrell Griffith and Ricky Gallon, help the U.S. team to gold.

"Winning the World Games was a thrill," Crum said, "but getting home to good food and comfortable living was a thrill for all of us, too."

■ January 22, 1980: Amid a school-record 18-game winning streak, Crum picks up victory No. 200 as the Cards beat Marquette, 76-63. The Cards turn a one-point deficit into a 13-point lead at one point as seventh-ranked Louisville won its 14th game in 16 outings.

"There's a spurt like that in every game," Crum said. "If you're lucky, it's your team that gets it, and you get it at the right time."

■ March 24, 1980: Led by Most Outstanding Player Darrell Griffith's 23 points, Crum guides Louisville to its first NCAA Championship with a 59-54 victory over UCLA at Market Square Arena in Indianapolis.

"There was something about that team," Crum said. "They loved each other. They played hard. And they played together."

■ March 14, 1981: After Louisville won 19 of its last 20 games to earn an NCAA Tournament berth, Arkansas' U.S. Reed buries a 49-foot shot to send Louisville home, 74-73.

"That's one I'll never forget," Crum said. "Some years, it's just not meant to be."

■ March 20, 1982: Louisville survives a physical battle and a homecourt advantage for its opponent as the Cards post a 75-68 victory over Alabama-Birmingham for Crum's fourth Final Four berth—and the second in three years. Georgetown eliminates the Cards in the national semifinals in a defensive struggle, 50-46.

■ March 26, 1983: The Cardinals earn their third NCAA Final Four appearance in four years with a classic Mideast Regional Championship victory over Kentucky in the first "Dream Game." After the two teams battled to a 62-62 tie, Louisville explodes in overtime for an 80-68 win at Knoxville, Tenn.

"The overtime was spectacular," Crum said. "It's one of those things you can't quite explain."

Louisville goes on to fall 94-81 to Houston in the national semifinals in Albuquerque, New Mexico as "Phi Slamma Jamma" defeats "The Doctors of Dunk"—other than the national championship contests, it was the highest-rated college basketball game of all time.

■ December 16, 1983: Crum signs a 10-year contract extension with the Cardinals which includes a $1 million completion bonus.

"I'm very pleased with the contract, especially since I had no intention of leaving," said Crum, who was in his 13th year at Louisville. "It's gratifying to know that the university appreciates my efforts enough to warrant this kind of commitment."

■ December 28, 1983: Crum picked up win No. 300 as Louisville defeated Hawaii-Pacific, 89-71, in Maui, behind Lancaster Gordon's 18 points.

"We've been blessed with a lot of great athletes and great athletes make you a great coach," Crum said. "Give the players the credit for those milestones. They're the ones that go out and play."

■ March 31, 1986: Led by Most Outstanding Player Pervis Ellison's 25 points and 11 rebounds, Crum guides the Cardinals to their second NCAA Championship with a 72-69 victory over Duke at the Reunion Arena in Dallas, Texas.

"Those guys had no quit in them," Crum said. "They were the best team, and they were determined to prove it."

It was Crum's sixth Final Four appearance and an unmatched fourth time in the Final Four in the 1980s.

"There was an enormous difference in my feelings toward winning the first championship and the second one," Crum said. "During the first one, I felt pressure because we had been to two previous Final Fours and come up short. I was not as relaxed then and did not enjoy the title as I probably should have. It was more of a feeling of relief when we won it. I had more fun with the second title in 1986 because the pressure had been lifted."

■ August 23, 1987: Crum coaches the U.S. basketball team to a silver medal in the Pan American Games in Indianapolis. Brazil's Oscar Schmidt pours in 46 points as the U.S. team falls, 120-115, in the gold medal game.

"The difference was Brazil's experience and their ability to hit three-pointers, even under pressure," Crum said, noting Brazil scored 39 points from 3-point range while the U.S. was limited to just 9. "Coaching the team was a great experience and a lot of fun."

■ February 3, 1988: The Cardinals hand Crum his 400th win with a 68-53 victory over South Carolina in Freedom Hall. Playing its ninth game in 18 days and nursing a number of injuries, Louisville uses a smothering defense for the win.

"Over the years, I've had a lot of reason and opportunity to be pleased with the way my teams have played," Crum said. "But I've never been prouder of the way my team played as I am tonight. It was a gutty, gutty performance."

■ February 20, 1988: Louisville stages the quickest rally of Crum's career with a victory at South Carolina. The Cards trailed 72-58 with 1:06 remaining, and fought back to tie the game at 74-74 on a buzzer-beating, 33-foot three-pointer by Craig Hawley, and Louisville won 98-88 in double overtime.

"I guess that shows that anything can happen," Crum said.

■ March 18, 1989: The Cardinals defeat Arkansas 93-84 in

Indianapolis to advance to their seventh NCAA Sweet 16 appearance in the 1980s under Crum. Only North Carolina has more appearances in the Sweet 16 than Louisville in the 1980s (nine). Louisville had the top winning percentage in the NCAA Tournament that decade (23-6, 79.3 percent).

■ March 9, 1991: Despite a sub-par campaign, Louisville falls just short of reaching its sixth straight NCAA Tournament with a 76-69 loss to Florida State in the championship of the Metor Conference Tournament in Roanoke, Va. The loss and 14-16 record that year ended the Cardinals string of 46 consecutive winning seasons that had started with the 1944-45 season.

"I was very proud of this team," Crum said. "We might have come up short, but our effort was fantastic. They were short on talent, depth and experience. But that didn't deter them from working hard and becoming a real competitive team."

■ January 7, 1993: Crum becomes the second fastest coach to reach 500 career victories by reaching that mark in the eighth game of his 22nd season, a 98-75 win at South Florida.

"It's a good achievement," Crum said, "but I'm glad it's behind me. There was a lot of anticipation for it, but now we can focus on more important things."

■ May 9, 1994: Crum is enshrined in the Naismith Memorial Basketball Hall of Fame, one of just three active collegiate coaches in the Hall.

"It's a feeling I really don't know how to express," Crum said when he learned of the honor. "It's a lifetime of experiences that go much deeper than winning or losing a game. It makes you feel really good down deep inside."

■ Jan. 11, 1997: Crum picks up win No. 600 with a 60-56 win over Georgia Tech, one of only 20 coaches in NCAA history (just nine active) to reach that plateau.

LETTERMEN UNDER CRUM

Abram, Mike (1984-85, 1985-86, 1986-87, 1987-88)
Akridge, Matt (1995-96, 1996-97, 1997-98)
Alberston, Bob (1977-78, 1978-79)
Alexander, Rick (1971-72)
Bacon, Henry (1971-72)
Bailey, Quintin (1998-99)
Best, Travis (1997-98, 1998-99)
Bond, Phillip (1972-73, 1974-75, 1975-76, 1976-77)
Bradley, Ken (1971-72, 1972-73)
Branch, Tony (1976-77, 1977-78, 1978-79, 1979-1980)
Brewer, James (1988-89, 1990-91, 1991-92, 1992-93)
Bridgeman, Ulysses (Junior) (1972-73, 1973-74, 1974-75)
Brown, Danny (1973-74, 1974-75, 1975-76, 1976-77)
Brown, Wiley (1978-79, 1979-1980, 1980-81, 1981-82)
Bufford, Randy (1977-78, 1978-79, 1979-80, 1980-81)
Bugg, Steve (1977-78, 1978-79)
Bunton, Bill (1971-72, 1972-73, 1974-75)
Bunton, Stanley (1973-74, 1974-75, 1975-76, 1976-77)
Burkman, Roger (1977-78, 1978-79, 1979-80, 1980-81)
Butler, Bill (1972-73, 1973-74)
Calhoun, Doug (1991-92, 1992-93, 1993-94)
Carter, Larry (1971-72)
Case, Mike (1989-90, 1990-91, 1991-92, 1992-93)
Clark, Rick (1982-83, 1983-84)
Clark, Steve (1979-80, 1980-81)
Cleveland, Daryl (1977-78, 1978-79, 1979-80)
Cooper, Tim (1971-72, 1972-73)
Cosby, Wayne (1975-76)
Cox, Wesley (1973-74, 1974-75, 1975-76, 1976-77)
Crook, Herbert (1984-85, 1985-86, 1986-87, 1987-88)
Dantzler, Damion (1994-95, 1995-96, 1996-97, 1997-98)
Deuser, Greg (1977-78, 1979-80, 1980-81, 1981-82)
Eaves, Jerry (1978-79, 1979-80, 1980-81, 1981-82)
Edward, Dion (1998-99)
Ellis, Jim (1977-78)
Ellis, John (1971-72, 1972-73)
Ellison, Pervis (1985-86, 1986-87, 1987-88, 1988-89)
Farmer, Craig (1994-95, 1995-96, 1996-97, 1997-98)
Flynn, B.J. (1994-95, 1995-96, 1996-97)
Forrest, Manuel (1981-82, 1983-84, 1984-85)
Fraley, Shannon (1987-88, 1988-89, 1989-90)
Frazer, Joey (1980-81)
Gallon, Rick (1974-75, 1975-76, 1976-77, 1977-78)
Gilstrap, Curt (1975-76)
Gordon, Lancaster (1980-81, 1981-82, 1982-83, 1983-84)

Griffith, Danny (1980-81)
Griffith, Darrell (1976-77, 1977-78, 1978-79, 1979-80)
Haas, Danny (1983-84, 1984-85, 1985-86, 1986-87)
Hall, Jeff (1982-83, 1983-84, 1984-85, 1985-86)
Harmon, Bill (1973-74,1974-75, 1975-76, 1976-77)
Harmon, Jerome (1989-90)
Hawley, Craig (1986-87, 1987-88, 1988-89, 1989-90)
Hecht, Bobby (1982-83, 1983-84, 1984-85)
Holden, Cornelius (1988-89, 1989-90, 1990-91, 1991-92)
Hopper, Tobiah (1998-99)
Hopgood, Brian (1991-92, 1992-93)
Howard, Terry (1972-73, 1973-74, 1974-75)
Howard, Todd (1989-90, 1990-91)
Jackson, Troy (1996-97, 1997-98)
Jeter, James (1981-82, 1982-83, 1983-84, 1984-85)
Johnson, Eric (1994-95,1996-97, 1997-98, 1998-99)
Johnson, Jerry (1996-97, 1997-98)
Johnson, Nate (1996-97, 1997-98, 1998-99)
Jones, Charles (1980-81, 1981-82, 1982-83, 1983-84)
Jones, Kent (1981-82, 1982-83, 1983-84, 1984-85)
Kimbro, Tony (1985-86, 1986-87, 1988-89, 1989-90)
King, Jimmy (1992-93, 1993-94, 1994-95, 1995-96)
Kinnaird, Tony (1973-74, 1974-75, 1976-77)
Kiser, Brian (1992-93, 1993-94, 1994-95, 1995-96)
Lawhon, Mike (1971-72)
LeGree, Keith (1991-92, 1992-93)
Lester, David (1981-82, 1982-83, 1983-84)
Loehle, Larry (1972-73)
Marshall, Avery (1986-87)
Martin, Jeff (1984-85, 1985-86)
Maybin, Marques (1997-98, 1998-99)
McCray, Rodney (1979-80, 1980-81, 1981-82, 1982-83)
McCray, Scooter (1978-79, 1980-81, 1981-82, 1982-83)
McKinley, Jeff (1997-98, 1998-99)
McLendon, Jason (1990-91, 1991-92)
McSwain, Mark (1983-84, 1984-85, 1985-86, 1986-87)
Meiman, Joe (1971-72, 1972-73)
Meiman, John (1975-76)
Miles, Rick (1972-73)
Minor, Greg (1991-92, 1992-93, 1993-94)
Mitchell, Danny (1981-82, 1982-83, 1983-84, 1984-85)
Morton, Dwayne (1991-92, 1992-93, 1993-94)
Murphy, Allen (1972-73, 1973-74, 1974-75)
Murray, Cameron (1997-98, 1998-99)
Olliges, Will (1984-85, 1985-86, 1986-87, 1987-88)
Osborne, Jason (1993-94, 1994-95)
Payne, Kenny (1985-86, 1986-87, 1987-88, 1988-89)
Price, Jim (1969-70, 1970-71, 1971-72)

Protenic, Jim (1972-73, 1973-74)
Pulliam, Marty (1977-78, 1979-80, 1980-81, 1981-82)
Robinson, David (1985-86, 1986-87, 1987-88)
Rogers, Tick (1992-93, 1993-94, 1994-95, 1995-96)
Rozier, Clifford (1992-93, 1993-94)
Sanders, Alex (1996-97, 1997-98, 1998-99)
Schreiber, Benny (1984-85, 1985-86, 1986-87)
Simons, Matt (1993-94, 1994-95)
Sims, Alvin (1993-94, 1994-95, 1995-96, 1996-97)
Smiley, Kevin (1998-99)
Smith, Beau Zach (1993-94, 1994-95, 1995-96, 1996-97)
Smith, Dave (1975-76, 1976-77, 1977-78)
Smith, Derek (1978-79, 1979-80, 1980-81, 1981-82)
Smith, LaBradford (1987-88, 1988-89, 1989-90, 1990-91)
Smith, Troy (1989-90, 1990-91, 1991-92, 1992-93)
Spencer, Felton (1986-87, 1987-88, 1988-89, 1989-90)
Stallings, Ron (1971-72)
Stone, Kip (1990-91, 1991-92)
Sullivan, Everick (1988-89, 1989-90, 1990-91, 1991-92)
Sumpter, Barry (1983-84, 1984-85)
Taylor, Charlie (1995-96)
Thomas, Ron (1971-72)
Thompson, Billy (1982-83, 1983-84, 1984-85, 1985-86)
Turner, Bobby (1976-77, 1977-78, 1978-79)
Valentine, Robbie (1982-83, 1983-84, 1984-85, 1985-86)
Vilcheck, Al (1971-72)
Wagner, Milt (1981-82, 1982-83, 1983-84, 1985-86)
Walker, Samaki (1994-95, 1995-96)
Wayne, Jeff (1973-74)
Webb, Derwin (1989-90, 1990-91, 1991-92, 1992-93)
West, Chris (1982-83, 1984-85, 1985-86, 1986-87)
Wheat, DeJuan (1993-94, 1994-95, 1995-96, 1996-97)
White, Chris (1985-86, 1986-87)
Whitfield, Ike (1973-74, 1974-75)
Williams, Keith (1986-87, 1987-88, 1988-89, 1989-90)
Williams, Larry (1975-76, 1976-77, 1977-78, 1978-79)
Williams, Tony (1996-97, 1997-98, 1998-99)
Wilson, Rick (1974-75, 1975-76, 1976-77, 1977-78)
Wine, Robby (1992-93, 1993-94, 1994-95, 1995-96)
Wingfield, Tremaine (1990-91, 1991-92)
Witt, Jeff (1984-85, 1985-86, 1986-87, 1987-88)
Woods, Chris (1974-75)
Wright, Poncho (1979-80, 1980-81, 1981-82)
Yaden, Paul (1996-97)